W9-CHF-985

NATIONAL GEOGRAPHIC

TRAVELER

Washington D.C.

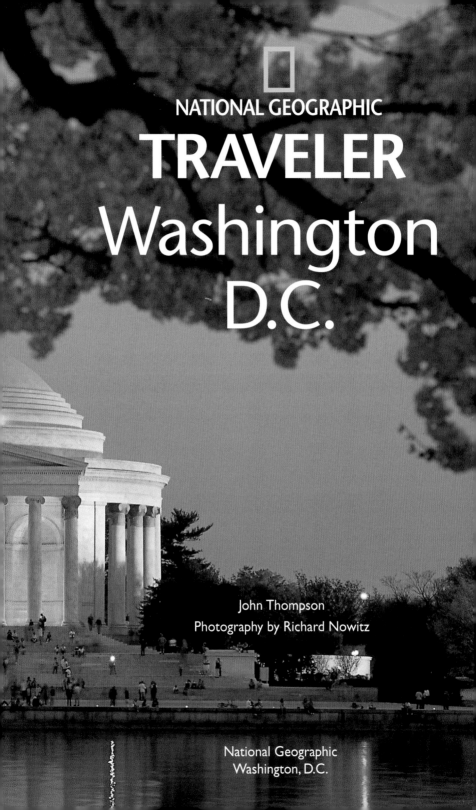

NATIONAL GEOGRAPHIC

TRAVELER
Washington D.C.

John Thompson
Photography by Richard Nowitz

National Geographic
Washington, D.C.

Contents

How to use this guide 6–7 About the author & photographer 8
The areas 49–232 Travelwise 233–264
Index 265–269 Credits 270–271

**Page 1: Snapshot of the
Washington Monument
and the Reflecting Pool
Pages 2–3: The Jefferson
Memorial and cherry
blossoms draw crowds
on a spring evening.
Left: Colorful kayaks await
their turn on the water
beneath Key Bridge.**

How to use this guide

See back flap for keys to text and map symbols.

The *National Geographic Traveler* brings you the best of Washington, D.C., in text, pictures, and maps. Divided into three main sections, the guide begins with an overview of history and culture.

Following are ten area chapters with featured sites selected by the author for their particular interest. Each chapter opens with its own contents list for easy reference. A map introduces the parameters covered in the chapter, highlighting the featured sites and locating other places of interest. Walks, plotted on their own maps, suggest routes for discovering the most about an area.

Features and sidebars offer intriguing detail on history, culture, or contemporary life.

The final section, Travelwise, lists essential information for the traveler—pre-trip planning, special events, getting around, practical advice, and emergency contacts—plus provides a selection of hotels and restaurants arranged by area, shops, activities, and entertainment possibilities.

To the best of our knowledge, all information is accurate as of July 2004. However, it is always advisable to call ahead or check information online when possible to find out about any changes.

Color coding

282

Each area of the city is color coded for easy reference. Find the area you want on the map on the front flap, and look for the color flash at the top of the pages of the relevant chapter. Information in **Travelwise** is also color coded to each region.

Corcoran Gallery of Art

www.corcoran.org

🅰 Map p. 106

✉ 500 17th St., N.W., between E St. & New York Ave.

☎ 202-639-1700

🕐 Closed Tues.

💲 $ Wed., Fri., Sat., Sun.; free Mon. (all day) & Thurs. after 5 p.m.

🚇 Metro: Farragut West; Bus: 80

Visitor information

Practical information for most sites is given in the side column (see key to symbols on back flap). The map reference gives the page number of the map and grid reference. Other details are address, telephone number, days closed, entrance charge in a range from $ (under $5) to $$$$$ (over $25), and nearest Metro station and most important bus routes for sites in Washington. Other sites have information in italics and parentheses in the text.

TRAVELWISE

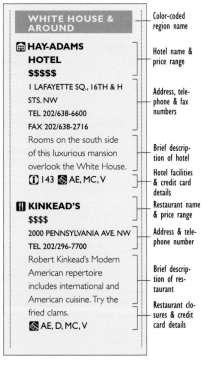

WHITE HOUSE & AROUND — Color-coded region name

🏨 **HAY-ADAMS HOTEL** — Hotel name & price range
$$$$$

I LAFAYETTE SQ., 16TH & H STS. NW — Address, telephone & fax numbers
TEL 202/638-6600
FAX 202/638-2716

Rooms on the south side of this luxurious mansion overlook the White House. — Brief description of hotel

🛏 143 💳 AE, MC, V — Hotel facilities & credit card details

🍴 **KINKEAD'S** — Restaurant name & price range
$$$$

2000 PENNSYLVANIA AVE. NW — Address & telephone number
TEL 202/296-7700

Robert Kinkead's Modern American repertoire includes international and American cuisine. Try the fried clams. — Brief description of restaurant

💳 AE, D, MC, V — Restaurant closures & credit card details

Hotel & restaurant prices

An explanation of the price bands used in entries is given in the Hotels & Restaurants section (beginning on p. 240).

AREA MAPS

- A locator map accompanies each area map and shows the location of that area in the city.

WALKING TOURS

- An information box gives the starting and ending points, time and length of walk, and places not to be missed along the route.

REGIONAL/EXCURSION MAPS

- Cities and sites described in the Across the Potomac and Excursions chapters (p. 201 & p. 215) are bolded and highlighted in yellow on the map. Other suggested places to visit are also bolded and are shown with a red diamond symbol.

NATIONAL GEOGRAPHIC
TRAVELER
Washington D.C.

About the author & photographer

John Thompson has written or contributed to more than a dozen National Geographic books. His latest Society publications include *Wildlands of the Upper South* and *America's Western Edge*. A former resident of Washington, D.C., he now lives in Charlottesville, Virginia.

Richard Nowitz was a contract photographer for National Geographic *WORLD* (now *Kids*) magazine for 10 years and is now a contributing photographer to the National Geographic Image Collection. He has been the principal photographer of more than 20 large-format photo and travel guides; in 1968 he was honored by the Society of American Travel Writers as Travel Photographer of the Year. He lives in Maryland with his wife and three children.

Diana Parsells updated the 2005 edition.

With contributions by:
David Montgomery, a reporter with the *Washington Post* Style section, wrote "Washington today" on pp. 10–17.
Thomas Head, *Washingtonian* magazine's Executive Wine and Food Editor, wrote the Travelwise section.
Sean Groom, "City on the river" feature on pp. 32–33
Mark Rogers, "Politics at work" feature on pp. 58–59
James Yenckel, "Famous denizens of Georgetown" feature on pp. 158–159

History & culture

The gold-leaf eagle has landed—atop Union Station.

Washington today

A HEADY SELF-CONFIDENCE IS SWELLING IN WASHINGTON, D.C., AS THE CITY demonstrates it is a city, not some unclassifiable zone dubbed the District of Columbia—a phrase that appears in speeches but never in conversation.

To natives and long-time transplants, home is just Dee-Cee, thank you, or Wahr-shington in soft Southern-accented tones slightly edged by the oddly Elizabethan flint of dialects around the Chesapeake Bay. Washington never forgets that the government is the reason this once marshy lowland was reclaimed and the federal city was planted at a twinkling bend in the Potomac River. Yet the city defiantly transcends its role as a bland backdrop to the grandeur of the monuments, museums, and great American history hereabouts. Those things are why many people come—but not why they stay.

The map looks as if something took a ragged bite out of the once perfect 100-square-mile diamond-shaped District. That happened in 1846, when Virginia reclaimed its share of the land donated to create the capital. The remaining 68 square miles, originally part of Maryland, make an intimate city of 572,000 people.

The other physical dimension of the intimate city is up, and in Washington ambition soars higher than architecture. No building stands taller than the Capitol dome; in the densest part of town—the K Street canyon populated by lawyers and lobbyists—offices top out at the 12th floor. This architectural homage to the Capitol means the typical Washington street has one of the biggest skies in urban America. It makes walking a pleasure in a city designed with walkers in mind, with wide avenues and breathtaking sight-lines anchored by Pierre Charles L'Enfant's ceremonial circles. Turn a corner and you might see the upper quarter of the Washington Monument peeking above the modest roofline of a modern office building—a juxtaposition of the monumental capital and the working city that is quintessentially Washington.

The dual nature of the city's soul is reflected in myriad ways as power Washington and workaday Washington mingle serendipitously. Spend time shopping on Connecticut Avenue, lunching on Wisconsin, or talking politics on Pennsylvania, and you'll be startled to see motorcycle police appear out of nowhere and block traffic. Next you'll hear the sirens and see the speeding motorcade: The President on his way to some engagement. Look through the limo's tinted glass and you might catch a wave in return. Then the police vanish—maestros of that Washington ballet, the rolling blockade.

Washingtonians always know when someone important has moved down the block. Suddenly fit-looking men and women in plain clothes wearing earpieces linger about. Several years ago, Capitol Hill residents reported that the U.S. attorney general, John Ashcroft, was an excellent piano player, after they heard his baby-grand renditions of show tunes and classical melodies floating out the windows of his row house. In Glover Park, trying to guess which neighbor's house conceals the entrance to a secret FBI tunnel under the old Soviet Embassy has been a favorite parlor game.

Not that the privilege of being the nation's capital isn't sometimes a burden. When that happens, Washington, ever the gracious Southern hostess, can also play the irreverent Northern wag. The lack of a vote in Congress is a sore point. Washingtonians pay 2.5 billion dollars a year in federal income taxes—more per capita than in 49 of the states—yet have no say in how the money is spent. The Constitution dictates that the District cannot be a state, but Congress could grant it a vote in the federal legislature. In 2000, the city's 200th anniversary as the capital, a resident came up with a new license plate motto, a cheeky civics lesson: "Taxation Without Representation."

As Washington strides into the future, its aspirations rise in glass and limestone amid the marble totems of its past. Construction cranes hover throughout the downtown like a new kind of Washington monument while layers of

A rosy dawn catches a mirror image of the U.S. Capitol and an equestrian statue of Ulysses S. Grant in the waters of the Capitol Reflecting Pool.

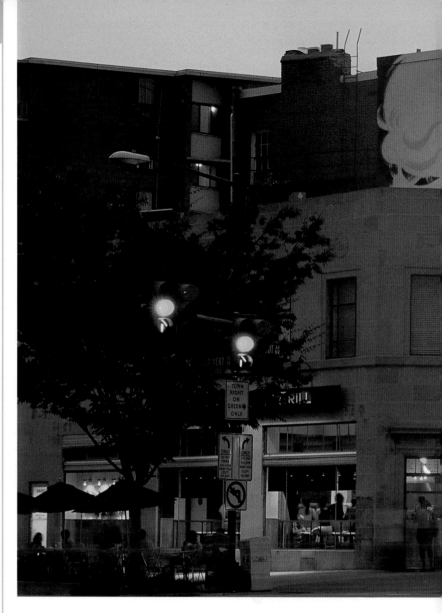

scaffolding signal exciting new uses of old spaces: a buzzing Seventh Street corridor, luxury hotel rooms inside the 19th-century Tariff Building, and welcome makeovers of august institutions such as the National Portrait Gallery and the National Archives.

Preservation guidelines are intended to ensure that development travesties don't mar the best of the old, but there's always a fear that shiny new facades and high rents will doom quirky neighborhood joints. A buttoned-down town like Washington needs as many of these places as it can get. People take infinite comfort that Ben's Chili Bowl on U Street continues to purvey the best chili dogs in the free world. All around Ben's, the street once known as the "Black Broadway," where Duke Ellington used to perform, is throbbing again with energy beneath the soulful gaze of Ellington himself—painted larger

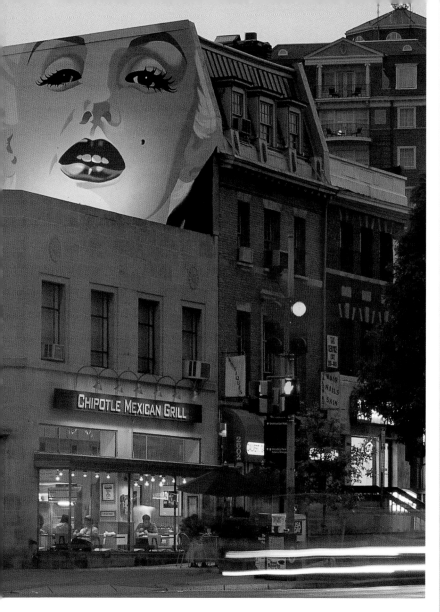

than life on the exposed side of a building.

Postcard Washington is a vision of famous buildings, but the people make the city. Contrary to reputation, this is not a population of transients, a capital of people from someplace else getting ready to leave. When a presidential administration changes, or a new Congress is seated, only a few thousand people arrive to replace the few thousand on their way out.

Most Washingtonians don't work for the

Marilyn Monroe is a regular on the busy corner of Calvert Street and Connecticut Avenue, popular for its ethnic restaurants.

government. Many settled here for opportunities in technology, education, public policy, international affairs, and journalism. A large core of native Washingtonians, particularly African American families, moved here from the South generations ago when jobs in the federal government afforded one of the few avenues of advancement for blacks. Now about 60 percent of the population is black, 31 percent white. The growing Hispanic community is about 8 percent.

In the late 1990s Washingtonians began hearing real estate agents use an unaccustomed term for the city: "Hot!" Suburban traffic congestion, falling crime, and an improving economy merged to make city living fashionable

again. Decades of population loss subsided, replaced by slight annual gains. The newcomers are busy restoring row houses in once-neglected neighborhoods and discarding at least one of their two cars for sensible shoes and the clean comfort of the Metro.

Even longtime Washingtonians can afford to be choosy about how they savor monumental Washington. They stand at the top of the Capitol steps and try again to absorb the perfect landscape geometry lesson that is the Mall. They visit their favorite Smithsonian exhibits religiously. They wait to see the Washington Monument at sundown, when the marble turns rose and gold. The Franklin Delano Roosevelt Memorial is popular for late-evening romantic interludes amid the mood-lit waterfalls.

But Washingtonians would just as soon leave the Mall and zip up to the National Arboretum in Northeast to study the exquisite bonsai tree

Downtown sidewalks such as this one on 17th Street fill with folks on lunchtime errands or simply taking a break from work.

exhibition. Or take the kids on an excursion to the remains of the Civil War forts that once ringed the city. Or catch a home baseball game, as the national pastime returned to the capital in 2005 after a 34-year hiatus. Or disappear into the wilds of Rock Creek Park, where you can forget you are in a city. It is places like these—beyond the Mall—where the heart of the living city beats in four quadrants. The perfect coda to seeing the Lincoln Memorial is a visit to the Frederick Douglass house in Anacostia. During the Potomac springtime, when the perfume of Southern blooms intoxicates even the most hopeless workaholic, by all means see the cherry blossoms suspended like pink breath around the Tidal Basin—but also don't miss the less

crowded and still spectacular blossom display at Dumbarton Oaks in Georgetown.

Spanish will get you as far as English in Adams Morgan, where club music blares until 2 a.m. and the cuisine runs from El Salvador to Afghanistan to Ethiopia to Lebanon and back again. Hop a Metro to the southwest waterfront and find the latest Pulitzer Prize-winning play being presented at Arena Stage or the freshest catch from the Chesapeake being sold on the Maine Avenue docks.

In the neighborhoods Washington comes most clearly into perspective. Climb the hill in Anacostia that John Wilkes Booth crossed when escaping after he assassinated Abraham Lincoln, and take in the view from the parking lot of Our Lady of Perpetual Help Church. Or find a perch on the Brookland heights occupied by the Basilica of the National Shrine of the Immaculate Conception. The bitten-off

Weekly jam sessions add a beat to beautifully landscaped Meridian Park.

diamond city spreads before you—the low downtown skyline slipping into rings of row house neighborhoods stretched along the long lines of L'Enfant's broad boulevards.

And there, too, are the white dome and the obelisk—still grand at this distance, but not so dominating, and part of a larger picture. ∎

History of Washington

GEORGE WASHINGTON, PIERRE CHARLES L'ENFANT, AND THE MANY OTHERS involved knew they were engaged in something momentous when they set out to design the capital of the United States. In an age when preplanned cities of this scale were unheard of, here was a chance to lay out a worldwide center of culture, commerce, and learning. Somewhat like the Constitution, the resulting city design was the product of a lively give-and-take among some of 18th-century America's greatest minds. Awkward and unattractive at first, the city has matured into a metropolis of unfinished grace and beauty—a reflection of the imperfect and ever evolving democracy it governs.

DOING IT ON PURPOSE

Seven years had passed since the Revolutionary War when, in July 1790, Congress agreed on the location of a new capital. Until that time, citizens of the new nation had identified primarily with their home state, thinking of themselves as Virginians or New Yorkers rather than Americans. Local ties would continue to command the loyalties of many, but it was clear that establishing the seat of a central government was essential to holding the loosely joined republic together.

One key was to avoid the mistakes of the European empires that had failed the very people who were here now. This was to be a government of the people, so the placement and design of the capital would set the tone for a federal government that aspired to be strong but not domineering. The capital, by extension, must be grand yet welcoming.

The first step in that tall order was to pick an appropriate place. With the 13 Colonies strewn the length of the eastern seaboard, it was logical to locate the capital about halfway down. In a classic display of democratic compromise, Secretary of the Treasury Alexander Hamilton agreed to urge northern states to vote for a southern capital if Virginia Representative James Madison would support federal assumption of state war debts (he did). So despite occupying the approximate midpoint of the coast, Washington was deemed a "Southern" town from the outset. This characterization had much to do with the fact that Washington lay (and lies) 60 miles south of the Mason-Dixon Line—the Maryland-Pennsylvania border that also divides the North from the South.

As for the precise size and site of the city, Congress left President Washington somewhat in the dark. The representatives decreed only that the capital was not to exceed 10 miles square, and that it must be positioned on the Potomac River somewhere between the mouth of the Eastern Branch (now the Anacostia River) and Conococheague Creek, some 70 miles upriver. The rest was up to Washington.

In January of 1791, Washington selected a swatch of land at the highest navigable point on the Potomac River, where it was joined by the Eastern Branch. The site was partly a marriage of convenience: The preexisting riverport towns of Alexandria, Virginia, and Georgetown, Maryland, could easily receive shipments of the lumber and foodstuffs the city would need to sustain construction.

Laid out in a square carved from Maryland (mostly) and Virginia, the capital was named "City of Washington" to honor America's first President. Surveyor Andrew Ellicott and Benjamin Banneker—his self-taught, freeborn black assistant—delimited a square 10 miles on a side, with the corners pointing in the cardinal directions.

Though President Washington had trained as a surveyor, like any good leader he was quick to recognize those moments when he needed expert advice. For his chief engineer he chose a well-connected young Frenchman who had fought against the British during the Revolutionary War and had gone on to design a temporary headquarters for the federal government in New York. The idea of creating an important city out of nothing appealed mightily to the brilliant Pierre Charles L'Enfant—and apparently daunted him not at all.

Charles Willson Peale's "George Washington" (1772) portrays the future president as a young colonel in a Virginia regiment.

Angling for the job, he wrote these words to President Washington in 1789: "No nation, perhaps, had ever before the opportunity offered them of deliberately deciding on the spot where their Capital City should be fixed."

L'Enfant got the job.

Throughout 1791, he could be seen standing high atop Jenkins Hill (now Capitol Hill) or striding the woods of Tiber Creek (modern-day Constitution Avenue), his surveying instruments in hand, measuring distances and elevations. By contrast, L'Enfant's motivation —a vision of a grand city of broad avenues, monumental government edifices, and stirring vistas—remained invisible to all but himself. "I see the capital city as something more than a place to live and work," he wrote. "I see it as a symbol…. [W]e should plan now with the realization that a great nation is going to rise on this continent…. Right now, we have a chance which no nation has ever given itself…. How can America plan for less than greatness?"

L'ENFANT TERRIBLE

L'Enfant's extraordinary prescience and pride were voiced at a time when the country's most populous city, Philadelphia, claimed only 28,522 residents. Yet here was L'Enfant, imagining a capital of 800,000 citizens— larger than many of the European cities such as Paris that had served as his models.

As it turned out, L'Enfant was dead on: At its population peak in 1950, Washington was home to 802,000 people. (That number is now about 570,000.)

Standing a mile apart but joined by Pennsylvania Avenue, the Capitol building and the President's House formed a barbell at the core of L'Enfant's design. (The presidential residence would not be officially named the White House until 1901.) Several broad streets would radiate from these two powerhouses, signifying their openness and accessibility. The avenues would unspool at length before ending at circular intersections atop existing hills, thus creating views of "magnificent distances."

The Capitol would divide the city into quadrants, while a grid of numbered and lettered streets would be superimposed on the radiating avenues. The Mall, extending about 1 mile west from the Capitol to the Potomac River, would be a grand esplanade similar to

the one L'Enfant had beheld in Marly, near Versailles. The Frenchman foresaw fine baroque houses lining it on either side.

Within a year, L'Enfant had been fired by President Washington for insubordination and refusal to compromise. Even so, his plan was largely enacted: Trees and buildings may veil several of those hoped-for views of "magnificent distances," yet Dupont and Scott Circles, among others, still clearly display the beauty of the original design.

Despite its ambitious origin, the city hardly sprang up overnight. Congressmen arriving for the Inaugural session in 1800 looked out upon a dismal scene. The streets were muddy. Mosquitoes and snakes bred in abundance. Hogs and cattle roamed at will, while the unfinished Capitol and President's House had spawned attendant clusters of huts and shacks resembling refugee villages. One newly minted statesman dubbed this hardship post "a mud-hole equal to the great Serbonian bog."

With no property tax on government buildings, the city relied on real estate speculation for funding. Yet buyers were scarce: By 1800, less than 10 percent of city lots had been sold. Washington grew from 8,208 people by 1810 to 18,826 by 1830, a rate far below the national average. Gazing upon these wide, uncluttered avenues going nowhere, Charles Dickens would dub Washington "the City of Magnificent Intentions."

WAR COMES TO WASHINGTON

The War of 1812 proved to be a turning point in the city's fortunes, which mirrored those of the country at large. In August 1814, with the British victory sealed, redcoats landed in Maryland and marched on Washington, where they torched the Capitol, the President's House, and all federal buildings except the old Blodgett's Hotel, which housed both the Post Office and the Patent Office at the time.

Afterward, Congress came close to voting that the capital be relocated. But with local bankers promising to help rebuild the city—and galvanized by the strong sense of community that often follows a disaster—Washington

Two years into the War of 1812, British soldiers gut the White House with fire in this undated Washington drawing.

"The Peacemakers" (1868) by George P. A. Healy depicts William Sherman, Ulysses S. Grant, President Lincoln, and David Porter dicussing peace terms just before the Civil War's end.

dug in and bounced back. President Madison repaired to the Octagon (see p. 122), Congress moved to the Patent Office (and from there to a temporary building on the site of the present-day Supreme Court), and life went on.

The third of the District lying west and south of the river was ceded back to Virginia in 1846. Not only did the federal government have no need for the land on that side of the Potomac River, but Alexandria—having lost political advantages by its inclusion in the District—had petitioned the state to re-embrace it. This reduced Washington City to a parcel of land covering just 68 square miles.

A SECOND CITY

History's most bitter irony may be that this bastion of freedom was built on slave labor. Beginning in the 1790s, plantation owners in Maryland and Virginia were paid for the use of their slaves to supplement the meager supply of skilled workers constructing the capital.

In a parallel development, this city of solons became a magnet for the disenfranchised. Situated at the northern extreme of the upper South, Washington was a natural gateway for runaway slaves. Though slavery would not be

outlawed in the city until 1862, by 1830 Washington contained more free blacks than slaves. A "second city"—one composed largely of African Americans—sprang to life within the federal city.

Lacking an entrenched society but rich with a transient mix of foreigners and congressmen, Washington was generally more tolerant of blacks than were other Southern cities. From 1807 to 1861, more than 15 private black schools flourished in the district.

Occasionally, however, race riots erupted. On the heels of the Nat Turner rebellion in 1831, the Snow Riot of 1835 was ignited by two unrelated events: A slave allegedly tried to murder the widow of the U.S. Capitol designer, William Thornton, and a white physician was arrested for possession of abolitionist tracts, whose publication or distribution was forbidden in D.C.

Rebuffed from lynching the doctor, a white mob turned its fury on Mr. Beverly Snow, the free black owner of a local restaurant. Though Snow escaped, roving bands attacked black churches, schools, restaurants, and tenements for the next week. Before long the city had tightened its black codes—discriminatory

Federal troops parade from the Capitol to the President's House to commemorate the end of the Civil War in April 1865.

laws governing the behavior of free blacks.

In the 1830s and '40s, Congress heard numerous petitions to banish slavery in Washington—the only place over which it exercised total control. Each time, shamefully, Georgetown's Southern-leaning aristocracy joined with the proslavery segment of Congress to keep the issue from being seriously debated.

In April 1848, 77 Washington slaves boarded the schooner *Pearl* at a city wharf and tried to escape to freedom down the Potomac River. Captured within a day, the slaves—many of them privileged house servants with only a few years' bondage remaining—were sold off to agents in Louisiana and Georgia. The deep passions stirred by the affair led the House of Representatives to pass a resolution that year calling for an end to the slave trade in Washington.

The resolution was nothing but paper. Slavery itself continued. Free blacks were only marginally better off. Black or white, poor neighborhoods were plagued by violent crime. The seedier areas of town included Swampoodle (now the area north of Massachusetts and New Jersey Avenues) and Murder Bay (today's Federal Triangle). The latter—located between President's Park (the Ellipse) and the fetid Washington City Canal (since covered by Constitution Avenue)—was especially notorious. "Crime, filth, and poverty seem to vie with each other in a career of degradation and death," a police superintendent characterized Murder Bay in 1866. "Whole families…are crowded into mere apologies for shanties."

BROTHER AGAINST BROTHER

Monumental Washington started to take shape in the years leading up to the Civil War. Work began on the Washington Monument in 1848, but within six years funds had dried up, the monument was mired in political controversy, and construction was suspended with the building just 152 feet tall. By the time work resumed in 1880, white marble from the original quarry was no longer available; the white marble furnished by the second quarry has weathered differently from the base, yielding the two-tone tower in evidence today.

In 1855 the distinctive red-sandstone Smithsonian Castle rose beside the Mall, paving the way for several national museums. A forerunner to the National Theatre was in place on Pennsylvania Avenue by 1835. The

Willard and other fine hotels popped up in the neighborhood by the 1850s. Amid the statuary and posh town houses of Lafayette Square, the White House had settled into a state of manorial dignity, complete with greenhouses, flower gardens, and fruit trees.

Destined to tower above it all, the Capitol's cast-iron dome (replacing its wood dome of 1822) was under way by the Civil War's outbreak in April 1861. Despite an absence of building funds during that conflict, Lincoln ordered the Capitol's construction to go forward as a sign that the Union would endure.

Considered a remote and somewhat sleepy town before the war, Washington now entered the national consciousness as the staging ground for Union forces and the embattled capital of a divided nation. With the Confederate capital of Richmond just 100 miles distant, the war's major battles—Fredericksburg, Antietam, Gettysburg—formed an arc within easy striking distance of Washington. The first and second battles of Bull Run, for example, took place just 30 miles west of city limits.

To keep the Rebels at bay should they outflank the Union Army, a ring of 68 forts was hastily thrown up around Washington. These installations proved their worth in July 1864, when a large Confederate force led by Gen. Jubal Early dashed through Maryland and reached the city's northern portal of Fort Stevens. Early's assault was repulsed within a day, but it gave the President a vivid taste of combat: Observing the skirmish from the fort's parapet, the 6-foot-4-inch top-hatted Lincoln made such a tempting target for enemy sharpshooters that a Union officer reprimanded him, "Get down, you damn fool, before you get shot!" The words were out of his mouth before the speaker—Lt. Col. (and future Supreme Court justice) Oliver Wendell Holmes, Jr.—realized he was upbraiding the President.

Washington was eventually overwhelmed—by its own troops. Bone-weary soldiers arrived by ship and rail, thronging the streets, falling asleep on vacant lots and sidewalks.

A time-lapse photograph of Dupont Circle on a winter's night (below) shows that L'Enfant's vision of central circles and radiating streets (opposite) is alive and well.

Horse-drawn guns and caissons rutted the muddy streets; livestock grazed on the Mall; a bakery and barracks opened in the Capitol.

With more than 4,000 prostitutes in residence, a newspaper reported, the "majority of the women on the streets were openly disreputable." Troops under Gen. Joseph Hooker were such constant patrons of the red-light district southeast of the Treasury Department that the area was dubbed "Hooker's Division."

As battle casualties poured into Washington, the city scrambled to treat as many as 50,000 sick or injured soldiers at once. Practically every church, public building, and large private home in the city was pressed into service as military housing.

HAPPY DAYS AGAIN

The population explosion unleashed by the war—during which the city grew from 60,000 to 140,000 inhabitants, including 40,000 former slaves—continued to boom in peacetime. Freedmen's Village in Arlington and Barry Farm in Anacostia received federal aid to

Politics as unusual

If it is true that all politics is local, Washington seems more than happy to oblige. Native Washingtonians, fueled by the injustice of being deprived of full congressional representation, often focus on the local political scene to the point of obsession.

Except for a brief flowering of self-governance from 1812 to 1871, Congress and the President have always controlled the city government and appointed its officials. In 1970, Washington was finally allowed to send a delegate to the House of Representatives, yet that deputy (in common with emissaries from Puerto Rico and other U.S. territories) could not vote, except in committees.

In 1973 Civil Rights and home rule activists won Washington the right to elect its own mayor and city council. Unwilling to cede power completely, Congress retained the right to interfere in local government whenever it deemed necessary.

That's exactly what happened in April 1995: With district finances in a shambles, Congress created a presidentially appointed D.C. financial control board to manage city spending. Two years later, Congress stripped Mayor Marion Barry of most of his authority—a move Barry lambasted as a "rape" of democracy—and the control board took over the city reins.

After the 1998 election of Mayor Anthony Williams, who previously served as the city's chief financial officer, the overall health of the city improved dramatically and the control board eventually released its grip. ∎

Washington had elected its own mayors and aldermen since 1820. With the city in debt and apprehensive about the power of the newly granted black vote, Congress scrapped that system in 1871 and replaced it with a territorial government headed by a presidentially appointed governor. Other parts of the new city government included boards of public works and health; a nonvoting delegate to Congress; an elected house of delegates; and a president-appointed council, with Frederick Douglass one of three blacks among its 11 members.

President Ulysses S. Grant wanted to hand the governorship of this newborn political entity to his crony Alexander R. "Boss" Shepherd. He backed down when the city's conservative old guard protested his choice, but Shepherd wormed his way into power nonetheless: He was named vice president of public works, a post that allowed him to run the entire city.

"How is our new governor like a sheep?" went a riddle of the time.

"He is led by A. Shepherd" was the answer.

By hook but mostly by crook, Boss Shepherd led the way for the next three years. During his reign the city added miles of sewers, water lines, gas lines, sidewalks, and roads, as well as 60,000 trees and more than 1,000 houses and buildings. Most important, Shepherd saw to it that miles upon miles of streets were leveled and paved. Working people adored him for the jobs and civic improvements; blue bloods despised him for raising their taxes.

As it turned out, citizens were amply justified in feeling fleeced. Authorized to spend four million dollars on the city, Shepherd approved the expenditure of 20 million instead. This put the city in hock but landed Shepherd in a mansion on Farragut Square, two blocks from the White House.

Armed with Grant's tacit approval, Shepherd bullied the city into submission. When the Baltimore & Ohio Railroad delayed removing its tracks from the Capitol grounds, Shepherd loyalists materialized at midnight to rip up the offending ties and rails. He invited critics of such tactics to "git up and git."

Shepherd's undoing was the financial panic of 1873. The next year, Congress dissolved the territorial government and installed three presidentially appointed commissioners. The

house northward-migrating blacks.

With the help of radical Republicans bent on Reconstruction, black Washington enjoyed a sudden (if short-lived) heyday in the late 1860s and early 1870s. Howard University and the nation's first black high school—both staffed by top-notch instructors turning out well-educated graduates—were founded during this period. At the same time, blacks moved into jobs as officials and clerks, launched newspapers and other businesses, and mingled in white society.

Servicemen and friends form a conga line in front of the Red Cross Building on 17th Street to celebrate the end of World War II.

Organic Act of 1878 abolished home rule for good, giving the three commissioners "near-absolute power." It also set up the system, still in place today, whereby the district receives an annual operating subsidy from the federal government, compensating the district for the costs that the federal presence places on the city. (In 1997, however, that federal payment was suspended; in return, D.C. got tax breaks and a guarantee that the federal government would cover the district's substantial pension shortfall.)

INTO THE 20TH CENTURY

In Washington as in many other American cities, the final quarter of the 19th century was a fin-de-siècle free-for-all. Hotels, public buildings, and arriviste villas mushroomed along the city's main avenues. Though industry was confined to a handful of gristmills and breweries in Georgetown and Foggy Bottom, Washington's main employer—the federal government—provided thousands of jobs. In addition to the clerks needed to run the many newly born government agencies, construction workers were in demand to complete the long-delayed Washington Monument (1884),

to construct the Library of Congress (1897), and to erect many other buildings that are city landmarks today. The National Zoological Park (1889) and Rock Creek Park (1890) were also created around this time, putting the pleasures of nature within easy reach of downtown museums and monuments.

Even as official Washington flourished, the city was nurturing seeds of discontent. Thousands of poor people had gravitated to the capital, lured by the simple notion that the President's adoptive home town would welcome them as well. Rarely was that the case. Washington's alleys, home to more than 17,000 residents, were notorious incubators of filth, crime, and disease. Most of these alleys would ultimately be torn down or gentrified, driving the poor underclass from one neighborhood to another.

To help the growing city realize the beauty envisioned by L'Enfant, in 1901 Senator James McMillan proposed a commission that would upgrade the Mall, expand the White House and the park system, and place judicial and congressional office buildings facing the Capitol. McMillan recruited four brilliant designers—architects Charles McKim and

Daniel Burnham, landscape architect Frederick Law Olmsted, and sculptor Augustus Saint-Gaudens—whose plans, drawn up free of charge, would be transformed into reality by the U.S. Army Corps of Engineers.

With Burnham leading the way, the city beautiful began to take shape. Railroad tracks crisscrossing the Mall were torn out. The Mall was extended to stretch all the way from the Capitol to the site of a planned memorial to Abraham Lincoln at its far west end. Gardens, fountains, and a reflecting pool were slated for the Mall as well. An opulent Union Station, designed by Burnham himself, rose north of the Capitol.

Not every aspect of the plan was enacted, yet it furnished a blueprint for future growth of the city core. It's fair to say that the McMillan Plan made possible the Mall's current status as a national showpiece.

STRUGGLES FOR FREEDOM

During the 1910s, the city's population swelled again as workers flooded in to support America's role in World War I. By decade's end, nearly 450,000 people called Washington home—a 32 percent increase since 1910. The Mall, which had begun to feel like a park, became a vast parking lot for hundreds of new automobiles that suddenly appeared in Washington.

With the proliferation of relief agencies during the Great Depression and President Franklin D. Roosevelt's New Deal, the number of workers on Washington's federal payroll rose from 70,261 in June 1933 to 108,673 in June 1935. Construction added many new facades to the cityscape: the Supreme Court building, the Federal Triangle buildings, the Library of Congress Annex (now called the John Adams Building), the Longworth House Office Building, and nearly 5,000 houses, apartment buildings, and office buildings.

As the city focused on winning World War II, the early 1940s brought yet another influx of new Washingtonians. Thousands of female office workers and servicemen descended on the city, and many of them stayed on after the war. By 1950, the district's population would peak at just over 800,000.

Once again, the Mall became a warehouse for the nation's needs. A beehive of "tempos"—temporary government office buildings

made of cement and asbestos board—were built along both sides of the Mall, adding to those thrown up during World War I.

By war's end in 1945, Washington found itself the capital of the most powerful nation on Earth. It had evolved from a provincial Southern town to a world leader in little more than half a century. The city seemed to be flexing its new muscles, spearheading a Cold War against communism worldwide.

On a local level, however, the story of Washington was increasingly a tale of two cities. More and more, white and black Washingtonians led separate lives in separate parts

Dr. Martin Luther King, Jr., salutes a crowd of Civil Rights activists during the August 23, 1968, March on Washington.

of town. Throughout the 1940s, D.C.'s schools, parks, playgrounds, restaurants, theaters, and water fountains remained as segregated as those in any Southern town.

Then, in 1954, came the U.S. Supreme Court ruling, in *Brown v. Board of Education,* that "separate but equal education facilities are inherently unequal." The ensuing rapid integration of D.C. public schools served as a model for the nation.

In the late 1950s, blacks outnumbered whites for the first time in Washington's history. The far reaches of the city's Northeast and Southeast quadrants had drawn a raft of new residents ever since World War II, most of them from rural backgrounds. Now, with whites leaving the severely overcrowded city for new housing in the suburbs, middle-class blacks moved en masse into such upper Northeast neighborhoods as Fort Totten and Brookland. From 1950 to 1975, the city's black population rose from 35 percent to more than 70.

With the appointment of Walter Washington as mayor-commissioner in 1967, black

Washington gained a degree of control over its affairs for the first time since the dissolution of the territorial government nearly 100 years earlier. Congress, however, retained final say over city governance—and it continues to wield that power today. This has created a troubling and inequitable political quirk: Washingtonians are the only modern Americans who suffer "taxation without representation," as some city vehicle licenses protest. D.C. voters can elect only nonvoting delegates (as opposed to representatives) to Congress, yet that body holds veto power over Washington's laws and budgets—a bone of lingering local contention and resentment.

THE PEOPLE'S PARADE GROUND

The Mall—the country's unofficial forum—has long been a rallying point for social causes. The women's suffrage movement, for example, demonstrated here in the 1910s; two decades later, thousands of Bonus Marchers descended on the Capitol to demand veterans' benefits, only to be run off by Gen. Douglas MacArthur's cavalry.

On August 28, 1963, more than 200,000 people marched on Washington to demand jobs and freedom for blacks. The event culminated in the rousing "I Have a Dream" speech delivered by Dr. Martin Luther King, Jr., on the steps of the Lincoln Memorial. Television cameras caught the historic moment on film, projecting it into living rooms and minds across the nation.

This encouraging progress was brought to a tragic end in April of 1968, when Dr. King fell to an assassin's bullet on a motel balcony in Memphis, Tennessee. Around the country, grief erupted in spasms of violence. In Washington, rioting, burning, and looting broke out near the intersection of 14th and U Streets and spread outward from there. Eventually the conflagration gutted 57 blocks in the heart of the city, crippling the once-thriving retail district downtown. Twelve people died and several hundred were injured amid the chaos.

It took 4,000 U.S. Army and National Guard troops three days to restore the peace. The scars lingered for years. Not until the late 1990s did some areas recover. The U Street corridor, for instance—once the epicenter of Washington nightlife—has been spruced up and now draws visitors from all backgrounds.

A FRESH START

The seeds of the city's rejuvenation had been planted several years before the 1968 riots. In 1961, President John F. Kennedy and his wife, Jackie, initiated improvements to the city core. They applied a mix of historic preservation and urban renewal to Lafayette Square and to the part of Pennsylvania Avenue from the White House to the Capitol. A few years later, the urban landscape received another official facelift from Lady Bird Johnson and her "Beautify America" campaign, which added tulips, daffodils, and flowering trees and shrubs to the banks of Rock Creek and the Potomac River.

1971 was pivotal in the city's growing emphasis on aesthetics. The Mall's tempos (see p. 28) were finally removed to make way for Constitution Gardens—a 50-acre park north of the Reflecting Pool—and the John F. Kennedy Center for the Performing Arts opened on the Potomac River just above the Theodore Roosevelt Memorial Bridge. Inscribed on a wall of the Kennedy Center are the words of arts patron JFK: "This country cannot afford to be materially rich and spiritually poor."

As of 2000, the first of Kennedy's conditions remained elusive: Per capita income for the District of Columbia's 572,000 residents was nearly $40,000, but close to 17 percent were below the poverty line. That number contrasts starkly with statistics for the larger metropolitan area, which reveal that the world's richest country is led by the nation's richest megalopolis.

Poking fun at Washington politics has become a national pastime, yet the city possesses a beauty and grandeur that can win over the most hardened cynic. After Lincoln's assassination in 1865, Congressman James Garfield reportedly assured a mob in New York City: "Fellow citizens! God reigns, and the Government at Washington still lives!" Sixteen years later, Garfield, by then President himself, would be assassinated. But Washington's business went on, as it still does—through wars, deaths, financial crises, and administrations good and bad. As long as we have a United States, we will have a Washington, D.C. ■

A candlelit vigil held at the Lincoln Memorial soon after the Sept. 11, 2001, terrorist strikes in the United States honors those who died.

Washingtonians soak up sunrays at Georgetown's Washington Harbour against a background of Watergate, the Kennedy Center, and Memorial Bridge.

City on the river

Most people don't think of Washington as a riverside city, yet the Potomac is the wildest watercourse running through any major metropolis. To experience this contradiction yourself, explore Washington by water. In the process you'll leave a world of traffic, concrete, and crowds for a realm where turtles bask on logs, an osprey wings low over the water with a fish flashing in its talons, and your only neighbor glides by in a scull.

The Potomac River has been the heart of Washington since Georgetown was founded as a shipping center in 1751. By the 1790s the harbor was exporting more tobacco than any other port in the country. Later, the Chesapeake & Ohio Canal (whose towpath you can still amble) connected Georgetown to villages inland, fueling both their growth and that of the capital city.

With affluence came effluence: The Potomac was declared unfit for bathing as early as 1894, and even touching the bacteria-laden water was deemed unwise as late as 1971. The 1970s brought a concerted, community-wide effort to clean up the river, with the result that today it has been reborn. The fish are back, the birds have returned, and the water bobs with all manner of recreational craft: canoes, kayaks, rowing shells, sailboats, and—alas—jet skis.

Washington's iconic landmarks appear grander and more intimate from the water. You can get especially close-up views of the Lincoln Memorial, Kennedy Center, and Jefferson Memorial. As you glide beneath one of the nine graceful arches of Memorial Bridge, Robert E. Lee's home, Arlington House, looms above Arlington Cemetery on the Virginia shore. Opposite Washington Harbour, heavily wooded, 88-acre Theodore Roosevelt Island makes a delightfully natural destination teeming with geese, snapping turtles, and beaver.

Many visitors take to the river aboard narrated cruises for a monumental view of the city or a leisurely trip to Mount Vernon. Brunch, lunch, dinner, and moonlight cruises are available, but schedules vary daily and seasonally. Options include Capitol River Cruises (301-460-7447); Potomac River Boat Company (703-548-9000); the *Spirit of Washington II* (866-211-3811); and the luxury *Odyssey* (888-822-5991). For a quirky alternative, check out the land/sea tour of D.C. Ducks (202-832-9800), which carries you past the Mall and museums in a DUKW (an amphibious military personnel carrier in World

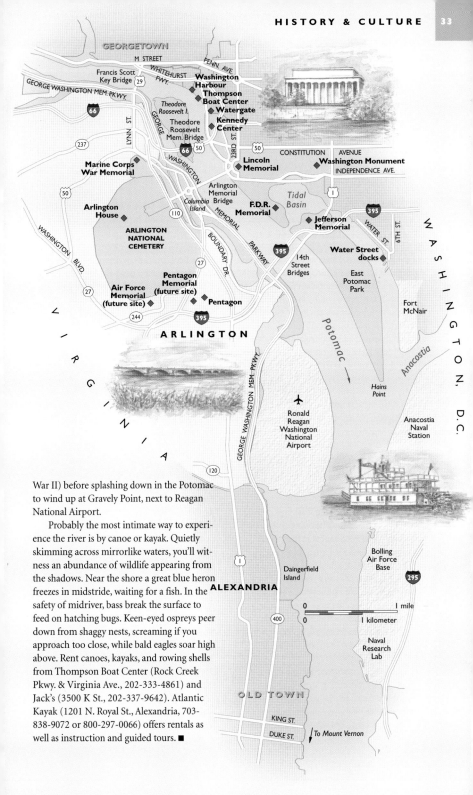

GEORGETOWN

M STREET

PENN. AVE.

Francis Scott Key Bridge 29

WHITEHURST FWY.

Washington Harbour

GEORGE WASHINGTON MEM. PKWY.

Thompson Boat Center

66

Theodore Roosevelt I.

Watergate

LYNN ST.

Theodore Roosevelt Mem. Bridge

Kennedy Center

237

66 50

WASHINGTON

23RD ST.

50

CONSTITUTION AVENUE

Marine Corps War Memorial

Lincoln Memorial

Washington Monument

INDEPENDENCE AVE.

50

Arlington Memorial Bridge

Tidal Basin

I

Arlington House

Columbia Island

F.D.R. Memorial

395

MEMORIAL

WASHINGTON BLVD.

110

ARLINGTON NATIONAL CEMETERY

BOUNDARY DR.

PARKWAY

Jefferson Memorial

WATER ST.

6TH ST.

Water Street docks

27

14th Street Bridges

East Potomac Park

W A S H I N G T O N,   D. C.

Pentagon Memorial (future site)

27

Air Force Memorial (future site)

244

Pentagon

395

Fort McNair

ARLINGTON

Potomac →

Hains Point

Anacostia

Anacostia Naval Station

V I R G I N I A

120

✈

Ronald Reagan Washington National Airport

War II) before splashing down in the Potomac to wind up at Gravely Point, next to Reagan National Airport.

Probably the most intimate way to experience the river is by canoe or kayak. Quietly skimming across mirrorlike waters, you'll witness an abundance of wildlife appearing from the shadows. Near the shore a great blue heron freezes in midstride, waiting for a fish. In the safety of midriver, bass break the surface to feed on hatching bugs. Keen-eyed ospreys peer down from shaggy nests, screaming if you approach too close, while bald eagles soar high above. Rent canoes, kayaks, and rowing shells from Thompson Boat Center (Rock Creek Pkwy. & Virginia Ave., 202-333-4861) and Jack's (3500 K St., 202-337-9642). Atlantic Kayak (1201 N. Royal St., Alexandria, 703-838-9072 or 800-297-0066) offers rentals as well as instruction and guided tours. ∎

I

Daingerfield Island

ALEXANDRIA

400

Bolling Air Force Base

295

0   1 mile

0   1 kilometer

Naval Research Lab

OLD TOWN

KING ST.

DUKE ST.

To Mount Vernon

The arts

WASHINGTON IS A RELATIVELY RECENT ARRIVAL ON THE BIG-LEAGUE ART scene. Despite the city's status as the birthplace of many gifted musicians and actors—among them John Philip Sousa, Duke Ellington, Helen Hayes, and Pearl Bailey—an artistic community of note did not really coalesce here until 1971, when the John F. Kennedy Center for the Performing Arts welcomed the first music and theater patrons to its riverside venue. Since then, Washington has distinguished itself in just about every field of artistic endeavor, making it a leading center of the arts worldwide.

CLASSICAL MUSIC

One of the nation's finest orchestral companies, the National Symphony Orchestra was officially incorporated in 1931. At the opening of the Kennedy Center 40 years later, the NSO premiered Leonard Bernstein's "Mass," a work commissioned for the occasion. The orchestra now has a busy year-round season that includes local performances in the Kennedy Center Concert Hall, tours in this country and abroad, televised Independence Day and Memorial Day concerts on the West Lawn of the U.S. Capitol, and programs for visiting heads of state and other occasions.

Its fifth music director, Leonard Slatkin, has guided the NSO since 1996. "The status of contemporary music is probably in better shape now than it's been in the last 25 years," says Slatkin. "What I think is coming in new compositions is a real infusion of the Americans from other cultures who are here—the Latino Americans, the Asian Americans."

From a regional company struggling to make its name in 1956, the Washington Opera has evolved into a world-class organization playing to sellout audiences in the Opera House at the Kennedy Center. In the early 1980s, the company scheduled 16 performances of four operas every year; it now stages 70 performances of eight operas a year. The Washington Opera has been under the artistic direction of Placido Domingo since 1996.

A commitment to staging new American operas, bringing out lesser known important works, and nurturing young talent keeps this company in the mainstream of the opera world. A 1984 innovation—projecting surtitles above the stage—helped attract a wider audience. The 1980s were also important growth years because of the enthusiastic support of local philanthropist David Lloyd

Kreeger and the inventive direction of Martin Feinstein. Among the outstanding talents that have worked on Washington Opera productions are Gian Carlo Menotti, Franco Zeffirelli, Bruce Beresford, and Werner Herzog. Conductors have included Daniel Barenboim, Rafael Fruhbeck de Burgos, Mstislav Rostropovich, and Max Rudolf.

Washington music lovers can find a concert any night of the week, whether performed by a D.C.-based or visiting group. The Kennedy Center has hosted renowned companies from around the world, including the Berlin Philharmonic Orchestra, the Metropolitan Opera, and La Scala, while the Millennium Stage program brings free daily performances of all sorts of musical genres to the Kennedy Center's Grand Foyer.

Nor is the Kennedy Center the only game in town. Nearby Lisner Auditorium at George Washington University is a comfortable 1,490-seat hall, and other area universities feature classical music by local and guest artists. Downtown churches and museums often schedule musical events: Concerts at the National Gallery of Art, the Corcoran Gallery of Art, the Phillips Collection, and Dumbarton Oaks can be wonderfully intimate occasions. The 670-seat auditorium at the National Academy of Sciences, with its excellent acoustics, occasionally offers free concerts, often of new music. Another small venue, the Folger Shakespeare Library, presents medieval, Renaissance, and baroque music in an Elizabethan setting.

Many music aficionados consider the District of Columbia to be the nation's capital of

A ballerina performs the Washington Ballet's *Carmen* at the Kennedy Center, which presents touring companies and solo artists.

**D.C. native and jazz maestro Duke Elling-
ton gazes from a painting on sale at
Eastern Market.**

choral music. Prominent groups include the
Master Chorale of Washington (formerly the
Paul Hill Chorale) and the Choral Arts Society
of Washington. Both frequently perform in
concert with the National Symphony Orchestra and touring orchestras.

In the summer, the place to go with a picnic and a group of friends is Wolf Trap Farm
Park, off the Dulles Toll Road or Va. 7. You can
sit on the lawn or in the Filene Center—the
open-air auditorium of this delightful park—
and enjoy al fresco programs of the National
Symphony Orchestra, touring opera companies, jazz, rock, or blues.

POPULAR MUSIC
Washington has historically excelled at military band music. The U.S. Marine Band received a great boost in 1868 when a local
13-year-old boy signed up as an apprentice.
His name was John Philip Sousa, and within
12 years he would assume leadership of the

band. Dismayed by the band's outdated and
poorly arranged music, Sousa sent off to Europe for scores by Wagner, Berlioz, and other
modern composers of the day. He also began
writing music of his own. Demanding excellence from others as well as from himself,
Sousa drilled the band into shape. Many
members quit within a year, but those who
stayed became a well-honed and disciplined
unit. In 1892 Sousa formed his own band and
toured the United States and abroad. His tune-
ful lifetime outpouring ultimately included
140 original military marches, among them
"The Washington Post" march (1889) and
"The Stars and Stripes Forever" (1896).

Heart-poundingly patriotic performances
of the illustrious U.S. Marine Band and other
military combos are staged free of charge on
summer evenings at the Sylvan Theater (on
the grounds of the Washington Monument)
and on the East Terrace of the Capitol. Alter-
natively, you might enjoy an evening tattoo at
the Marine Barracks on Capitol Hill.

Another local musician who made good
was jazz legend Edward Kennedy "Duke" Ellington. Born at 1217 22nd Street, N.W., in

1899 and raised in the Shaw neighborhood, Ellington studied classical music with a neighbor who taught music at Dunbar High School. At 24 he headed off to New York City—and thence into the Big Band and Jazz Hall of Fame. Washington jazz has enjoyed a devoted following ever since. When the Howard Theatre opened at 7th and T Streets in 1910, it marqueed such standouts as W. C. Handy, Fletcher Henderson, Bessie Smith, and Count Basie. Duke Ellington and Pearl Bailey were among the local talents who debuted at the Howard. Another star-studded black showcase, the 1922 Lincoln Theater on U Street, N.W., closed for a short while but reopened as a movie theater in the 1970s; renovated in 1994, the 1,250-seat theater today features a mixture of concerts, dance recitals, plays, and movies.

Blues Alley in Georgetown has long worn the crown as the best—sometimes the only—place in town to catch big-name jazz acts. This comfortable den has low ceilings, high cover charges, and a serious and sophisticated clientele. Other reliable spots for hearing live jazz most nights of the week include Georgetown's One Step Down, which promotes local artists, and City Blues Café on Connecticut Avenue.

Various venues host the occasional jazz concert. The most popular acts take the stage at DAR Constitution Hall, the Kennedy Center's Concert Hall, and Wolf Trap; others show up in smaller locales such as the Terrace Theater in the Kennedy Center or Baird Auditorium in the National Museum of Natural History.

If you get a chance to catch local piano virtuoso John Eaton in concert, don't pass it up. One of the country's leading exponents of classic jazz, Eaton played the piano bar circuit for years before graduating to his current trademark lecture-concerts. They are high-order entertainment.

An endless number of options exist for rock and other popular music. These range from headliner concerts at the 20,000-seat MCI Center downtown to eclectic local acts (and some up-and-coming national ones) at popular hangouts such as the 9:30 Club on V Street and the Black Cat on 14th Street. On the east side of Rock Creek Park, Carter Barron Amphitheatre is a fun summer weekend place for watching pop, rock, blues, and jazz.

Acoustic folk and bluegrass have also carved out solid niches in the Washington area; the Birchmere in Alexandria, which nurtured Grammy-winner Mary Chapin Carpenter and bluegrass pioneers The Seldom Scene, is the top choice.

THEATER

Home to more than 78 active theaters as of early 2002, the Washington metro area can boast more playhouses than any city besides New York. Whether the show is a classic drama, a local original, off-Broadway, pre-Broadway, or post-Broadway, the best of standard and contemporary theater captivates Washington audiences on a nightly basis.

Most prominent is the Kennedy Center, with two large theaters: The 1,100-seat Eisenhower Theater is a plush venue for touring productions of dramas and comedies, while the adjacent 2,200-seat Opera House presents elaborate musicals and performances of the Washington Ballet and other dance troupes.

Washington theater does not begin and end at the Kennedy Center, however. A theater has operated continuously on the Pennsylvania Avenue site of the National Theatre, rebuilt in the early 1920s, since 1835. In 1845 fire destroyed the building during a performance of *Beauty and the Beast*—the first of five such conflagrations in the theater's history.

Until 1873, blacks were confined to the balcony; after that, they were not admitted at all. Finally, in 1948, local Civil Rights activists campaigned to desegregate the National. They picketed the facility, and the actors playing at the time in a touring production of *Oklahoma!* voted to honor the picket lines; for the next four years, as a result, the theater staged only movies (it reopened as a live theater in 1952).

John Wilkes Booth, Jenny Lind, Helen Hayes, John Barrymore, Sarah Bernhardt, Vivien Leigh, and Katharine Hepburn have all trod the boards of the National, which has premiered such groundbreaking productions as *West Side Story, M. Butterfly,* and many other shows. The National also continues its tradition of offering big glittery Broadway and pre-Broadway productions.

Half a block away on 13th Street, the Warner Theatre opened in 1924 as a silent-

Putting on arias: Opera—in this case, a performance of "Figaro"—is just one of the musical offerings on tap at Wolf Trap Farm Park for the Performing Arts in Vienna, Virginia.

movie palace and vaudeville stage. From 1945 to the late 1960s, it presented movies only. It then deteriorated, as did much of downtown Washington, but stayed alive with a menu of porn films and rock concerts. After closing for three years, the Warner reopened in 1992 with its rococo finery intact. It now offers a mix of musicals, dramas, and concerts.

About three blocks east of the Warner, Ford's Theatre on 10th Street had been in business for only four years when, in 1865, it became notorious as the scene of Lincoln's assassination. Restored to its 1860s appearance, it reopened in 1968 with a staging of *John Brown's Body*. Ford's Theatre now offers contemporary plays and musicals.

Probably the city's best program of serious and innovative drama is offered at the Arena Stage, on the waterfront in Southwest Washington. Since its 1950 founding by Zelda and Thomas C. Fichandler and Edward Mangum, the Arena has pioneered the resident theater movement; part of the fun is seeing your favorite local actors perform a wide variety of roles. Arena Stage also owns the distinction of being the first playhouse outside New York City to win a Tony award (the 1976 Regional Theatre Tony Award). James Earl Jones, Ned Beatty, Jane Alexander, and other notable actors cut their teeth here. Three theaters in one, the Arena holds the Fichandler Stage, a theater in the round with 827 seats sloping down to the stage; the 514-seat Kreeger Theater; and the cozy 200-seat Old Vat Room, which often presents new and local works.

After 20 praiseworthy years in its original home at the Folger Shakespeare Library, the Shakespeare Theatre moved in 1992 to a larger, 451-seat theater in the Lansburgh on Seventh Street, N.W. Richard Thomas and Kelly McGillis are among the luminaries who have played in this acclaimed local company, which performs works by Shakespeare and other dramatists. The group also stages the "Shakespeare Free For All," a summer Shakespeare play at Carter Barron Amphitheatre that is presented free to the public.

Two theaters in the Logan Circle area have garnered outstanding reputations. The Source Theatre on 14th Street presents the work of new or local playwrights, as well as a more orthodox slate of classic plays by the likes of Anton Chekhov and Arthur Miller.

Known for its offbeat contemporary plays, the Studio Theatre on P Street has claimed many Helen Hayes awards. These homegrown awards for theatrical excellence recognize the formative contributions to local drama of Hayes, a Washington native who first appeared on a D.C. stage at the age of six and later won an Academy Award for her portrayal of the title character in 1932's *The Sin of Madelon Claudet.*

Perhaps seeking deliverance from the real-life hams on Capitol Hill, Washingtonians are flocking to comedy clubs. Two well-established companies spin out partially improvised political satire on a regular basis. The Capitol Steps, consisting of current and former congressional staffers, offer witty, well-polished songs and skits every Friday and Saturday night at the Ronald Reagan Building on Pennsylvania Avenue. Inside the Naval Heritage Theater farther east on Pennsylvania, the no-holds-barred Gross National Product presents a wilder, almost guerrilla-style lampoonery, whether skewering Democrats in "All the President's Women" or Republicans in "Son of a Bush." The Connecticut Avenue comedy club known as Improv features headliners as well as promising locals doing traditional stand-up.

FINE ARTS

In a city of monumental buildings and larger-than-life statuary created by some of the nation's finest architects and sculptors, D.C. art has tended to be powerful and realistic, depicting powerful people and real events. With a preponderance of these pieces being commissioned—and with many of them requiring committee approval—it's a wonder the city holds so many truly fine works of art.

The U.S. Capitol, for example, is a trove of officially sanctioned art. Its chief muralist, Italian artist Constantino Brumidi (1805–1880), was known as the Michelangelo of the Capitol; his 1865 "Apotheosis of George Washington" graces the ceiling of the Rotunda. Acclaimed artist John Trumbull (1756–1843) painted the eight large historical scenes hanging in the Rotunda.

Much of the city's great painting and sculpture is housed in established museums: the National Gallery of Art, the Corcoran Gallery of Art, the Phillips Collection. Significant works of art created on site in Washington have tended to be in portraiture and open-air sculpture (see pp. 44–45).

Early painting in Washington was documentary as well as aesthetic: Public figures, it was agreed, should have their portraits painted for posterity. Thus locals such as George Washington, James Madison, and the wife of Capitol designer William Thornton sat for eminent portrait painter Gilbert Stuart (1755–1828), who lived in Philadelphia and Boston.

Another leading portrait painter, Charles Willson Peale (1741–1827), completed seven life paintings of George Washington, as well as portraits of Benjamin Franklin, Thomas Jefferson, and John Adams. His son Rembrandt Peale (1778–1860) parlayed his family connections into a precocious start in painting: At age 17 he produced a life portrait of George Washington. The younger Peale studied under his father, whose sharply modeled neoclassic style exerted a strong influence; Rembrandt Peale's 1805 portrait of Jefferson, now owned by the New-York Historical Society, is considered his masterpiece—and our best likeness of the third President.

The White House, too, has a Rembrandt Peale oil of Jefferson, as well as other important portraits. The Reception Rooms of the Department of State hold several portraits by the Peales, Stuart, and Thomas Sully (1783–1872). Other places to look for early Washington faces include the National Portrait Gallery and the National Gallery of Art.

What did the city look like in its infancy? Thanks to the efforts of several minor artists, we have a fairly good idea. Sketches by surveyors and architects show the lay of the land around the Capitol, the White House, and other government buildings as they were going up. Views of Washington by painter George Jacob Beck depict the Georgetown waterfront in the 1790s as a Constable-style landscape, where a country lane stands sprinkled with little houses.

City views by August Kollner in the 1830s show a Potomac busy with sailboats and the new steamboats. The latter owed their existence to engineer and painter Robert Fulton (1765–1815), who in 1807 invented the first commercially successful steamboat; in the

early 1800s Fulton had stayed with friends who owned a country estate that would become the Kalorama neighborhood, and he painted its pastoral scenes.

An 1832 lithograph of the west front of the Capitol by Hudson River artist Thomas Doughty (1793–1856) is a decidedly bucolic setting; the wooded hills and cultivated fields around Jenkins Hill (now Capitol Hill) make the government structure seem almost comically out of place. Washington's rural aspect would continue to be emphasized as late as the 1880s in the sketches and drawings of isolated cabins by DeLancey W. Gill (1859–1940), an illustrator for the Smithsonian Institution's Bureau of American Ethnology. Perhaps these were in wistful lament for a town changing into a city?

An artists' salon blossomed in Washington at the turn of the 20th century. It met at the studio-home of painter and playwright Alice Pike Barney (1857–1931), at 2306 Massachusetts Avenue, next to the current Turkish Embassy. Overlooking Sheridan Circle, Barney's Studio House became the venue for poetry readings, plays, art shows, and other creative undertakings of the sort now associated with a multitude of Dupont addresses. Barney helped establish the Sylvan Theatre on the Mall. Both George Bernard Shaw and Alice Roosevelt Longworth sat for portraits by her hand.

Nowadays the homes of the rich and au courant are graced by abstract art turned out by Washington Color School artists, who rose to prominence in the 1960s. Gene Davis (1920–1985), known for his boldly striped canvases, worked as a White House correspondent during the Truman years before settling down to abstract art. Sam Gilliam (1933–) stepped into the limelight with his "drape paintings" in the late 1960s—stained, unframed canvases thrown over sawhorses and furniture, hung from ceiling beams, or draped on walls. The *Washington Post*

Mary Cassatt's "Little Girl in a Blue Armchair" (1878) gazes in eternal ennui from a wall of the National Gallery of Art.

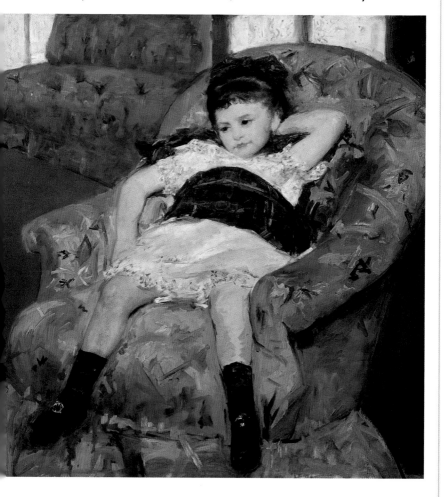

described a 1999 show of his glass-enclosed collages of acrylic on birch plywood as "cubist African kimono sculptures." Gilliam's work has been commissioned for the Washington Convention Center and Ronald Reagan National Airport. He has also been honored with solo exhibitions at the Corcoran Gallery of Art and other showcases.

tings by tackling the city's major industry: politics. The first classic "Washington novel"—an insider's look at the political machinations of the federal government—was probably *The Gilded Age*, an 1873 satire of political and financial shenanigans coauthored by Mark Twain and newspaper editor Charles Dudley Warner. It was followed in 1880 by *Democracy, an American Novel*, a mysterious and anony-

At Kramer Books & afterwords café, a literary landmark just north of Dupont Circle, browsers converge to flip pages, sip coffee, and, on weekends, listen to live music.

LITERATURE

In more than two centuries as the nation's capital, Washington has embraced a succession of bards—writers who have succeeded in capturing this elusive power spot in prose or verse. The district's standout chroniclers have included Henry Adams, Allen Drury, and Gore Vidal.

Unlike literature set elsewhere, Washington novels often aspire to capitalize on their set-

mously authored exposé that became wildly popular for blowing the lid off corruption in the Grant Administration. Despite widespread public and private conjecture about the identity of the crusading novelist, not until the author's death in 1918 would it be revealed that *Democracy* had been written by Henry Adams.

Published more than 40 years ago but still relevant today, Allen Drury's *Advise and Con-*

sent (1959) broke new ground for its startling portrayal of backroom politics. Focusing mainly on the U.S. Senate and a controversial nominee for secretary of state, the book won the former newspaper reporter a Pulitzer Prize in 1960; the 1962 movie version, starring Henry Fonda and Charles Laughton under the direction of Otto Preminger, remains one of Hollywood's more intelligent treatments of Washington.

Many consider Gore Vidal to be Washington's modern laureate, though the erudite author of *Washington, D.C.: a Novel* (1967) and more than 25 other books seems determined to flee that distinction; Vidal has lived in Ravello, Italy, since the early 1970s. Born in West Point, New York, in 1925, Vidal spent much of his childhood inhaling politics at the Rock Creek Park home of his grandfather, Thomas P. Gore, a populist senator from Oklahoma. Vidal himself ran for Congress (unsuccessfully) in 1960 and for the Senate (with identical results) in 1982. He was already a novelist by his first campaign, but his most popular work was still decades away: *Lincoln* (1984) painted a balanced and human portrait of a President who

Novelist Gore Vidal frequently based his fiction on events in Washington history.

had been only canonized until then. Vidal's novel *1876* puts recent political history into perspective: In that year Republican Rutherford B. Hayes stole the election from Democrat Samuel J. Tilden, who had won the popular vote; one of the states whose election returns were contested was Florida.

In a city of often secret doings, those who bring them to light can achieve near-mythic acclaim. Bob Woodward and Carl Bernstein, who broke the scandalous story of the Watergate break-in and burglary in the early 1970s, are but two of the many Washington reporters who have used journalism as a springboard to

literary fame. The 1976 film version of their book *All the President's Men* was a real-life political thriller. Woodward riveted readers around the world in 2004 with the publication of his book *Plan of Attack*, a behind-the-scenes account of the White House's decision to wage war against Iraq.

Another scribe-turned-literary lion, Ward Just, reported for the *Washington Post* until the late 1960s. While covering Richard Nixon's 1968 presidential campaign, Just concluded that fiction was the only medium capable of conveying the true nature of politics. His acclaimed work includes *The Congressman Who Loved Flaubert,* a 1973 collection of political short stories, and *Echo House,* a 1997 portrait of D.C. government that spans eight decades and three generations.

Newsweek columnist Joe Klein hit the jackpot with his first book, the 1996 best-seller *Primary Colors.* In common with Henry Adams's *Democracy* of a century earlier, Klein's book—a thinly veiled fictionalization of Bill Clinton's 1992 campaign—was first published anonymously.

Carrying a book by any of four other leading local lights—satirical novelist Christopher Buckley, hard-boiled detective writer George P. Pelecanos, espionage master Charles McCarry, or journalist Stanley Karnow—should mark you instantly as a Washingtonian in the know.

Poets, too, have been pivotal in the city's literary life. Walt Whitman, who helped care for wounded soldiers in Washington during the Civil War, wrote one of his greatest poems here: the moving elegy to Lincoln, "When Lilacs Last in the Dooryard Bloom'd." Its lines let the reader see the slain President's funeral cortege clatter by: "With the tolling tolling bells' perpetual clang, / Here, coffin that slowly

Stories in stone

Filled with monumental architecture and heroic statuary, Washington is a city that can be read even by the illiterate. The pediment of the Supreme Court's west facade, for example, shows an enthroned Liberty holding the scales of justice. The busy scene depicted on the pediment of the National Archives uses winged horses, rams, and papyrus flowers as classical symbols of aspiration, parchment, and paper.

The more somber the structure, the less evident the signage. Nowhere on the outside of the Supreme Court is the building's function identified. Nor will you find the words "Abraham Lincoln" until you walk inside the Lincoln Memorial.

Yet building exteriors cannot narrate the welter of stories that Washington has to tell. As you walk around the district, you'll encounter more equestrian statues than in any other North American city. These sculptures—most of them depicting military men astride horses in various stances—came into vogue in the late 19th century, when the nation's compulsion to honor its Civil War heroes dovetailed with the rapid growth of its capital city. It's an urban myth, by the way, that a horse with one hoof raised denotes its rider was wounded in battle; nor is it true that both hooves in the air denote the rider died in battle.

Befitting its wartime role as the Federal capital, Washington bristles with Union generals in bronze. Only one Confederate officer is so honored: Even then, the statue of Brig. Gen. Albert Pike—at Third and D Sts., N.W.—recognizes his service not as a soldier but as a Mason. Otherwise you'll have to cross the river to Alexandria, Virginia, to find the nearest Confederate statue—the Rebel soldier who stands at Prince and South Washington Streets in Old Town, head downcast, arms crossed, back turned resolutely on the North.

Washington's late 19th-century renaissance in statuary also coincided with America's emergence as an environment favorable to artists. A nation of growing affluence and power demanded artists to document its glory. As a result, many world-renowned sculptors have work on display in Washington. One of them was Augustus Saint-Gaudens (1848–1907), a Dublin-born artist who grew up in New York City. His 1890 Adams Memorial (see p. 190), commissioned by author Henry Adams to honor his wife, Clover, is one of the most beautiful, moving, and remote pieces of sculpture in the city: It is tucked away in a grove of Japanese yews in Rock Creek Cemetery.

The most famous sculpture in Washington, if not the entire country, is Daniel Chester French's 1922 marble figure of Lincoln, who sits in brooding majesty 19 feet high inside the rectangular marble Lincoln Memorial at the east end of Memorial Bridge. Lincoln clenches his left hand to show strength and resolve; his right lies open to signal compassion (it's another urban myth that he is signing "A.L.").

Thanks to the lobbying efforts of certain groups and the personal fortunes of certain individuals, tributes to elusive or lost causes dot the cityscape as well. The Temperance Fountain (ca 1880) at Pennsylvania Avenue and Seventh Street, for example, is a mini-temple surmounted by a long-legged crane; a San Francisco dentist donated the drinking fountain to advocate the salutary effects of water over spirits. Though the fountain no longer functions, a bar across the street stays busy.

So what does it take to get yourself memo-

The 19-foot-high marble statue of Abraham Lincoln dominates the open-air Lincoln Memorial, built from 1914 to 1922 in the likeness of a Doric temple.

rialized in the nation's capital? First, you must form a citizens' group to petition Congress. A vote must then be taken, a sculptor commissioned, an approval granted by the Commission of Fine Arts, and funds raised. Only a fraction of proposals make the long journey from paper to stone.

For a guide to more than 400 of the city's open-air sculptures, take a look at James M. Goode's *Outdoor Sculpture of Washington, D.C.* (Smithsonian Institution Press, 1974). ■

passes, / I give you my sprig of lilac." Ironically, 1865 was the same year that Whitman was fired from his job as a clerk in the Indian Bureau. The charge: writing offensive poetry.

Another world-class poet served a Washington sojourn, but not by choice. Indicted for treason in 1945 for having broadcast Fascist propaganda during World War II, Ezra Pound was remanded to the care of St. Elizabeth's Hospital (formerly St. Elizabeth's Lunatic Asy-

wise created a capital context for her capital crimes, strewing corpses around tourist sites from the Kennedy Center to the Smithsonian.

ARCHITECTURE

Conceived as a grand capital, Washington has attained a unifying look about its core. One of the main proponents of a neoclassic-style capital was architect-philosopher-statesman Thomas Jefferson. The great buildings and

The restrained symmetry of the Georgian Carlyle House (left) in Old Town Alexandria sets off the 1800 federal-style Octagon (right), a house museum and national historic landmark.

lum). Upon his release in 1958, Pound proclaimed: "All of America is an insane asylum."

Nicer surroundings were in store for the many writers who have stayed at the Willard Hotel on Pennsylvania Avenue, among them Mark Twain, Emily Dickinson, and Charles Dickens. Julia Ward Howe wrote the "Battle Hymn of the Republic" during an 1861 stay. Martin Luther King, Jr., penned parts of his "I Have a Dream" speech here in August 1963.

In the capital's quirkiest epistolary pattern, presidential progeny have written a host of murder mysteries with a Washington locale. FDR's son Elliott Roosevelt set a number of his books in the White House, where characters meet untimely ends in various locations. Margaret Truman, daughter of Harry S., like-

monuments, harking back to ancient Greek and Roman models, were designed to impress with their massiveness and their references to earlier democracies. Weighty columns of marble and pediments embellished with allegorical scenes are the general rule for these early (and many later) federal buildings.

Precious few 18th-century edifices remain. The White House and the Capitol were started in the early 1790s, but both were burned in 1814—and both have undergone many alterations and renovations since they were rebuilt. The Capitol recalls the Pantheon in Rome, begun in 27 B.C. as a temple for worshiping the gods. A less grandiose style was chosen for the executive mansion: Its Georgian format was popular in many manor houses of the day, among them Mount Vernon, Woodlawn, and Gunston Hall, all in Virginia. All three abodes feature porticoes, cornices, steep roofs pierced by several chimneys, and near-perfect symmetry.

The federal style flourished in tandem with Washington's growth in the 19th century. Alexandria and Georgetown, already well established, built scores of elegant brick town houses and row houses for prosperous local

breathtakingly cavernous interior. It was nearly razed in the 1960s.

The Old Executive Office Building—the world's largest office building at the time of its 1888 construction—was ridiculed and likewise threatened with demolition. Harry S. Truman, for one, called it the "greatest monstrosity in America." Apparently the 33rd President's appreciation of architecture did not match his statecraft; the Gilded Age building,

The Mediterranean façade of an 1868 Italianate villa (left) looms bright on Cooke's Row of Q Street in Georgetown; Victorian eclecticism reigns along a P Street block (right).

merchants. Residences from the early 1800s tend to be unadorned, while those built after the Civil War betray unmistakable Victoriana: They sport rosettes, urns, swags, and decorative ironwork. The finest examples of the federal style in Washington are the 1800 Octagon at 1799 New York Avenue, N.W. and the 1816 Tudor Place at 1644 31st Street, N.W. The latter, despite its name, blends neoclassic and federal elements. Conceived as private homes by Capitol designer, William Thornton, both are now national historic landmarks.

Other building styles began to appear later in the 1800s, but architects risked opprobrium if they strayed too far from the city's neoclassicism. Completed in 1887, the redbrick Pension Building (National Building Museum) has a

with its mansard roofs and hundreds of window pediments and columns, is now recognized as an outstanding American example of French Second Empire-style architecture.

Daring and exuberant, the Old Post Office (1899) was likewise slated for obliteration until it was saved in the late 1970s and converted into a retail-office complex. Though it hunkers uneasily among its sedate neighbors on Pennsylvania Avenue, the castlelike building has become a beloved landmark.

Popular in the first half of the 20th century, the beaux arts style, with its use of columns and other classical elements, meshed well in Washington. Union Station (1908) by Daniel Burnham and John Russell Pope's National Archives (1935) and National Gallery of Art

(1941) are grand without ostentation.

Many downtown buildings were razed in the mid-20th century and replaced with concrete cubes, a few of them noteworthy. Though boxy, Edward Durell Stone's National Geographic Society 17th Street building (1964) and Kennedy Center (1971) have an interplay of columns and white stone well suited to Washington.

Other styles have made their way into the cityscape, yet they send symbolic nods to their

Since its 1988 restoration, Union Station has been a hub of shopping, dining, partying, and transportation.

forerunners. Architect I. M. Pei's radically modernist East Building (1978) of the National Gallery, for instance, is faced with the same pink marble as the traditional West Building (1941). In general, no city building is allowed to rise more than 20 feet higher than the width of the street on which it stands. ∎

Grand marble halls of law, justice, and knowledge top Washington's most prominent hill. But here, too, you'll discover a more prosaic world of lively markets, soothing parks, and flower-filled gardens.

Capitol Hill

**The Capitol Rotunda
from below**

Capitol Hill

"A PEDESTAL WAITING FOR A MONUMENT" CITY PLANNER PIERRE CHARLES L'Enfant called the swell of land then known as Jenkins Hill, on the city's southeastern side. Today beautiful monuments grace this hill, including the Capitol and the Supreme Court. Humanizing the grandeur of marble buildings and plazas are tree-lined residential streets. The heart of Washington, Capitol Hill is a good place to begin your tour.

For nearly one hundred years, the Capitol was the only building created for the use of the nation's legislature. To the east spread an orderly neighborhood of brick row houses. But by the end of the 19th century, the Library of Congress's Jefferson Building had risen across from the Capitol, followed shortly by architect Daniel H. Burnham's imposing Union Station and adjacent City Post Office. The early 1900s saw construction of the Cannon Building (1908) and Russell Building (1909), the first House and Senate office buildings. In the 1930s, the Supreme Court, the Folger Shakespeare Library, and the Adams Building of the Library of Congress added more density to Capitol Hill.

By the mid-20th century, much of the residential area was in decline as middle-class families abandoned the city for the suburbs. Then in the 1970s, urban pioneers, lured by low real estate values and the convenient location, began moving in and revitalizing the area. With the Eastern Market *(7th & C Sts., S.E.)* as an anchor, Capitol Hill became a vibrant neighborhood once again. Spruced up historic houses, shops, and restaurants from the Capitol to Lincoln Park make this a pleasant and lovely place to live in and visit.

You will need a full day to see all the sights here, two days to see them in detail. Union Station and Capitol South Metro stops are about equidistant from the Capitol. If you start from one, you can work your way to the other or do a leisurely loop back to your starting point. Either way, plan on getting some exercise—the area was designed on a grand scale. Walking gives you a chance to savor the magnificent architecture from various points.

As you walk, bear in mind that these buildings are both historical museums and working halls of democracy. Touring them gives you a sense of the great enterprise upon which the Founding Fathers embarked. If the free world has a geographical center, it is Capitol Hill. ∎

Row houses cluster in the desirable Capitol Hill neighborhood.

U.S. Capitol

U.S. Capitol
www.aoc.gov

Map p. 51

Capitol Hill, between Independence & Constitution Aves.

202-225-6827

Metro: Capitol South or Union Station; Bus: 30-36, , A11, J11-13, N22, 96-7

ONE OF THE MOST RECOGNIZED LANDMARKS IN THE world, the marble white U.S. Capitol, rising in domed and columned splendor at the Mall's east end, defines the center of Washington. South, East, and North Capitol Streets and the Mall radiate out from the Capitol in the cardinal directions, dividing the city into quadrants. In this vaulted location, Presidents are inaugurated, national issues debated, and new laws made.

EVOLUTION

The Capitol you see today looks almost nothing like its original conception. From the laying of the cornerstone by George Washington in 1793 to the placing of the statue of "Freedom" atop the dome in 1863, some half dozen major designers and architects put their visions and efforts into the final image. Erecting an edifice as important as the Capitol was about as easy as enacting a controversial new law. The egos of architects, engineers, and congressmen often clashed; funding grew scarce at times; and disputes drove major players into resigning their positions. Like the nation's early history, the history of the Capitol is one of false starts, compromises, and ultimate triumph.

Pierre Charles L'Enfant stubbornly refused to come up with an architectural plan for the Capitol, declaring that he had it "in his head." His dismissal in 1792 led to a national competition to design the building, the winning architect to receive $500 and a city lot. The 16 known entries were so poor that the contest had to be extended. An amateur architect named William Thornton finally came up with a winning design—a Pantheon-like dome flanked by symmetrical wings for the Senate and the House. Though greatly modifying and extending the design over the years, later architects generally followed

Paintings by John Trumbull (1756–1843) hang in the echoing cavern of the Capitol's Rotunda, depicting important moments in the American Revolution.

this basic layout; they also incorporated the Corinthian pilasters, seven-bay portico, balustrade, and other neoclassic details Thornton had envisioned. The beauty of his plan lay in the fact that it was both grand and simple, as George Washington said, yet also flexible enough to accommodate a growing nation.

In 1800 the government moved from Philadelphia to Washington, and President John Adams addressed the Congress in the Capitol's brick-and-sandstone north wing, the only completed part of the building. During these early years, Thornton resigned, and two out of the three other architects were fired over their attempted design alterations. Fortunately, in 1803 the government hired the brilliant British architect Benjamin Henry Latrobe, and his collaboration with President Thomas Jefferson, himself an amateur architect, made for substantial progress.

Then in August of 1814, British troops marched on Washington, and torched many buildings, including the Capitol. The fire destroyed much of the building's interior, though the walls remained standing. For the next few years, Latrobe worked at restoring the damage. Cost overruns and a dispute about vaulting the ceilings of the House and Senate Chambers finally led to his resignation. Boston architect Charles Bulfinch stepped in. Quieter and more conservative than Latrobe, Bulfinch ingratiated himself with Congress and President James Monroe. Bulfinch served until 1830, completing the building with a copper-covered wooden dome and an east portico.

By 1850, an expanding Congress had outgrown its chambers, necessitating the addition of new grand wings to the original building. The Capitol expansion project was still underway when the Civil War broke out. Construction went on, culminating in the addition of the current cast-iron dome, which replaced a leaky, wooden predecessor. On Dec. 2, 1863, the magnificent nine-million-pound dome, rising from a circular portico, was crowned with "Freedom," the 19.5-foot-tall bronze figure of

Tulips highlight the beauty of the Capitol at night. The nation's leading landscape architect, Frederick Law Olmsted, designed the grounds in the 1870s.

a woman dressed in flowing robes. A 35-gun salute (for each of the states, including those that had seceded) greeted "Freedom's" ascent. An interesting historical footnote concerns her headgear. The original plan had her in a liberty cap, worn by freed slaves in ancient Greece. Then Secretary of War Jefferson Davis—president of the Confederacy by the time the statue was placed atop the Capitol— objected, saying the cap was "inappropriate to a people who were born free." A helmet with eagle feathers was substituted.

In the 1870s, renowned landscape architect Frederick Law Olmsted added terraces to the north, south, and west sides. Congress again outgrew the building in the early 20th century, scattering to the nearby Senate and House office buildings. A major addition in 1958–62 added 32 feet to the east front, leaving the sandstone west facade as the only original exterior not covered with a marble addition.

VISITING

A new Capitol Visitors Center on track for completion in spring 2006 has required the excavation of 196,000 square feet at the east front of the Capitol. Three levels of space will provide improved screening, orientation, and amenities for the thousands of visitors who line up early for tickets to enter the building. Until the project is complete, free timed-entry passes are issued beginning at 9 a.m. on a first-come, first-served basis at a kiosk on the southwest corner of the Capitol grounds (*1st St. & Independence Ave., S.W.*), opposite the Botanic Garden. Entry passes are not available in advance. Many members of Congress have tour information available on their websites; check with your representative or senator about the possibility of special tours. Keep in mind that Congress is usually in recess in August and in the fall during elections.

At the heart of the Capitol, the **Rotunda** soars 180 feet to a round ceiling fresco, "The Apotheosis of

Washington" (1865), by Italian-American artist Constantino Brumidi. A berobed George Washington stares down from on high, surrounded by a swirl of clouds and figures that represent the 13 Colonies and American democracy. Encircling the Rotunda, a 300-foot-long frieze begun by Brumidi but not completed until 1953 depicts more than 400 years of American history, from Columbus to the Wright brothers.

On the Rotunda's west side hang the four huge scenes from the American Revolution painted by Washington's aide-de-camp John Trumbull. Across from them, on the east side, are canvases portraying the discovery and settlement of the United States. A small white marble stone marks the center of the Rotunda's floor; here eminent Americans such as Abraham Lincoln and John F. Kennedy have lain in state.

One room south of the Rotunda is the **National Statuary Hall,** where the House of Representatives met from 1807 to 1857. In 1864 Congress first invited each state to send a bronze or marble statue of two prominent citizens. Some have been moved elsewhere, but among the notables on site are Henry Clay (Kentucky), Daniel Webster (New Hampshire), Robert E. Lee (Virginia), and King Kamehameha I (Hawaii).

North of the Rotunda is the **Old Senate Chamber,** which served the Senate from 1810 to 1859 (except between 1814 and 1819, when senators had to meet across the street after the British burned the Capitol). Here such famous men as Clay, Webster, and John C. Calhoun hotly debated the issues of slavery and economics prior to the Civil War. Today the Senate uses this chamber for closed-door conferences, including a 1999 session on the impeachment trial of Bill Clinton. Rembrandt Peale's famous portrait of George Washington (1823) hangs on the chamber's east wall, above the Vice President's dais.

On the first floor, directly beneath the Rotunda, awaits the **Crypt.** George and Martha Washington were to be entombed here, but family members objected, so the two remain at Mount Vernon, in Virginia. Ringing the room, 40 Doric sandstone columns help support the Rotunda. Gutzon Borglum, who carved Mount Rushmore, created the marble head of Lincoln displayed here. The statue's missing left ear symbolizes the slain President's incomplete life.

North of the Crypt, through the small Senate Rotunda and to the right, stands the **Old Supreme Court Chamber.** The Senate

Capitol views

One of the earliest travel books about America was written by Frances Trollope, mother of English writer Anthony Trollope and herself a prolific novelist. In her popular *Domestic Manners of the Americans* (1832), written after a three-year journey to the fledgling United States, she found much to disparage. But she was impressed by the Capitol:

"None of us, I believe, expected to see so imposing a structure on that side the Atlantic. I am ill at describing buildings, but the beauty and majesty of the American capitol might defy an abler pen than mine to do it justice. It stands so finely too, high, and alone.... The view from the capitol commands the city and many miles around, and it is itself an object of imposing beauty to the whole country adjoining." ∎

When the white light shines in the dome, Congress is in session.

Senate Chamber

U.S. CAPITOL

West Front

originally met in this vaulted room designed by Latrobe; the Supreme Court used it from 1810 to 1860. In the early 1970s, restorers armed with mid-19th-century descriptions returned the chamber to its earlier appearance. Half of the furnishings, including justices' desks and chairs, are original.

On the first floor of the north wing, the colorful Brumidi Corridors boast a wealth of frescoes

and other paintings by Constantino Brumidi, who worked in the Capitol for 25 years in the late 1800s. Sometimes called the Michelangelo of the Capitol, Brumidi based his designs for the corridors on the Raphael loggia in the Vatican, where he had done some restoration work. The historical scenes and heroes, along with depictions of flora and fauna in trompe l'oeil frames, provide a rich summary of early

The heart of American democracy, the U.S. Capitol is also the geographic center of Washington; the city's four quadrants radiate from the middle of the building.

Rotunda room

National Statuary Hall
(Old House Chambers)

House Chamber

Speakers Lobby

America. Later paintings include scenes of the first moon landing and a tribute to the crew who died in the 1986 explosion of the *Challenger* space shuttle.

On the other side of the Crypt, in the south wing, are the **First Floor House Corridors** containing more statuary as well as murals by contemporary American artist Allyn Cox. Among the scenes are the Capitol in flames in 1814 and wounded Union soldiers lying in a makeshift hospital in the Rotunda.

The **Congressional Chambers** are in the Capitol's wings (the House south, the Senate north). The 435 House representatives are not assigned specific seats, though Democrats traditionally sit to the Speaker's right, Republicans to the left. The same arrangement holds for the more stately Senate, but here desks are based on seniority. ■

Politics at work

In the summer of 1787, following the successful rebellion of the 13 Colonies against England and the loosely structured "Confederation" period, 55 leaders from the newly independent states met in Philadelphia's State House (now Independence Hall) to revise the the the Articles of Confederation, the country's first constitution. Trying to strike a delicate balance between sufficient government power to rule a nation yet guarantee adequate liberty for its citizens, the delegates decided to toss out the Articles and create a new document. The result: the Constitution of the United States of America—the fundamental law of the U.S. federal system and a landmark document of the Western world.

This constitution, having been the product of secret deals and silent compromises, could not become the law of the land by fiat, so the Founders asked that it be ratified by the people of the 13 independent states. There were many heated state conventions, some producing violence, other producing eloquent words, that have helped Supreme Court Justices determine the meaning of this concise blueprint for the government we have today—living up to its preamble: "We the People of the United States of America…"

From the beginning Congress met to air differences and reach hard fought compromises. The reason the capital is in Washington, for instance, is because of the very public Compromise of 1790, in which northern congressmen and senators got their southern counterparts to approve funding our first national debt in return for placing the nation's capital in the south on the Potomac River, not far from George Washington's home. From the First Congress came the traditions of national debt and logrolling. And anyone who has tuned into

C-SPAN knows that political debate and compromise continue to be integral ingredients in making laws.

You can see the fireworks first-hand in Washington several different ways. The most obvious is go to the Capitol, where it may be possible to hear your senator give a speech or watch a debate about a current issue on the floor of the House. Contact your representative or senator before leaving home to find out about access and making special arrangements, such as stopping in for a chat with your hometown legislator. Many congresspeople have information on their individual websites. Or call your politician's office (202-224-3121).

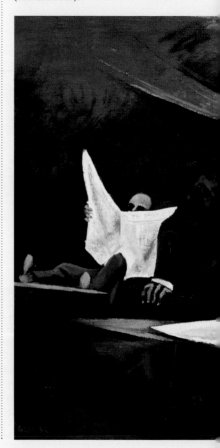

Right: "Senate Hearing" by William Gropper (1897–1977): Making fun of gasbag politicians is a 200-year-long tradition, but discord, as understood by James Madison, was effectively designed into our constitutional democracy to give voice to different groups.

While the work done on the Congress floor is well publicized, much of the real work goes on behind the scenes in committees and subcommittees—the first place where most bills being nominated as future laws are discussed and debated and picked apart. Most days the legislature is in session, a dozen or more committees and subcommittees meet—most of which are open to the public. Here you can watch the future of high-definition television being decided, hear an EPA administrator grilled about pollution enforcement, listen to debates about space exploration, or attend the confirmation hearing for a newly nominated federal judge. To find out what committees your local elected officials are on, visit *www.house.gov* or *www.senate.gov.*

If a bill is good and has powerful friends on the committee, it will be recommended to the House or Senate for debate and vote. Of the some 10,000 bills introduced every year, only about 10 percent ever make it to the floor of either the House or Senate to be voted on.

If passed, the bill is sent to the other chamber, referred to committee, and so on. If the bill makes it through the tortured path to passage in that chamber, then a "Conference" committee is set up to settle differences between the two bills, if there are any. The Senate and House vote again on the revised bill, and if that compromise bill passes it goes to the President for his signature—or veto.

Regardless of how a bill turns out, the process is interesting and fun to watch. You will be observing how that blueprint for a government hashed out in a steamy room centuries ago works every day on issues great and small. ■

Supreme Court

Supreme Court

www.supremecourtus.gov

 Map p. 51

✉ 1st & E. Capitol Sts., N.E.

☎ 202-479-3000 or 202-479-3211

🕐 Closed Sat.–Sun.

Ⓜ Metro: Capitol South, Union Station; Bus: 96-7, J11-13, A11, N22

THIS IMPOSING NEOCLASSIC BUILDING OPPOSITE THE Capitol makes a simple yet powerful statement with its wide marble stairway and its lofty portico rising on 32 Corinthian columns.

An architrave just below the pediment bears the inscription "Equal Justice Under Law," an echo of Justice John Marshall Harlan's famous dissenting opinion in 1896 in *Plessy v. Ferguson:* "In view of the Constitution, in the eye of the law, there is in this country no superior, dominant, ruling class of citizens. There is no caste here. . . . [A]ll citizens are equal before the law."

Here the nation's highest tribunal arbitrates cases involving the Constitution or the nation's laws. In this court of final appeal, decisions have been handed down that have profoundly influenced the country. In 2000 the Court showed its muscle again by effectively settling the controversial U.S. presidential race.

Surprisingly, the Supreme Court did not have its own building until 1935. Before then it sat in various places within the Capitol. In 1929 Chief Justice William Howard Taft, the only U.S. President (1909–1913) to serve on the Court (1921–1930), urged Congress to authorize the erection of a Supreme Court building. The neoclassic edifice designed by Cass Gilbert was constructed with 27,400 pieces of marble. Every feature lends a sense of gravity and dignity, from the 6.5-ton bronze doors to the seated marble giants out front— "Contemplation of Justice" (left) and "Guardian of Law" (right).

VISITING

You enter through the main (west) entrance on the building's second floor, which leads to the **Great Hall** and its long line of busts depicting former chief justices. At the end of the hall lies the actual **courtroom.** When the Court is not in session, you can visit the chamber, and learn about court procedure and the building's architecture, by attending a free lecture there, given on the half hour.

There is much for the eye to feast on in the nation's most important courtroom. Behind the raised mahogany bench stand the chairs of the nine justices, their height varying according to how tall the justice is (so that they all appear the same height when seated). Along the sides of the room rise 24 veined marble columns, above which sculpted marble panels depict such lawgivers as Moses, Confucius, and Napoléon. Above these friezes stretches the bright red and blue ceiling coffered with hand-carved wood and plaster rosettes and lined with gold.

When the court is in session (*Oct.–April Mon.–Wed.*), you can listen to oral arguments by lining up on the plaza in front of the building. Seating begins at 9:30 a.m. and 12:30 p.m. Some cases attract big crowds, with people even sleeping outside the court to ensure a place inside. You may have a better chance with the other line—for those who just want to hear a three-minute sample of the case. Seating begins at 10:00 a.m. and 1:00 p.m.

More than 7,000 petitions asking the Supreme Court to overturn a lower-court ruling arrive every year. Only 100 to 120 make it to the argument stage. Each side is given 30 minutes to argue its case; the justices then write their opinions. You can access these and other Court information via the internet.

Go down a flight of stairs to the ground level, where you'll find a small theater in the **Lower Great Hall;** a 24-minute film details the workings of the Court and includes interviews with current justices. The hall also has several exhibits on the Supreme Court. On the south side the famous Warren Court (1953–1969), presided over by Chief Justice Earl Warren, still sits in session, in a cast stone and aluminum sculpture. The Warren Court's progressive opinions included the outlawing of school segregation.

At the hall's east end rises a statue of the great fourth Chief Justice, John Marshall, who served 1801–1835. He is considered responsible for our system of constitutional law, including the doctrine of judicial review (*Marbury* v. *Madison*, 1803), by which the Court can declare acts of Congress unconstitutional. Follow signs for a view of two amazing marble-and-bronze freestanding spiral staircases; the ascending ovals make the five-story building appear twice as tall as it really is. ■

**Opposite:
The neoclassic
Supreme Court
Building, with its
open courtyard
of Georgia marble,
was completed
in 1935.**

Library of Congress

Library of Congress

www.loc.gov

⚑ Map p. 51

✉ 1st St. & Independence Ave., S.E.

☎ 202-707-8000 or 202-707-5000

🕐 Closed Sun.

🚇 Metro: Capitol South; Bus: 30-36, A11, J13, N22

AFTER EXTENSIVE RENOVATION FROM 1986 TO 1997, THE Library of Congress—the world's largest library—has emerged as one of the most breathtaking buildings in the city. Inside and out, the Italian Renaissance-style Thomas Jefferson Building (main building) dazzles the eye with its opulent yet tasteful cornucopia of sculpture, murals, mosaics, and architectural flourishes. Whether you come here for serious research or just to wander around, you'll leave understanding why this temple of learning was considered, at its opening in 1897, the most beautiful public building in America.

Originally housed in the U.S. Capitol, the Library began in 1800 as a reference collection for Congress. After the British burned the Capitol in 1814, destroying the books, Thomas Jefferson sold his personal library of 6,487 volumes—one of the country's most extensive—to Congress. Larger than the original collection, Jefferson's contained law books, as well as works of literature, history, science, architecture, and philosophy. As he wrote at the time, "There is, in fact, no subject to which a member of Congress may not have occasion to refer." His unbounded interest in everything has set the tone for the Library ever since.

The Library suffered a second devastating blow in 1851 when fire destroyed two-thirds of the collection. Though most titles have since been replaced, almost 900 remain missing. The Library is now conducting a worldwide search for copies of the books.

Ainsworth Rand Spofford, Librarian of Congress from 1864 to 1897, took Jefferson's eclectic philosophy seriously and began amassing a huge collection, including two copies of every copyrighted work in the country. The flood of material led to the construction of the Thomas Jefferson Building, the first of the Library's three buildings.

Though the Library does not hold every book published in the U.S., it does acquire some 10,000 of the 22,000 items received every day.

You can request books at the central desk, then read them at one of the tables in the octagonal Main Reading Room.

The Library—an invaluable resource for legislators, students, scholars, and filmmakers—now holds some 120 million items, including more than 18 million books, 4.5 million maps, and the papers of 23 U.S. Presidents, housed on 530 miles of shelves. The National Digital Library Program is putting much of the collection on the Internet (*ww.loc.gov*).

VISITING

You can take an organized tour of the **Jefferson Building** or pick up a self-guided tour brochure at the visitor center just inside the west side's ground level entrance. A 12-minute film explains the Library's history. Several galleries in the building feature permanent and rotating exhibitions of American history and culture as well as important international materials from the Library's collection, such as a cuneiform tablet from 2400 B.C. and a copy of Ptolemy's *Geographica* (1480).

In the **Great Hall** on the first floor, you will feel as though you have entered a Mediterranean palazzo. Grand staircases lead up through carved marble arches; brilliant mosaics and paintings honor music, poetry, astronomy, and other disciplines; and columns and sculptures add to the vertical effect, as if to emphasize man's lofty aspirations. In the east corridor two Library treasures rest behind glass cases: the Giant Bible of Mainz and the Gutenberg Bible, both made in Germany in the mid-1450s.

On the second floor, an arcade makes a square around and above the Great Hall, offering unobstructed views of the first floor and the high ceiling. From the **Treasures Gallery,** a collection of exhibit halls at the south end, the east stairway leads up to the **Visitors' Gallery,** which has a wonderful view of the

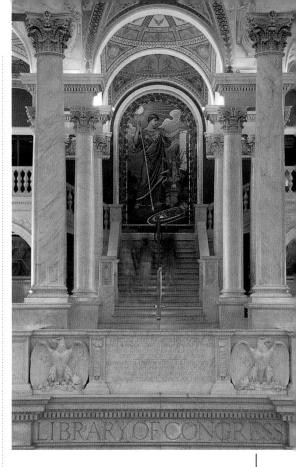

Main Reading Room, the sanctum sanctorum. A splendid coffered dome rises to a cupola 160 feet above the floor. Farther down, 16 bronze statues in balustrades represent such luminaries as Beethoven and Newton. Below, library patrons work at concentric circles of desks.

To use the library, you need a reader's pass, available at the **Madison Building,** across Independence Avenue. The Madison opened in 1980 and holds photos, prints, and a film archive; on the third floor, the **Mary Pickford Theater** (*202-707-5677*) screens free classic films. The 1939 deco-style **Adams Building,** behind the Jefferson on Second, has a business and science reading room. ■

A grand marble staircase in the Library of Congress's exquisite Great Hall

Folger Shakespeare Library

**Folger
Shakespeare
Library**
www.folger.edu

🅰 Map p. 51

✉ 201 E. Capitol St.,
S.E., between 2nd &
3rd Sts.

☎ 202-544-4600

🕐 Closed Sun.

🚇 Metro: Capitol South;
Bus: 96-7

**The Folger's
Reading
Room evokes
an Elizabethan
great hall.**

THIS UNIQUE LIBRARY HOLDS THE WORLD'S LARGEST collection of William Shakespeare's works. Originating from a gift by Henry Clay Folger, the library opened in 1932 and now houses 280,000 books and manuscripts; 27,000 paintings, drawings, prints, and engravings; and many musical instruments, costumes, and films.

In 1879 a lecture on the Bard by Ralph Waldo Emerson fired the interest of Folger, then a 22-year-old student at Amherst College. A decade later, he bought his first Shakespeare folio. With the money he made in the oil business (as president of the Standard Oil Company of New York), he went on to buy thousands of rare books, manuscripts, and paintings. In the early 1900s, he began casting about for a site to build a library; he finally chose one adjacent to the Library of Congress (see pp. 62–63). But just after the cornerstone was laid, in 1930, he died; his wife, Emily, saw the project to completion.

The bold lines of this art deco-inspired neoclassic marble building make it a fitting presence among its neighbors. Nine bas-reliefs on the north side depict scenes from the Bard's plays. A statue of Puck (from *A Midsummer Night's Dream*) graces a fountain on the west side. On the east lawn lies an **Elizabethan flower and herb garden.**

For more details on the Folger, take one of the daily tours, which start at the docent's desk directly inside the library's entrance. Or wander on your own through the wood-paneled 30-foot-high **Great Hall,** which displays a copy of the Bard's first folio and changing thematic exhibits from the library's collection. You may peer through an iron gate into the adjacent Tudor-style **Reading Room,** where a stained-glass window depicting the "Seven Ages of Man" (*As You Like It*) adorns the west end. A Shakespeare bust is mounted on the east wall. The room is open to scholars and graduate students for research.

At the building's eastern end, the **Folger Theatre** offers an intimate venue for seeing the Bard's plays, or hearing 16th-century music performed or readings by award-winning authors. The oak columns, tiered balconies, and sky canopy contribute to the atmosphere of an Elizabethan courtyard. ∎

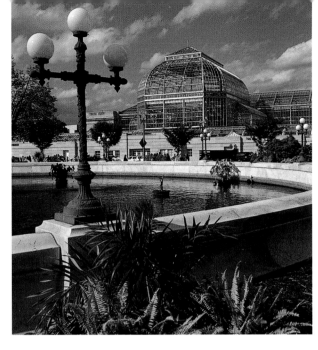

The renovated Conservatory as seen from across Independence Avenue

United States Botanic Garden

IF YOU'RE SURPRISED TO SUDDENLY FIND YOURSELF IN THE thick of a tropical rain forest or surrounded by a soothing oasis in the middle of downtown Washington, then you've stumbled onto the U.S. Botanic Garden in the shadow of the U.S. Capitol.

Congress established the garden in 1820 for the collection, growing, and distribution of important plants. Through the decades, parts of the facility fell into disrepair. Eventually the site was closed for several years for repairs and restoration. In 1997 a 33.5-million-dollar renovation project was launched; the expanded and up-dated garden reopened in 2001 with a significantly enlarged plant collection.

Today, more than 4,000 plants are on view at any one time in the glass-paneled **Conservatory**. They are selected from many thousands of plants grown at a facility off-site. You can stroll through the various areas devoted to desert, jungle, and oasis flora, and explore exhibits on medicinal and economically useful plants, primeval vegetation, and plant exploration, among others. Don't miss the outstanding collection of orchids. A new National Garden is scheduled to open in 2006.

Across Independence Avenue (at 245 First Ave., S.W.) is the garden's **Bartholdi Park**. Fre´de´ric-Auguste, who created the Statue of Liberty, sculpted the park's 30-foot-high cast-iron fountain for the Centennial Exposition of 1876 in Philadelphia—the first world's fair. The sculpture's large upper basin is borne by three upright sea nymphs, as water jets from the mouths of fish and turtles. ∎

U.S. Botanic Garden
www.usbg.gov
🅐 Map p. 51
✉ 100 Maryland Ave., S.W.
☎ 202-225-8333
🚇 Metro: Federal Center S.W.; Bus: 30-36, P17-19, W13

More places to visit on Capitol Hill

CAPITAL CHILDREN'S MUSEUM

For more than 25 years, children have loved visiting this educational fun place with activities such as lab experiments, a prehistoric cave, and an animation studio. In 2004 plans were underway for an ambitious expansion and relocation to a new site near L'Enfant Plaza.
Map p. 51 ✉ 800 3rd St., N.E. ☎ 202-675-4120 $ $$ Ⓜ Metro: Union Station

EASTERN MARKET

This 1873 block-long building holds scores of bustling stalls selling everything from meats and cheeses to seafood and baked goods. On Saturdays farmers sell vegetables, fruits, and flowers; this is also festival day, with its street performers, artists, and clothes designers. A flea market operates on Sundays. Map p. 51

One of the many fresh fruit and produce stands at Eastern Market

✉ 7th & C Sts., S.E. ☎ 202-544-0083 ⊙ Closed Mon. Ⓜ Metro: Eastern Market

NATIONAL POSTAL MUSEUM

The building that formerly housed the Washington City Post Office makes an elegant home for this museum, which is part of the Smithsonian Institution complex. The galleries explore topics such as the history of mail delivery, stamp collecting, and the art of personal correspondence. Among the artifacts on display in the 90-foot-high atrium are suspended prop planes and a railway car,

modes of mail conveyance in the past. Map p. 51 ✉ 2 Massachusetts Ave., N.E. (just W of Union Station) ☎ 202-633-5555 Ⓜ Metro: Union Station

NATIONAL GUARD MUSEUM

Opened in February 2003, this small but engrossing museum at the National Guard Memorial uses memorabilia, light and sound effects, and dramatic narratives to chronicle the experiences of citizen soldiers who have served America at home and abroad for nearly 400 years. The museum's aim was to provide a factual history of the country's oldest military organization, which traces its roots to colonial militias. But the displays and interactive programs are especially poignant given the Guard's major role in homeland security and war in the Middle East following the September 11, 2001, terrorist attacks on the United States.
Map p. 51 ✉ 1 Massachusetts Ave, N.W. ☎ 202-789-0031 ⊙ Closed Sat.-Sun. Ⓜ Metro: Union Station

SEWALL-BELMONT HOUSE

Robert Sewall built this two-story brick house in 1799–1800. In the 20th century, Alva Belmont helped purchase it for the National Woman's Party, headquartered here since 1929. The house contains memorabilia of women's rights leaders.
Map p. 51 ✉ 144 Constitution Ave., N.E. ☎ 202-546-1210 ⊙ Closed Sun.–Mon. Ⓜ Metro: Union Station

UNION STATION

Completed in 1908 and beautifully restored in the 1980s, this grand beaux arts-style building is worth visiting just for its architecture. Faced in white Vermont granite, the station's huge Romanesque arches give way to a triumphal, echoing Main Hall where 36 larger-than-life Roman legionnaires preside on the gallery level. A barrel-vaulted ceiling with gold-leaf coffers soars 96 feet above the station's bustle. There are more than 130 shops and restaurants.
Map p. 51 ✉ 40 Massachusetts Ave., N.E. ☎ 202-289-1908 Ⓜ Metro: Union Station ∎

The vast expanse of the Mall, with its Smithsonian museums and stately monuments, is the Washington everyone comes to see. But this is also a laidback place for picnicking, afterwork softball and soccer games, and just taking a stroll.

National Mall

Annual Smithsonian Folklife Festival, a summer highlight on the Mall

National Mall

LINED AND DOTTED WITH THE MOST SIGNIFICANT GROUP OF MUSEUMS AND monuments in the country, the National Mall is a long avenue of green grass edged by shade trees. You could spend a week, and more, visiting this world-famous tourist mecca.

One day hundreds of colorful kites are flying near the Washington Monument, on another a crowd is shouting and waving banners, and on yet another day the Mall is just a peaceful stretch of green. From the U.S. Capitol to the Lincoln Memorial, America's grand promenade extends for more than 2 miles between Constitution and Independence Avenues. Walkers, joggers, soccer players, and Frisbee throwers regularly take to the inviting lawns.

In summer, thousands flock to the Smithsonian Folklife Festival *(late June–early July)*, the Fourth of July celebration, and the Sylvan Theater's outdoor concerts. Numerous other events are held on the Mall, including a kite festival *(late March–early April)* and the Black Family Reunion *(Sept.)*. The Mall is also the stage for rallies by many national groups.

Pierre Charles L'Enfant's city plan of 1791 included a "vast esplanade" lined with magnificent residences. But by the end of the 1800s, the Mall was very different from his vision: Coal piles, sheds, tracks, and a railroad station made it less than appealing. In 1901 the MacMillan Commission recommended reviving L'Enfant's plan. Tracks and debris were removed, vistas were opened up, and

marshy areas were filled. With the addition of the Lincoln Memorial, the Mall stretched to the Potomac River, making it the east–west axis of a memorial park area. The White House and Jefferson Memorial form the north–south axis, with the Washington Monument in the middle.

By the late 1980s, the Mall's eastern part held nine Smithsonian museums and two National Gallery of Art buildings. In 2004 the National Museum of the American Indian opened near the National Air and Space Museum, and the new World War II Memorial opened just west of the Washington Monument. ■

Freer Gallery of Art

**Freer Gallery
of Art**

www.asia.si.edu

- Map p. 69
- Jefferson Dr. &
  12th St., S.W.
- 202-633-1000
- Metro: Smithsonian;
  Bus: 13A & G,
  52-3

**Artist James M.
Whistler painted
the sumptuous
Peacock Room
as though it were
an enormous
lacquer box.**

DATING FROM THE FOURTH MILLENNIUM B.C. TO MODERN times, the objects in the Freer make a comprehensive sweep of Asian art. The collection, donated by Detroit businessman Charles Lang Freer (1856–1919), now numbers more than 28,000 individual works and is considered among the finest in the world. It is complemented by a large collection of 19th- and 20th-century American pieces, including many works by James McNeill Whistler.

Opened in 1923, the Italian Renaissance-style building has a pink granite exterior and polished white marble floors. Its galleries surround a hallway where large windows look out onto a refreshing inner courtyard. The lighting and exhibit space combine to lend a refined, contemplative atmosphere.

Of the 19 galleries, 16 are devoted to Asian art, including Indian sculpture, Japanese lacquerware, Chinese paintings, Korean ceramics, and Islamic metalware. The Freer does not host traveling exhibitions or lend any of its objects; the gallery rotates pieces from its permanent collection.

Among the Asian works are the 10th-century Indian bronze "Queen Sembiyan Mahadevi as the Goddess Parvati" and a 12th-centu-

ry wood sculpture, "Bosatsu," from the late Heian period of Japan.

American treasures include the exquisite **Peacock Room,** which is a must-see. Whistler painted the room, called "Harmony in Blue and Gold," for a rich London shipowner. Recently restored to its original elegance, the room features antique gilded leather walls, a metal ceiling painted in a feather pattern, and a painting known as "The Princess in the Land of Porcelain." The opposite wall has a painting of two peacocks, a reference to a quarrel between Whistler and his patron over the fee. Freer bought the room intact from a London dealer and installed it in his Detroit home; it was moved to Washington in 1919.

The Freer's lower level connects to the Arthur M. Sackler Gallery. ■

Arthur M. Sackler Gallery

HOUSED ALMOST ENTIRELY BELOW THE GROUND, THIS 1987 museum has at its core the Asian collection of research physician and medical publisher Arthur M. Sackler. Among its many treasures are Chinese bronzes and jades, Persian manuscripts, ancient Iranian silver, and works from Tibet and Japan. The museum exhibits items from its growing permanent collection as well as from other collections in the United States and elsewhere. Visiting the Sackler and the Freer, which are administered jointly, gives you a comprehensive overview of traditional and modern Asian art.

Arthur M. Sackler Gallery

www.asia.si.edu
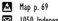 Map p. 69
⊠ 1050 Independence Ave., S.W.
☎ 202-633-1000
🚇 Metro: Smithsonian; Bus: 13A & G, 52-3

The **first level**—one level below ground—contains works from a variety of cultures. The treasures are artfully displayed, enhancing their beauty and viewers' appreciation. Many of the rooms feature only half a dozen or so objects in glass cases, with subtle lighting and just enough information to keep you interested but not overwhelmed. Wander through the galleries and see a wide array of objects such as a beaten brass incense burner from 13th-century Syria; a ceramic, gazelle-shaped drinking vessel from 4th-century B.C. Iran; and 10th- to 14th-century granite deities from India.

In the **Arts of China galleries,** also on the first level, the Ancient Chinese Art section displays 12th- to 13th-century B.C. jade knives crafted by incredibly skillful artisans—not a fact that one always associates with pieces from the Neolithic period. Another section, the Arts of Six Dynasties and Tang in China, holds Tang dynasty tomb guardians adorned with brilliant horns and flames. The guardians look as fierce and original as they must have 13 centuries ago.

The **second level** of the gallery houses mainly administrative offices. Do not overlook the **third level** of the Sackler, where displays of contemporary Japanese bowls and vases, colorfully glazed, are enhanced by a small pool and bubbling fountains.

From the third level visitors can find access to the **S. Dillon Ripley Center,** which features temporary exhibits, and then continue on to the National Museum of African Art. ∎

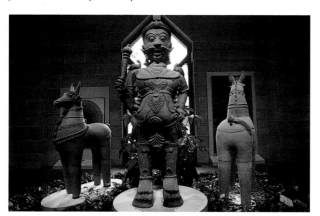

Terra-cotta festival statues from India dating from 1984–85

National Museum
of African Art

**National
Museum of
African Art**
www.nmafa.si.edu
🏛 Map p. 69
✉ 950 Independence
Ave., S.W.
☎ 202-633-1000
🚇 Metro: Smithsonian;
Bus: 13A & G,
52-3

THIS MUSEUM TRACES ITS ROOTS TO A TOWNHOUSE ON
Capitol Hill once owned by Frederick Douglas, a former slave who
became a noted abolitionist. In 1964 Warren M. Robbins founded the
Museum of African Art there as a private educational institution that
mainly displayed some Douglas memorabilia.

The museum's early holdings also
included a donated collection of
19th-century paintings by African-
American artists, but for exhibitions of African works Robbins had
to rely on loaned objects.

In 1979 the museum became
part of the Smithsonian Institution.
Three years later it was officially
renamed the National Museum of
African Art, and in 1987 the steadily growing institution moved to its
present location on the Mall. Its
permanent collection has grown to
include more than 7,000 objects.
They represent
nearly every area
of the continent
and a variety
of media and
art forms—tex-
tiles, photos,
sculpture, pot-
tery, painting,
and jewelry—
dating from
ancient to con-
temporary times.
For years the
museum displayed
samples from its collec-
tion in three main dis-
plays on the underground
first level, but the galleries
were revamped in 2004 for a
fresh look. In their place is a changing exhibition that highlights treasures from the museum's collection
along with pieces from public and
private collections, dating from the
14th to the 20th centuries.

The new displays are being
designed with the aim of illuminat-
ing the high aesthetic and technical
craftsmanship that is not always
readily apparent in African art.
They show, for example, how
Africans often fashion all kinds of
materials—from simple household
utensils to ceremonial objects to
monumental sculpture honoring
the living and the dead—in ways
meant to embody expressions of
an "ideal" that reflects standards of
beauty, moral behavior, leadership,
intelligence, and fertility.

A long-running exhibit of traditional hand-crafted **African
ceramics** shows the dexterity and
artistry of the continent's master
potters—mainly women. Included
are 20th-century pieces from
Algeria, Democratic Republic of
the Congo (formerly Zaire),
Malawi, Rwanda, and Tanzania.

The new permanent exhibit
Playful Performers shows how
children use masks, costumes, performances, and other forms of play
as both entertainment and a means
by which to learn important life
lessons and skills.

The museum also houses a
major library and research center
and offers many cultural programs.
Its **Eliot Elisofon Photographic
Archives,** named for the famed
Life magazine photographer, has an
expanding collection of 300,000
photo prints and transparencies
and 120,000 feet of unedited film
footage. ∎

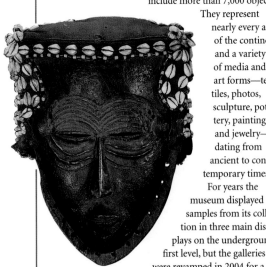

**Face mask from
Democratic
Republic of Congo
(early to mid-
1900s)**

Hirshhorn Museum &
Sculpture Garden

IN A WHITE, HATBOX-SHAPED BUILDING, THE HIRSHHORN exhibits modern works of art. A substantial gift (nearly 12,000 works between 1974 and 1981) from philanthropist Joseph H. Hirshhorn (1899–1981) forms the core of the rotating collection. The 82-foot-high building surrounds an open courtyard featuring a bronze fountain, while across Jefferson Drive on the north lies a lovely recessed sculpture garden. Designed by Gordon Bunshaft, the museum was considered daring when it opened in 1974; it has since become an accepted fixture of the National Mall and the Smithsonian.

Works from the permanent collection and on loan are displayed on two circular floors and a basement level. Modern art masters such as Picasso, Matisse, Giacometti, de Kooning, and Warhol are well represented, but the museum also has devoted much attention to acquiring works created in the last 25 years. The collection has grown by more than 5,000 works since the museum opened.

In the past, the Hirshhorn presented its holdings in more or less conventional fashion, arranged in chronological progression with paintings and sculpture often displayed in separate areas. Recently, the museum adopted a more innovative approach intended to help viewers better navigate the often mystifying world of modern art—hence the project's name, **Gyroscope**. Now, diverse works from the permanent collection are shown in rotating exhibits installed throughout the museum.

The pieces are arranged in groupings by era, medium, genre, or theme to provide insight into how and why particular artworks are made. One recent exhibit, for

Hirshhorn Museum & Sculpture Garden
www.hirshhorn.si.edu

Map p. 69

Independence Ave. & 7th St., S.W.

202-633-1000

Metro: L'Enfant Plaza; Bus: 30-36, 54, 13B & F

The Hirshhorn's circular courtyard often serves as a setting for receptions.

What was there before

Before the Hirshhorn took shape on the Mall, the U.S. Army Medical Museum (now the National Museum of Health & Medicine; see p. 190) occupied the site from 1887 to 1968. More than 25,000 specimens of diseased or wounded flesh and bones were kept here, and morbidly fascinated tourists could see preserved gunshot wounds, a vertebra from John Wilkes Booth, and disfigured and diseased organs. Over the years the tastes of the public changed, and the museum was moved to the Walter Reed Army Medical Center at 6900 Georgia Avenue, N.W. Meanwhile, the Hirshhorn delivers its own provocative, if not gross-out, punch. ■

focused on representations of the human form and universal themes of human experience and ideas, ranging from science to spirituality.

Prized works from the museum's collection are showcased alongside recent acquisitions. Some galleries are devoted to a single artist or feature single works from the museum's collection, including contemporary art that evades the categories of painting and sculpture. In Ann Hamilton's "At Hand" (2001), sheets of white paper drift from the ceiling and accumulate in piles on the floor. A gallery on the third floor, **Directions,** brings the work of emerging artists from around the world to Washington.

Outside, the **sculpture garden** features some 60 large-scale works of art dating from the 1880s to the 1960s. Included are Rodin's dark and brooding masterpiece, "Monument to the Burghers of Calais" (1884-89); biomorphic figures by Henry Moore and Barbara Hepworth; abstract works by Henry Moore and Claes Oldenburg; and kinetic sculptures by Alexander Calder and Mark di Suvero.

Tours covering the art collection and related topics are offered (202-633-3382), as are films, lectures, workshops, and concerts. ■

example, offered a study in formlessness and structure. Works such as Jackson Pollack's action paintings and Jean Dubuffet's encrusted surfaces were juxtaposed with pieces in which physical and spatial boundaries are more rigidly observed. Other exhibits have

An angular ode to modern art: "Are Years What? (for Marianne Moore)" (1967), composed of industrial I-beams with a suspended, moving V element, is considered one of Mark di Suvero's greatest works.

National Air and Space Museum

THE EXCITEMENT OF AERONAUTICAL AND SPACE-FLIGHT technology has made the National Air and Space Museum the most-visited museum in the world. More than nine million people a year roam the nearly four acres of its flagship building. The opening of a second, huge facility in suburban Virginia to house hundreds of additional artifacts in the museum's collection has swelled interest even more (see Steven F. Udvar-Hazy Center, pp. 220-21).

The Smithsonian's involvement in air and space goes back to 1857, when it began using balloons to collect weather data. Later, during the Civil War, the first secretary of the Smithsonian, Joseph Henry, won President Abraham Lincoln's support for making military observations from balloons. The third secretary, Samuel Pierpont Langley (1887–1906), was an astronomer and airplane pioneer. He experimented successfully with heavier-than-air craft on the Potomac in the 1890s, but the first actual manned, controlled flight was made by the Wright brothers in 1903.

During the first half of the 20th century, the Smithsonian participated in or funded major rocket research and astrophysical observation projects. In 1971, Apollo astronaut Michael Collins was appointed director of the new

National Air & Space Museum

www.nasm.si.edu

Map p. 69

Independence Ave. & 7th St., S.W.

202-357-2700

Metro: L'Enfant Plaza; Bus: 30-36, 54, P1-6

RT shuttle service available to Steven F. Udvar-Hazy Center in Chantilly, Va. ($$)

A mural showing the Milky Way galaxy highlights the "Explore the Universe" exhibit.

Lindbergh

Perhaps more than any other aviator, Charles Lindbergh (1902–1974) captured the public's admiration. Son of a Minnesota congressman, he spent many of his early years in Washington, D.C. Later he attended a Wisconsin college but dropped out to enroll in a Nebraska flying school. For a few years he was a stunt flyer and an airmail pilot. Then he competed for a $25,000 prize offered to the first person to fly from New York to Paris nonstop.

On May 20, 1927, the aviator took off in the *Spirit of St. Louis,* named for the city where he received financial backing. Because the large fuel tank partially blocked his view, Lindbergh relied on a periscope or tilted the plane to see forward. He flew for 33.5 exhausting hours before landing at Le Bourget Field near Paris and

receiving a warm welcome by a cheering crowd of 100,000.

Back in Washington, Lindbergh stayed a few days at the Patterson House on Dupont Circle with President Coolidge, who lived there while the White House was being renovated. Later that year the U.S. Congress awarded him a Medal of Honor. The following year he gave his plane to the Smithsonian, where it is prominently displayed in the Milestones of Flight gallery.

In 1929, Lindbergh wed Anne Morrow, and together they made several flights to chart airline routes. When their son was kidnapped and killed in 1932, the unending publicity drove them abroad. Lindbergh advocated neutrality at the outbreak of World War II, leading to criticism by President Roosevelt, yet he quietly served as an aircraft consultant and flew on combat missions over the Pacific. He described his famous transatlantic flight in thrilling detail in *We* (1927) and *The Spirit of St. Louis* (1953), the latter winning a Pulitzer Prize. ■

Charles A. Lindbergh (1902–1974), with the *Spirit of St. Louis*

National Air and Space Museum, and construction began the next year. The Wright Flyer and other aircraft that had been on display in another Smithsonian facility on the Mall, the Arts and Industries Building, were moved to the new museum, which opened to the public in 1976.

Opposite: The *Spirit of St. Louis* took Charles Lindbergh across the Atlantic in 1927; 35 years later, Mercury Friendship 7 carried John Glenn into Earth orbit.

VISITING

A drawback to so large a space is that, depending upon where you are, you may have to walk the equivalent of a city block to get to a rest room or dining area. If you're with children, or anyone who tires easily, you'll have a more enjoyable time if you carefully plan

your visit (see the floor plan on pp. 78-79). If you decide to split up, determine a specific place and time to meet; otherwise you could spend a long time trying to locate members of your party. Purchase tickets to the IMAX and planetarium shows first, then tour the galleries that most interest you. Plan to spend about half a day for a quick overview of the whole museum or a thorough look at a few galleries.

Almost all the aircraft and most of the spacecraft are the genuine articles. Some space vehicles, of course, stay in space; in those cases backups, test vehicles, or authentic reproductions are shown. Labels highlight the differences.

FIRST FLOOR

Just inside the Mall entrance, the outstanding **Milestones of Flight gallery** holds aviation's greatest hits. A museum in itself, this is a gallery where almost everyone will want to linger. For years one of its centerpieces—suspended from the ceiling—was the wood-and-fabric plane that Orville Wright flew at Kitty Hawk, North Carolina, in 1903. To mark the centennial of the historic event, the plane was moved in 2003 to a new gallery on the second floor. In that exhibit, **The Wright Brothers and the Invention of the Aerial Age**, visitors can now see the Wright Flyer at eye level.

Included in the Milestones gallery is the *Spirit of St. Louis*, in which Charles Lindbergh made the first solo, nonstop flight across the Atlantic in May 1927. Another place of honor is given to Chuck Yeager's sleek orange Bell X-1, which in 1947 became the first aircraft to break the sound barrier. Nearby is the Mercury Friendship 7, the capsule in which John Glenn became the first American to orbit Earth in 1962. Then there's the Apollo 11 Command Module, which carried the first humans to the moon and back in 1969.

Examples of space probes are pretty close to the real thing: The Viking Lander, for example, is a copy used to simulate what Vikings 1 and 2 did on Mars from 1976 to 1982. You can also touch a four-billion-year-old moon rock, collected in 1972 during the Apollo 17 mission.

Past the museum shop, to the right, you come to the **Air Transportation gallery.** Its several planes from the 1920s and '30s illustrate strides in commercial aviation.

Across the hall just to the right is the **Golden Age of Flight.**

Sea-Air Operations

WWII Aviation

Air Transportation

Golden Age of Flight

Scratchy recordings of old torch songs set the tone for this exhibit of the glamour days, and a small theater continuously runs historic footage. Here you can see Howard Hughes's single-prop H-1 racer, in which he set a speed record of 352 mph in 1935. That same year the nearby *Gamma Polar Star* made the first transantarctic flight. Also on display is a Beech Staggerwing, a biplane flown by aviation pioneer Edwin Eugene Aldrin, the father of astronaut Edwin "Buzz" Aldrin.

In the adjacent **Jet Aviation gallery,** you can trace the development of jet technology. The plane with its wings folded up is a 1945 FH-1 Phantom, the first type to

SECOND FLOOR

- Albert Einstein Planetarium
- Langley IMAX
- Beyond the Limits
- WWI: The Great War in the Air
- Pioneers of Flight
- Apollo to the Moon
- Explaining the Planets

FIRST FLOOR

- Milestones of Flight
- Langley IMAX
- Rocketry & Space Flight
- Museum shop
- Space Race
- Lunar Exploration Vehicles
- Early Flight
- Info Desk
- Looking at Earth
- Jet Aviation
- How Things Fly
- Explore the Universe
- Cafeteria

Independence Avenue

take off from and land on an aircraft carrier.

The **Early Flight gallery** re-creates a 1913 aeronautical exhibition. An 1894 Lilienthal glider with batlike ribbed wings hangs at the entrance; farther along a mannequin makes a sales pitch for a Bleriot monoplane. The worn-looking 1909 Wright Military Flyer was the world's first military plane.

Step across the Independence Avenue entrance hall, pausing to admire the two tremendous murals. On one wall, Robert T. McCall's 1976 "The Space Mural: A Cosmic View" traces space history from the Big Bang to lunar exploration and beyond. On the opposite wall, Eric

Sloan's "Earthflight Environment" (1976) shows a western landscape beneath a sky filled with the kinds of weather pilots must fly through.

Children will especially take to the adjoining **How Things Fly gallery,** which contains about 50 hands-on exhibits. Learn about lift, drag, air pressure, wave action, and other principles, or climb into the cockpit of a Cessna 150, for example. Next door, the **Looking at Earth gallery** holds a de Havilland DH-4 surveying plane, a Lockheed U-2 spy plane, and model satellites. Touch a screen to view a Landsat image of any state.

At the east end of the first floor is the shiny Mylar-covered Lunar

Praised by pilots for its agility, a World War II Italian fighter plane—one of two remaining Macchi C.202s—hangs above a North American P-51 Mustang, a superb American fighting machine of the same vintage.

Module 2, a duplicate of one used on Apollo 5. It's the same kind of craft that went to the moon with Apollo 11.

The popular two-story-high **Space Race Hall** in the northeast corner harbors boosters and missiles. Especially interesting are the suspended Apollo and Soyuz docked together and a bell-shaped Soyuz landing module autographed by Russian cosmonauts. You also can stare up at a 42-foot-tall test vehicle of the Hubble Space Telescope; its 8,500 pounds make it only one-third the weight of the actual telescope. You can walk through a backup of the Skylab space station. Launched in 1973, its working counterpart fell to Earth in 1979, breaking up and landing in Australia and the Indian Ocean.

Displays in the nearby **Rocketry and Space Flight gallery** include rocket engines and the evolution of space suits. Down the hall, **Explore the Universe** offers a history of the tools that astronomers use for

studying the universe.

In the **Langley IMAX Theater** *(fee)*, you can see amazing films projected on a five-story-high screen with seat-rumbling effects. "To Fly!" is the long-running classic, while "Space Station: 3-D" is the new blockbuster.

At lunchtime, catch a bite at the two-story restaurant.

SECOND FLOOR

On the second floor, you can visit the **Einstein Planetarium** *(fee)* and see multimedia presentations on the planets and stars.

The **Sea-Air Operations gallery** next door holds carrier aircraft from 1911 to the present, including a 1930s F4B-4, a World War II FM-1 Wildcat, an SBD Dauntless dive-bomber, and an A-4 Skyhawk from the 1950s and '60s. Walking around the upper and lower decks, you can watch videos on the major Pacific aircraft carrier battles of World War II and learn about carrier missions in the atomic era. Across the hall, go into **World**

War II Aviation to learn more about the air history of World War II. Continue down the south side of the floor to the next exhibits.

The glory days of air fighting are examined in unromanticized detail in the **Great War in the Air gallery,** which tells the story of World War I aviation. On display are a German Fokker D.VII, a British Sopwith Snipe, and others.

Exploring the Planets gallery includes a duplicate of the Voyager spacecraft and a meteorite that might have come from Mars. In **Pioneers of Flight,** you'll find several famous aircraft: Amelia Earhart's Lockheed Vega, in which she became the first woman to fly solo across the Atlantic in 1932; the Lindberghs' 1930s Tingmissartoq, used for charting airline routes; and the Gossamer Condor, which made the first human-powered flight.

The **Where Next, Columbus? gallery** examines exploration possibilities of the future and includes a simulated Martian landscape and a hydroponic gar-

den. The heady years of manned spaceflight are examined in the **Apollo to the Moon gallery,** while **Flight and the Arts** features aeronautics and spaceflight in art, film, and popular culture.

Across the hall, design your own aircraft in **Beyond the Limits.** On display are a lightning-fast Cray-1 supercomputer, a robotic airplane, and the brains of a Minuteman intercontinental ballistic missile.

Finally, you'll need to wander outside to view the exhibit **Voyage: A Journey Through Our Solar System.** Depicting the solar system at one-ten-billionth of its actual size, it demonstrates the relative size of the planets and the great distances between them. The planets are porcelain balls mounted atop stainless steel posts. The Sun is about the size of a large grapefruit; Earth, like the head of a pin. The installation extends along the Mall from in front of the Smithsonian Castle all the way to the Air and Space Museum. ■

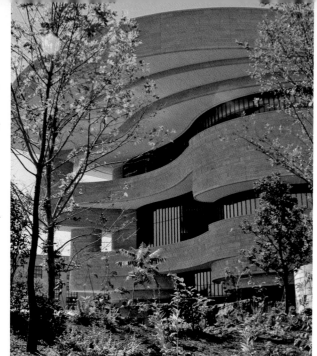

The museum's exterior has undulating curves and deep window ledges, giving it the appearance of a stratified stone mass that has been carved by wind and water.

National Museum of the American Indian

National Museum of the American Indian

www.nmai.si.edu

 Map p. 69

✉ Fourth St. & Independence Ave., S.W.

☎ 202-633-1000

 Metro: L'Enfant Plaza; Bus: 30-36, 54, Pl-6

STRIKING IN ITS ARCHITECTURE, WHICH WAS INSPIRED BY the rocky mesa cliffs of the American Southwest, the National Museum of the American Indian opened in September 2004 after 15 years of planning. It gives the nation a vibrant center for Native American events and educational programs as well as a showcase for outstanding Indian art and artifacts.

The museum got its start at the turn of the 20th century when a wealthy New York banker, George Gustav Heye, needed a place to house the objects he had obtained from North and South American Native cultures in a buying frenzy from 1903 to 1954—an astonishing collection of almost a million pieces spanning 10,000 years. He established a museum in what is now the restored Alexander Hamilton U.S. Custom House in lower Manhattan.

In 1989 Heye's collection was transferred to the Smithsonian Institution. Among the artifacts were human remains that had to be repatriated and buried in Native grounds. As the Smithsonian's Native American collection swelled to some 4 million objects, a campaign began to build a major museum for Indian art and culture. The original location in New York City is now a branch of this new 4.25-acre museum on the Mall, along with a 200,000-square-foot Cultural Resources Center in Suitland, Maryland, where a large bulk of the collection is preserved, documented, and researched.

Among the museum's treasures

are intricate carvings and masks from Pacific Northwest coastal tribes; embellished hides and feather bonnets from North American Plains Indians; pottery and basketry from the southwestern United States; 18th-century materials from the Great Lakes region; and early Navajo weavings. Artifacts from Mexico, Central and South America, and the Caribbean include jade carved by the Olmec and Maya and elaborate Amazonian feather works.

VISITING

Because of the museum's popularity, free timed-entry passes are required. They are available at the east entrance for same-day admission; or reserve passes in advance at www.tickets.com or by calling 866-400-6624 (*service fee*).

As you wander about the five-story museum, observe the many symbolic references to the cultures it honors. The curvy outside façade of Kasota limestone was made to appear like an ancient slab of stratified stone. Crystal prisms embedded in the south-facing wall create "light shows" when reflecting the mid-day sun, while the main doors bear Native sun symbols.

Inside, you first reach a central space called the **Potomac,** a Piscataway word for a place "where the goods are brought in." The overhead dome, 120 feet high and 120 feet wide, has an oculus offering views of the sky and celestial bodies—critical reference points in Native cultures. In the floor is an abstract fire design shaped from pipestone, and rings of black and red granite that map the solstices and equinoxes. A wall of copper bands woven to suggest Native baskets and textiles encircles the room.

Near the information desk, a **Welcome Wall** projects hundreds of Native American words for "welcome" onto a 23-foot screen. A the-ater on the ground floor features storytelling, music, dance, and other programs. An inaugural temporary exhibit in the Potomac area spotlights boat-building traditions of Native peoples.

Take the elevators to the exhibition areas on the upper levels. The 120-seat **Lewali Theater** on the fourth floor offers a short orientation program explaining the themes and messages emphasized throughout the exhibits.

The museum has three permanent exhibits. **Our Universes: Traditional Knowledge Shapes Our World** looks at the primary role of cosmology in the myths and everyday life of Native peoples, and their reverence for the spiritual rela-

"Lightening Strikes," a blown glass base by Tom Jojola (Isleta Pueblo), New Mexico, circa 1990

tionship between mankind and the natural world. The galleries show how various tribes interpret the order of the world and its meaning for harmony in their lives.

The exhibit **Our Peoples: Giving Voice to Our Histories** conveys events that have shaped the lives and outlook of American Indians from 1491 to the present. **Our Lives: Contemporary Life and Identities** examines how American Indians work to preserve and define their identities amid the challenges of the 21st century.

On the third and fourth levels, more than 3,500 objects from the museum's magnificent and wide-ranging collection are on display, arranged by categories in drawers and glass-fronted cases. ■

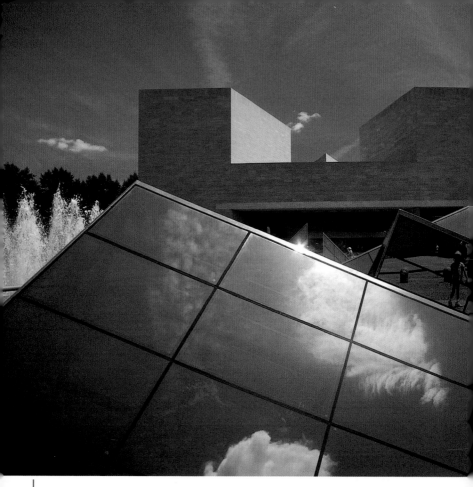

National Gallery of Art

National Gallery of Art

www.nga.gov

🅜 Map p. 69

✉ Constitution Ave. between 3rd & 9th Sts., N.W.

☎ 202-737-4215

🚇 Metro: Archives, Smithsonian; Bus: 30-36, 54, 13A & G

ONE OF THE COUNTRY'S TOP ART MUSEUMS, THE NATIONAL Gallery of Art holds a comprehensive collection of Western masterpieces. The West Building exhibits European painting and sculpture from the 13th to 19th centuries; American art; and prints, drawings, decorative arts, and temporary shows. The newer East Building, or East Wing, contains modern and contemporary art.

In the 1920s, financier Andrew Mellon began collecting great art with the idea of establishing a museum in Washington. In 1931 he completed a purchase of 21 paintings from Russia's Hermitage Museum, including Raphael's "Alba Madonna." Mellon died in 1937, the same year that construction began for the new museum designed by John Russell Pope and funded by the A.W. Mellon Educational and Charitable Trust.

Other major donors soon added to the holdings—including 375 Italian paintings and 18 sculptures from Samuel H. Kress, founder of a chain of five-and-dime stores. In March 1941, President Roosevelt

Under phased renovation plans various galleries in the two buildings are closed temporarily, so check the website before your visit if there's a particular masterpiece you want to see.

Also check for special exhibitions and new acquisitions. In 2004, for example, art scholar and collector John Wilmerding donated 51 notable works of 19th-century American art, such as George Caleb Bingham's "Mississippi Boatman" (1850). In recent years 22 new galleries were added on the ground floor of the West Building, featuring 900 works of art such as sculpture masterpieces from the Middle Ages through the late 19th and early 20th centuries; 18th-century French decorative arts; and Chinese porcelains. New photo galleries were due to open in October 2004.

WEST BUILDING

All entrances other than on the Mall put you on the ground floor. One level up is the **main floor,** where European art from the 13th to 19th centuries and American painting and sculpture from colonial times to the early 20th century are displayed. The spectacular **Rotunda,** ringed by Tuscan marble pillars, rises to a high oculus above a central fountain graced by a statue of Mercury. The dome is strongly reminiscent of John Russell Pope's other great Washington structure, the Jefferson Memorial.

Extending from either side of the Rotunda, the **West Sculpture Hall** contains works in bronze, while the **East Sculpture Hall** has works in marble. Each hall ends in a garden court, where free concerts are often held. Several cafés and coffee bars throughout the National Gallery facilities offer light fare.

The halls and courts are surrounded by galleries that are numbered 1 to 93 and generally proceed

Rising from the plaza between the East and West Buildings, glass tetrahedrons act as skylights for a lower concourse.

presided over a dedication ceremony attended by nearly 9,000 guests.

The holdings continued to grow, and in the late 1960s, architect I.M. Pei was hired to create a plan for a new building to accommodate the collection. Opened in 1978, the East Building had to fit a trapezoidal site, mesh with the neoclassic West Building, and be an appropriate receptacle for modern art. The resulting marble-faced monolithic surfaces, acute angles, and glass hyphens make it not only visually arresting but also a fitting counterpart to the nearby 1970s buildings— the Hirshhorn and the Air and Space Museum. An underground concourse connects the two buildings.

West Garden Court

West Sculpture Hall

Rotunda

East Sculpture Hall

East Garden Court

Main Floor

Ground Floor

West Building

NATIONAL GALLERY OF ART

chronologically, with nationalities grouped together.

Galleries 1–15 hold **13th- to 15th-century Italian paintings.** Representing the early Florentine and central Italian Renaissance, these works range from Byzantine iconography to the beginnings of the high Renaissance. Masterpieces include Leonardo da Vinci's "Ginevra de' Benci," a 1474 oil on wood; Giotto's "Madonna and Child" (ca 1320–1330); Fra Filippo Lippi's "Adoration of the Magi" (ca 1445); and Botticelli's "Giuliano de' Medici" (ca 1478).

You'll find **16th-century**

Italian and Spanish works in Galleries 16–28. Here is art from the northern Italian Renaissance, distinguished by allegorical and religious scenes within a colorful, sensual, pastoral setting. Especially outstanding are paintings by the Venetian master Tiziano Vecelli, or Titian, whose lovely "Venus with a Mirror" (1555) is vibrant with life. Raphael's "Alba Madonna" (1510) hangs here, as do works by Tintoretto, one of the great Mannerist painters. Don't fail to pause in Gallery 26 for Bernardino Luini's "Fresco Cycle," with the "Story of Procris and Cephalus" (1520-22). America's only Italian Renaissance

WEST BUILDING GALLERIES

▦ 12th- to 15th-century Italian	▦ 19th-century French
▦ 16th-century Italian and Spanish	■ British
▦ 17th- and 18th-century Italian, Spanish, and French Baroque	▦ American
▦ 15th- to 16th-century Netherlandish and German	▦ Special Exhibitions
▦ 17th-century Dutch and Flemish	▦ Photography
■ 18th- and 19th-century Spanish	▦ Prints and Drawings
▦ 18th- and early 19th-century French	▦ Non-Exhibition Space
	▦ Sculpture

East Building

fresco series recounts a myth in nine pastoral scenes around a villa-like room that's floored with mosaic tiles from third-century Tunisia. Gallery 28 has several works by El Greco.

Galleries 29–34 and 36–37 display **17th- to 18th-century Italian, Spanish, and French Baroque** paintings. Among the artists are Tiepolo—a Venetian master known for his handling of chiaroscuro, the interplay of light and shadow—and Velázquez, whose use of color foreshadowed Impressionism. Look for Georges de la Tour's "The Repentant

Magdalene" (1640) and Jacopo Manfredi's tavern scene, "Bravos Drinking and Making Music" (1615).

In Galleries 35, 35A, and 38–41A, **15th- to 16th-century Netherlandish and German** painters include Albrecht Dürer (the "Leonardo of the North") and Matthias Grunewald, whose relatively few works, mostly of religious subjects, were enough to secure his reputation as one of the greats of his time.

Among the most popular areas of the museum, Galleries 42–51 feature **17th-century Flemish**

Self-portrait by Vincent van Gogh

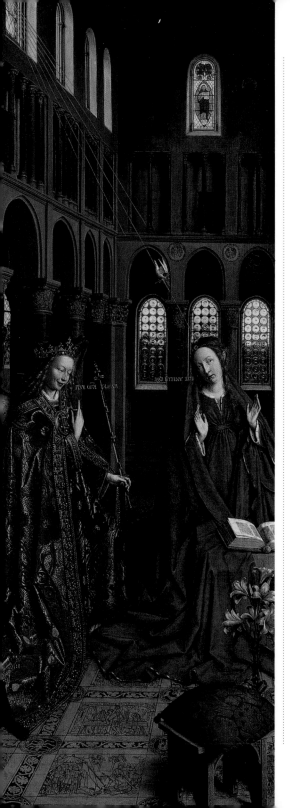

and **Dutch** paintings. From Rubens's "Daniel in the Lions' Den" (1613–15) to Rembrandt's "Portrait of a Man in a Tall Hat" (1663) and his dark "Self-Portrait" (1659), the possibilities of realism are pushed to an intensity that would influence art for generations. In "The Mill" (1650), Rembrandt demonstrates his expert handling of chiaroscuro.

Walk now to the east side of the rotunda, where Gallery 52 contains **18th- and 19th-century Spanish** paintings, notably by Francisco de Goya. **French art** from the **18th and early 19th centuries** lines the walls of Galleries 53–56, much of it in a florid style depicting lighthearted sophistication in French society. Among the treasures are Antoine Watteau's "Italian Comedians" (1720), Boucher's "Madame Bergeret" (1746), and Fragonard's "A Young Girl Reading" (1776).

British works fill Galleries 57–59, 61, and 63. Painters represented here include Hogarth, Reynolds, Romney, Gainsborough, Constable, and Turner. The landscapes of Constable and seascapes of Turner are particularly worth noting. **American** paintings are on view in Galleries 60A–B, 62, and 64–71. Gilbert Stuart's portraits of early U.S. Presidents vie for attention with the big mid-19th-century landscapes of Bierstadt, Cole, and Church. Other works are by Homer, Whistler, Bellows, Ryder, Sargent, and Cropsey. Galleries 72–79 are reserved for **special exhibitions.**

Impressionist and other 19th-century French painting is on exhibit in Galleries 80–93. These rooms are filled with the light and color of leading exponents Renoir and Monet, and the idiosyncratic styles of Cézanne and van Gogh. Also on display are Parisian nightlife scenes by Degas and Toulouse-Lautrec. Among the great works are Renoir's "Girl with a Watering Can" (1876), Manet's "The Railway" (1873), and Monet's "Woman with a Parasol— Madame Monet and her Son" (1875).

The ground floor showcases **photography and sculpture,** as well as **prints and drawings** by luminaries such as Michelangelo, Leonardo, Manet, and Cézanne. From here you can reach the East Building via a below ground concourse, or enter it from Fourth Street.

EAST BUILDING

The towering walls and angles of the East Building (or East Wing) are marvels in themselves. Gracing the entrance, Henry Moore's curvy bronze "Knife Edge Mirror Two Piece" (1977–78) mimics the shape of the building, in rounded form. The building itself consists of two triangular shapes; the one on the north exhibits works of modern art, while the other one has offices.

At the ground-floor information desk, you can check on current exhibits and the tour schedule. This floor opens to a soaring atrium that for years featured an untitled mobile by Calder. Other art is usually on view as well, such as small "postcards" of French people and scenes by masters of Impressionism and Postimpressionism. The **mezzanine** and **upper levels** hold several large exhibition rooms for permanent and temporary exhibits. On display are works that trace the evolution of modernism, and the artists include Picasso, Braque, Miró, Mondrian, Arp, Magritte, Stella, O'Keeffe, Lichtenstein, Kandinsky, Brancusi, and Giacometti.

Take the winding staircase to the **tower level** to view the Matisse cutouts (1950s), huge colorful paper collages the artist created near the end of his long life. The **concourse level** also has exhibit space for large canvases and installations.

SCULPTURE GARDEN

Opened in 1999, the 6-acre Sculpture Garden lies across Seventh Street from the West Building. Its 17 works include "Puellae" (1992), featuring 30 headless, shriveled, 3-foot-tall girls—Polish-born sculptor Magdalena Abakanowicz's eerie depiction of a Holocaust story. You can't miss Louise Bourgeois's 9-foot-tall "Spider" (1997), part of the artist's series that explores childhood memory and loss. Another large piece, "Aurora" (1992–93) by Mark Di Suvero, illustrates elegance and balance on a massive scale.

An attractive glass-sided café in the garden serves sandwiches, salads, and drinks. It is a pleasant venue for free "Jazz in the Garden" concerts held Friday evenings from Memorial Day to Labor Day. Nearby is an outdoor ice-skating rink that is open November to March. ■

Opposite: Jan van Eyck's "The Annunciation" (1434–36, oil on wood transferred to canvas) was probably once the left wing of a triptych. Below: Claes Oldenburg and Coosje van Bruggen's "Typewriter Eraser, Scale X" (1999, stainless steel and fiberglass), found in the Sculpture Garden, depicts one of Oldenburg's favorite childhood playthings from his father's office.

National Museum of Natural History

National Museum of Natural History

www.mnh.si.edu

🅰 Map p. 69

✉ 10th St. & Constitution Ave., N.W.

☎ 202-633-1000

🚇 Metro: Federal Triangle, Smithsonian; Bus: 13A-B & F-G, P1-2, A42-48

DINOSAUR FOSSILS, SPARKLING GEMS, A GIANT SQUID, AN insect zoo, and rare Native American artifacts—these are the kinds of things that make this such a popular museum. The Smithsonian's National Museum of Natural History explores in wondrous detail the natural world and our place in it. Housed in a green-domed beaux arts building from 1904, this was the third Smithsonian building, erected to hold the institution's bursting collection.

The teeming variety of nature continues to assert its importance: More than three-fourths of the Smithsonian's entire collection of artifacts, specimens, and works of art belongs to this museum alone. That's more than 125 million individual specimens and artifacts. Though most people won't see these specimens, researchers from around the world use the collection —much of it stored off-site—to carry out various systematic studies. Think of all the millions of bee-tles, butterflies, mosquitoes, sponges, mollusks, mineralogical samples, birds' eggs, microscopic organisms, and Native American baskets stored in drawers and on shelves.

VISITING

You can easily spend a day wandering through the museum, getting sidetracked from whatever it was you had set out to see. If you have only a few hours, pinpoint a couple exhibits and plot your route (maps available at information desks at both entrances). Entering from the Constitution Avenue side puts you on the **ground floor,** which has a **highlights** exhibit, a sampler of the treasures awaiting you within. Before you head up to the two exhibit floors, walk to the back of this floor, past the Atrium Café and Museum Shop, to the **Birds of D.C.** exhibit. Many people miss this compendium of taxidermed eastern birds, on display since the 1920s. Along with bald and golden eagles, swans, and warblers, the extinct Carolina parakeet and passenger pigeon are represented.

The museum features a number of special exhibitions. One new program, for example, examines the physical, biological, and cultural interactions that shape our world. Called **Forces of Change,** it shows connections between seemingly remote forces such as gas bubbles inside the Antarctic ice cap and famines in tropical Africa.

First floor

If you enter the museum from the Mall side, you'll step into the grand **Rotunda,** one of the city's great interior spaces. The eight-sided Rotunda rises to a dome 125 feet from the floor; columned galleries offer splendid views from above. But the sight in the middle of the Rotunda is what grabs most people's attention: Standing 13 feet 2 inches at the shoulder, the **African bush elephant** weighed 12 tons when it was killed in 1954. It is the largest mounted specimen of Earth's largest land animal, and its grassy savanna display has sound effects and other mounted animals.

You may want to begin your visit in the building's recently restored west wing, which features an exciting new attraction: the **Kenneth E. Behring Family Hall of Mammals.** The 25,000-square-foot permanent exhibition, which tells the story of mammal evolution through adaptation to

Crowds pass in and out of the Rotunda on their way to galleries, often pausing to view the mounted African elephant; the enormous animal was about 50 years old when killed in 1954.

A model of a salt crystal, enlarged nearly 1.5 billion times, bedazzles visitors to the Hall of Geology, Gems, and Minerals.

changing habitats, features 274 taxidermied specimens artfully posed in a variety of environments—from polar to desert, dry to humid. Interactive features enhance the displays by explaining aspects of the incredible diversity of mammals, including humans, and the processes by which they arose and continue to adapt. A short film traces mammal evolution.

Just to the right of the Mall entrance, the **Early Life** exhibit contains one of the oldest known fossils—a mass of fossilized microbes 3.5 billion years old—and presents a short animated film that outlines the origins of life. The rare fossils of 530-million-year-old soft-bodied animals, among the museum's most important finds, were discovered in 1909 by geologist Charles Walcott, the Smithsonian's fourth secretary.

The adjacent **Dinosaur Hall** exhibit showcases the skeleton of an 80-foot-long *Diplodocus,* a family member of the largest land animals ever. **Life in the Ancient Seas**

displays the curving, partially reconstructed skeleton of a 30-foot whale that swam the ocean about 39 million years ago. Before moving on to the next area, watch scientists and artists at work in the glassed-off **FossilLab.**

Just around the corner, the **Ice Age Hall** explores the beginnings of human influence on the world of animals and plants. Casts and composite skeletons of a woolly mammoth, mastodon, and giant ground sloth illustrate the large creatures that went extinct more than 10,000 years ago. Pleistocene survivors include a mounted wolverine, musk ox, and badger. You can't help pausing before the diorama of a Neanderthal burial, a re-creation of a ritual performed 70,000 years ago. In a compelling, intimate scene, the deceased lies bound in the fetal position while his family and a shaman look on.

The other exhibits on this floor explore various cultures. **African Voices** sports a jazzy look with world-beat music and touch terminals. By contrast, the older **Asian and Pacific Cultures Galleries** have the same terrazzo floors and glass display cases they have had for decades. There is something comforting about the older displays, and their longevity attests to their excellence; the totems and stone discs and vivid dioramas free the imagination to wander to faraway lands.

In the far corner, the **Discovery Room** *(closed Mon.)* holds a number of animals, fossils, shells, and minerals that visitors can handle. Also in this part of the museum, a 400-seat **IMAX Theater** *(fee)* shows large-format 2-D and 3-D films on a screen six stories high.

Second floor

On the second floor, many people head directly for the **Janet Annenberg Hooker Hall of Geology, Gems, and Minerals.** Here you can learn how a meteorite impact may have wiped out the dinosaurs, build a virtual volcano, touch a piece of limestone scarred by Ice Age glaciers, see fluorescent minerals, view a mock-up vertical mine shaft, and watch a film on plate tectonics. You will definitely want to ogle the dazzling **National Gem Collection,** starring the 45.5-carat Hope Diamond, the largest blue diamond in the world. Other outstanding riches include a thousand-diamond diadem given by Napoleon I to his wife Empress Marie Louise; a pair of Marie Antoinette's earrings; and the world's largest perfect quartz sphere, a magically clear 107-pound globe from China. Just beyond lies a hall of sparkling crystals in a myriad of colors, shapes, and sizes, including such oddities as twinned and twisted crystal formations.

Continuing on this floor, the **South America: Continent and Culture Hall** has life-size tableaus, detailed murals, and a number of weapons, tools, and other artifacts to present the life and history of four South American regions: the wide Patagonian grasslands, the lush tropical rain forests, the dry Pacific coastlands, and the high Andean mountain valleys.

Turn the corner and you'll see an interesting exhibit on the giant squid. Two preserved specimens, including a 9-foot female that washed ashore on Plum Island, Maine, in 1980. Earth's largest invertebrate animals, giant squid live from about 650 to 2,300 feet beneath the surface of the ocean. Scientists have never seen them alive in their natural environment.

The next-door **Western Cultures** exhibit covers the rise of Western civilization from the end of the Ice Age to about A.D. 500. Helping to tell the story of the emergence and spread of Western culture are a reconstructed Ice Age cave with flint tools; early Egyptian pottery; reconstructed Bronze Age tombs from Jordan's Bab-edh-Dhra, the City of the Dead (3000 B.C.); an Egyptian coffin; and a mummified bull.

Walk on to the **Hall of Bones and Reptiles,** where you can see mammal skeletons varying in size from the pocket mouse to the huge, extinct Steller's sea cow. The adjoining **O. Orkin Insect Zoo** is a storehouse of delights for anyone who appreciates the most abundant animals on Earth. Live exhibits, animated by buzzing and chirping sounds, give this exhibit an edge. Watch live bees, water striders, darkling beetles, centipedes, tarantulas, and whip scorpions. Labels indicate which species, such as scorpions and tarantulas, are "insect relatives." Here, you can add a bit of excitement to your life by walking through a simulated rain forest with giant cockroaches and cave arthropods. ■

National Museum of American History

National Museum of American History

www.americanhistory.si.edu

🗺 Map p. 69

✉ 14th St. & Constitution Ave., N.W.

☎ 202-633-1000

🚇 Metro: Federal Triangle, Smithsonian; Bus: 13A-B & F-G, 52-3, 11Y

THE NATIONAL MUSEUM OF AMERICAN HISTORY COLLECTS, cares for, and preserves more than 3 million artifacts, which together create a vast and fascinating mosaic of life in the United States. Dedicated to "inspiring a broader understanding of our nation and its many peoples," this bonanza of American history reflects the trends and events in the country's multifaceted history.

A museum visitor delivers an impromptu inaugural presidential address.

When it opened in 1964, the building was called the National Museum of History and Technology. The name was changed in 1980, however, to more accurately reflect the museum's expanded scope of interests and responsibilities.

The museum, after 40 years, recently embarked on a major revamping of its exhibits. Under these plans, the layout of separate halls devoted to various subjects is giving way to exhibits organized around themes. Objects large and small from the museum's vast collections are being incorporated into displays that are designed to provide a narrative framework on aspects of American life, from colonial times to the present.

Among the major changes, the **Hall of Transportation** has been completely refurbished, and a new **Military History Hall** was added. Several of the museum's longtime exhibits—including **Maritime Hall, Information Age, First Ladies, The American Presidency,** and **A More Perfect Union**—are being upgraded in stages, so some flexibility may be required when you arrive for your visit.

VISITING

With so much to see on three sprawling floors—some 30 exhibit areas on nearly twice the floor space of the National Air and Space Museum—you'll have a difficult time taking in the whole museum in one gulp. Spend a few hours on one floor, then come back another day. Or just hit a few highlights.

First floor

The Constitution Avenue entrance puts you on the first floor of the museum; the Mall entrance, on the second. The galleries on the east side of the first floor focus on agriculture and transportation.

In the **Agriculture** section, view artifacts such as a big red International Harvester that was driven 1,800 miles to Washington in 1979 as part of the American Agricultural Movement, and a monster 1924 Hyber Steam Tractor. The Maritime area has a 1920 Marine Steam Engine and model ships galore.

The major new transportation exhibit, **American on the Move,** is built on the idea that mobility is the defining experience in changing American life. Move from the railroad's arrival in a California town in 1876, up to modern life in auto-choked Los Angeles. Get your kicks on 40 feet of famed Route 66, commute on the Chicago "L" train, and marvel at a 92-foot Southern Railway locomotive. A companion exhibit, **On the Water: Stories From Maritime America,** is planned.

Nearby, **Engines of Change** explores the industrial revolution in America and how work-saving machines have changed our lives. The exhibit's 1836 *John Bull* is the world's oldest operable locomotive. **On Time** looks at the ways Americans have measured, used, and thought about time for 300 years,

through ingenious timepieces from sundials to atomic clocks.

On the west side of the first floor, science is the focus. The extensive **Science in American Life** exhibit examines issues in society affected by science, such as the birth control pill's effect on the sexual revolution, and ripples cast by experimental psychology, nylon, and atomic testing. In the **Hands on Science Center** (*closed Mon.*), perform experiments to learn about testing for radioactivity, conserving textiles, and protecting against ultraviolet rays.

The adjacent **Information Age** exhibit walks you through the history of telecommunications and computers. Starting with Samuel Morse's telegraph (invented

1835–37) and Alexander Graham Bell's original telephone (from 1876), you move on to the early computers — including a 1946 machine that would fill a modern office.

A temporary first-floor exhibit on **Julia Child's Kitchen** has been highly popular. The 14-foot-by-20-foot kitchen and 1,200 objects from it were moved to the museum from the Cambridge, Massachusetts, home where the late celebrity chef worked for 45 years

Magazine photographs and campaign buttons in the "First Ladies" exhibit

1875   1900   1925

BUCHAN...   LINCOLN   JOHNSON   GRANT   HAYES   GARFIELD   ARTHUR   CLEVELAND   HARRISON   CLEVELAND   McKINLEY   ROOSEVELT   TAFT   WILSON   HARDING   COOLIDGE   HOOVER   ROOSEVELT

A primer on the nation's leaders anchors the popular "American Presidency" exhibit.

demystifying the cooking process for Americans. (*The exhibit closes in September 2005.*)

Near the information desk, the Palm Court offers refreshments.

Second Floor

In a special lab on the second floor, you can watch experts working to preserve one of America's greatest treasures: the original **1813 flag** that inspired the national anthem (see box). Permanently donated to the Smithsonian in 1912, the banner has long been the museum's centerpiece, hanging for all visitors to see. Because of its poor condition, the flag underwent state-of-the-art treatment begining in 1998. When the work is complete, the famous icon will be showcased in a new gallery at the center of the museum, **For Which It Stands.**

Next door, the exhibit **Field to Factory** explores the massive migration of blacks from the rural South to the industrialized North from 1915 to 1940. View outfits and booklets of the Ku Klux Klan and read stories from black-run newspapers of the 1920s.

On the same side of the museum is the popular exhibit **First Ladies: Political Role and Public Image.** It showcases evening gowns worn by the Presidents' wives and chronicles their changing role and their accomplishments. The nearby exhibit **Within These Walls** features the largest artifact in the museum: a mid-1960s house from Ipswich, Massachusetts. The Georgian-style, timber-frame house serves to illustrate the lives of five ordinary families who lived in the house while experiencing changes and events in our nation's past.

itary uniform. A **Ceremonial Court** features mockups of some areas of the White House.

Other exhibits on the third floor highlight the role of women in politics and social reform from 1809-1925 and look at the 1800s as experienced by three communities. **Hands On History** lets you delve further into areas of interest. The small and eclectic **Icons of Popular Culture** features such items as a pair of Dorothy's Oz-enchanted ruby slippers, Indiana Jones's fedora and leather jacket, and Muhammad Ali's boxing gloves. Exhibits in the **Hall of Musical Instruments** include a tribute to Ella Fitzgerald. ∎

"What So Proudly We Hail'd"

The 30-by-34-foot flag known as the Star-Spangled Banner is fragile despite its size. Woven loosely to fly on a 90-foot flagpole, its expected life span was only two years. Flying over Fort McHenry, it incurred much damage. When the British attacked Baltimore in 1814, amateur poet Francis Scott Key was on a ship in the Chesapeake. Moved by the sight of the enormous flag still flying in "the dawn's early light" after a 25-hour bombardment, he scribbled the words that became the lyrics for a popular patriotic song; Congress made it the national anthem in 1931. As part of conservation efforts, specialists at the Smithsonian recently removed a cloth backing (and 1.7 million stitches) added decades ago for support. Photo images documented the original flag's condition close-up, guiding work to ensure the flag's survival for future generations. ∎

Third Floor

The museum's third floor now houses a new **Military History Hall,** with a permanent exhibition that tells the history of the U.S. military and explores America's wars not just as battles but in relation to political leadership, social values, and technological innovation. The artifacts include a regimental flag of Civil War black troops, a UH-1H Huey helicopter from the Vietnam War, and, from Operations Desert Storm and Iraqi Freedom, Colin Powell's uniform and a first-generation military robot.

The American Presidency: A Glorious Burden also has many fascinating objects on view. Among them are the portable desk Jefferson used in drafting the Declaration of Independence, the hat Lincoln wore the night he was assassinated, and Washington's mil-

A wreath adorns the black-granite wall of names at the Vietnam Veterans Memorial.

A walk around the monuments

The western end of the Mall, where you'll find the city's most significant monuments and memorials, is a delightful place for walking. A 3-mile loop taking you past a half dozen major memorials makes for a wonderful morning or afternoon; benches along the way offer rest stops. About two blocks from the start is the Smithsonian Metro stop. Parking during cherry blossom season *(late March–early April)* is nearly impossible.

Begin at the **Washington Monument ❶,** off 15th Street between Constitution and Independence Avenues. Set on a slight rise, this 555-foot marble obelisk is surrounded by flags from every state in the nation.

Begun in 1848, the monument rose slowly but steadily for five years to 152 feet; at that point funding ran out and building ceased for almost 25 years. Look about a third of the way up to see where the work stopped. Though taken from a nearby Maryland quarry, the more recent marble is of a darker color. The monument recently underwent a comprehensive restoration, which included installation of a new elevator system and security facility. You can ride the elevator to the 500-foot level for one of the best views of the city. If you wish, you can descend the 897 steps past the scores of memorial stones, but only on scheduled tours led by rangers. Visit the ticket kiosk near the monument for same-day tickets; to reserve advance tickets *(service fee)*, call 800-967-2283 or go online at http://reservations.nps.gov.

From the grounds of the Washington Monument, you can see the Lincoln Memorial directly to the west and the Jefferson Memorial across the Tidal Basin, but your next destination is hidden among the trees of **Constitution Gardens,** a memorial to the founders of this nation. Walk down the hill, cross 17th Street, and take the sinuous trail through lovely landscaping just north of the **Reflecting Pool.** On small **Signers Island,** a memorial honors the 56 signers of the Declaration of Independence.

On the pool's east end is the newest attraction, the **National World War II Memorial ❷.** Thousands of veterans were on hand for the Memorial Day 2004 dedication of the $174 million, privately funded memorial, which has drawn much criticism for its massive design and overwhelming presence amid the Mall's more graceful monuments. Around a fountain-spouting pool are two facing arcs of granite columns, each bearing two bronze wreaths; the 56 pillars represent U.S. states and territories during the war and the District of Columbia. The columns are

The FDR Memorial also remembers the Depression-era President's lovable dog, Fala.

anchored by a pair of 43-foot-high arches—one for the war's Atlantic theater and one for the Pacific. Two dozen bronze panels depict scenes from the war, and a Freedom Wall with 4,000 gold stars honors the 400,000 Americans

🗺 See area map pp. 68–69

▶ Washington Monument

🔄 3 miles

🕐 2 hours

▶ Jefferson Memorial

NOT TO BE MISSED
- Vietnam Veterans Memorial
- Lincoln Memorial
- Jefferson Memorial
- World War II Memorial

The newly opened World War II Memorial honors the 16 million who served in the U.S. armed forces during World War II and the more than 400,000 who died.

who were killed during World War II.

Just west, architect Maya Lin's stunning **Vietnam Veterans Memorial** ❸ presents a moving contrast to the classical-style monuments all about. A tremendous black-granite wedge, bermed into the earth instead of standing above it, is inscribed with the names of all the 58,209 Americans who died or were missing in action in the Vietnam War. Polished to a

reflective sheen, the walls of the wedge seem to project life as much as honor death. As you walk the path beside the memorial, the names of the dead increase dramatically as the walls reach their high point at 10.1 feet. The nearby bronze group of three soldiers, by Washington sculptor Frederick Hart, adds a dose of gritty realism. Dedicated in 1982, the memorial was supplemented in 1993 by another bronze group, the

Vietnam Women's Memorial, in tribute to the women who took part in the war.

Continue on to the magnificent **Lincoln Memorial** ❹ built from 1914 to 1922 to honor Abraham Lincoln, President during the Civil War. The 36 Doric columns represent the number of states at the time of Lincoln's death. Inside, facing the Mall, the 19-foot-tall statue of a seated Lincoln was carved from 28 blocks of white Georgia marble. The walls of the memorial are inscribed with words from the Gettysburg Address and Lincoln's second inaugural speech.

Just to the southeast is the **Korean War Veterans Memorial** ❺. Dedicated in 1995, it features 19 gray soldiers warily crossing a field of scrubby junipers. Next to this riveting stainless-steel group, a black-granite wall is etched with a mural of those who served, while another wall bears the simple message: "Freedom Is Not Free." Beside a "pool of remembrance" stands a stone carved with the war's toll—the numbers of killed, wounded, missing, and captured.

Walk east toward the **Tidal Basin** and cross West Basin Drive at the second traffic light, in front of the nearly hidden **D.C. WWI Veterans Memorial,** honoring the District's veterans.

Amid the trees of West Potomac Park on the Tidal Basin's west side is the **Franklin Delano Roosevelt Memorial** ❻, honoring the 32nd President. Four unroofed, granite-walled alcoves—one for each of his four terms—spread along the water's edge, surrounded by landscaped plazas, statuary, and waterfalls. After the memorial was dedicated in 1997, disability advocacy groups criticized the design for failing to publicly recognize FDR's regular use of a wheelchair, which he was confined to from age 39 when paralyzed by polio. Finally, in 2001, a statue of Roosevelt in a wheelchair was added.

On the south side of the Tidal Basin stands the impressive **Jefferson Memorial** ❼. The view from here, across the Tidal Basin with its gulls and paddleboats and springtime cherry blossoms, is not to be missed. Dedicated to the author of the Declaration of Independence and third U.S. President, the structure was designed by John Russell Pope in the style of the ancient Roman Pantheon and completed in 1943.

Inside the colonnaded building a 19-foot bronze of Jefferson stands beneath a towering dome. Among the quotes on the wall is one from a letter written in 1800: "I have sworn upon the altar of God eternal hostility against every form of tyranny over the mind of man." A lower lobby has exhibits, a gift shop, and a bookstore.

Behind the monument on Ohio Drive is the **George Mason Memorial Garden,** which opened in spring 2002. In keeping with the quiet patriot's love of his garden at Gunston Hall (see p. 222), the setting is a classical landscape designed as a peaceful, contemplative place. ∎

More to come

Since the 1990s there has been growing concern about overbuilding on the Mall. Yet several memorials have been added in recent years, and still more monuments and museums are in the air. A memorial to Martin Luther King, Jr., was announced in 2000, and others, such as one honoring Black Patriots of the American Revolution, are being considered. Despite the squeeze, advocates of a National Health Museum are pushing for a Mall site.

Taking shape across the Potomac River, in Virginia, the Pentagon Memorial honors the 184 people who died when American Airlines Flight 77 was hijacked on September 11, 2001. The design consists of a pool surrounded by benches bearing the names of each of the victims; halogen lights in the benches will glow at night, creating a deeply reflective atmosphere. Near a nearby Navy annex site, ground has been broken for a new U. S. Air Force Memorial—three soaring stainless steel spires. Also in Virginia, the National Museum of the Marine Corps opens in 2005 in Quantico; a campaign is underway to build a Cold War Museum in Lorton; and an $85 million expansion at Mount Vernon will feature a museum and visitor education complex. Other possible projects include a Museum of the Americas, with artifacts from the Aztecs and present-day Mexico, and a National Women's History Museum. ∎

U.S. Holocaust Memorial Museum

U.S. Holocaust Memorial Museum
www.ushmm.org
⬛ Map p. 69
✉ 100 Raoul Wallenberg Pl. (15th St.), S.W., just S of Independence Ave.
☎ 202-488-0400
🚇 Metro: Smithsonian; Bus: 52-3, 11Y, 13A-B & F-G, V7-9

The Holocaust Museum's first floor sets a somber tone for a visit to the galleries above.

OPENED IN 1993, THIS MUSEUM SERVES AS A MEMORIAL TO the millions of people murdered during Nazi rule in Germany from 1933 to 1945. The architecture—windowless recesses, brickwork guard towers, and obscured windows—suggests some of the themes and images documented within. Inside, the skylit first-floor atrium is overshadowed by heavy steel trusses. A factory-like brick wall on one side is where visitors enter and ascend, via a cargo-style elevator, to see the permanent exhibition, starting on the fourth floor.

VISITING

Pick up timed passes at the museum on the day of your visit, or call 800-400-9373 for advance passes (*service fee*). The exhibition is self-guided and takes two to three hours. Because there are several films, audio programs, and a lot of text on the three-floor exhibit, you may want to make a selective tour. The **Meyerhoff Theater** on the concourse level shows a 14-minute orientation film. Most of the exhibits are not recommended for children under 11; it's also a good idea to prepare older children for what they are about to see.

On the **fourth floor,** which covers the spread of Nazism from 1933 to 1939, visitors are funneled through hallways from one exhibit area to the next. The dim, quiet halls, with grated ceilings, reflect the museum's somber content. A theater, grim photographs, and monitors displaying silent footage bespeak the early years of the Third Reich and the start of its sanctioned violence toward Jews, Poles, Gypsies, homosexuals, political dissidents, the handicapped, and others.

On the **third floor,** the years 1940–45 are examined in grisly detail through displays on ghettos, deportations, slave labor, and extermination camps. Among the powerful artifacts are a cobblestone floor from a Warsaw ghetto, clothing, and a cemetery gate from Karnow where Jews were routinely shot. A walk-through tower is lined with family photos from a shtetl, a Jewish village; you later learn that this entire village of 4,000 was destroyed in 1941, bringing 900 years of continuous history to an abrupt and complete end. Perhaps most telling are the shelfloads of victims' belongings—rusty scissors, can openers, graters, razors, toothbrushes—and the huge piles of old shoes. There are bunks from Auschwitz and a scale model that shows how the gas chambers and crematoria worked. Video moni-

tors show unsettling images such as medical experiments, executions, and malnourished children. The monitors are shielded by walls so young children cannot see them; adults can elect not to watch.

Efforts at resistance and the ultimate liberation of survivors are documented on the **second floor.** In the **Hall of Remembrance,** an eternal flame honors victims of the Holocaust; visitors may light candles in their memory.

The **first floor** recounts the Holocaust from a child's point of view; this hands-on gallery is suitable for children eight years and older. Downstairs, the **concourse level** has changing exhibits and a **Wall of Remembrance** honoring the estimated 1.5 million children who died. Outside the museum, it's a relief to look across the Tidal Basin to the Jefferson and FDR Memorials and remember those who stood against tyranny and won. As one FDR Memorial donor put it, a man in a wheelchair beat Hitler. ■

More places to visit around the National Mall

ARTS AND INDUSTRIES BUILDING

The Smithsonian's Discovery Theater (*202-357-1500*), which offers live plays and performances for children, is based in this brick-and-sandstone edifice beside the Castle. Completed in 1881, it originally housed items from the first world's fair—the 1876 Centennial Exposition in Philadelphia. The building was closed indefinitely in January 2004 for renovation, but the theater is open. 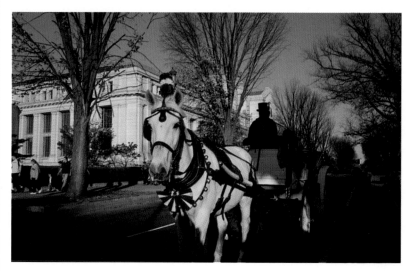 Map p. 69 ✉ 900 Jefferson Dr., S.W. ☎ 202-633-1000 🚇 Metro: Smithsonian

BUREAU OF ENGRAVING & PRINTING

One of the popular standards of Washington tourism, the bureau is the place to see a lot of money—up to 38 million dollars—being printed daily. To replace worn-out bills and keep up with economic growth, this facility and a similar one in Fort Worth, Texas, churn out about 7 billion notes a year in denominations from $1 to $100. The 24 high-speed presses run 24 hours a day, 5 days a week, turning out mainly $1 bills, which have a shelf life of only 18 months. You can see 32-note currency sheets rolling through

Visitors can tour streets near the National Mall in old-fashioned style.

production and 4,000-note "bricks" being prepared for distribution to the 12 Federal Reserve Banks around the country. You'll also learn about the latest techniques to prevent counterfeiting. A visitor center on the premises sells uncut sheets of legal tender and other currency-related novelties. www.moneyfactory.com 🅰 Map p. 69 ✉ 14th & C Sts., S.W. ☎ 202-874-2330 🕐 Closed Sat.–Sun. Call for summer and winter tour hours; obtain free tickets from booth on west side of the building 🚇 Metro: Smithsonian

VOICE OF AMERICA

This government-run news service has operated continuously since it went on the air in February 1942, soon after America entered World War II. Today, the service broadcasts 1,000 hours of news, educational, and cultural programs a week to 87 million people in 44 languages, transmitted by radio, satellite television, and the Internet. On 45-minute tours you can see 1940s murals by Ben Shahn and observe production in the radio stations and newsrooms. www.voa.gov 🅰 Map p. 69 ✉ 330 Independence Ave., S.W. ☎ 202-619-3919 🕐 Tours Mon.–Fri. 10:30, 1:30, 2:30. Call for reservations. 🚇 Metro: Federal Center, S.W. ■

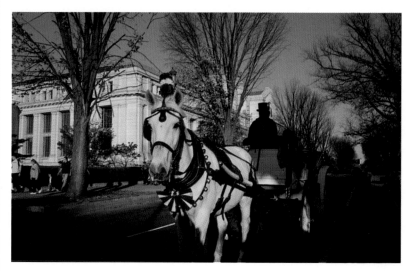

Although a certain famous residence at 1600 Pennsylvania Avenue gets most of the attention, the neighborhood around the White House overflows with art galleries, historic houses and hotels, churches, museums, and other stops of note.

White House & around

The south portico of the White House

White House & around

A LOCUS OF POLITICAL POWER THAT IS ALSO A MAJOR TOURIST ATTRACTION, the home of the Chief Executive is a living museum of the Presidency in downtown Washington. The immediate environs are rich in history, culture, and political excitement.

In 1791 a surveyor and an engineer picked the site for a presidential "palace," as the latter called it. The surveyor was George Washington, the engineer was Pierre Charles L'Enfant, and the site was a cornfield above a tidal marsh where hunters shot ducks and geese.

Just a mile from the site of the future Capitol, the manse they envisioned would be about four times the size of the current White House.

Thomas Jefferson, Secretary of State at the time, persuaded Washington to hold a competition for the design. Unimpressed by the mundane entries that resulted, Washington urged Irish-born architect James Hoban to have a go. Hoban's entry, selected in 1792, was an adaptation of the Duke of Leinster's palace near Dublin. Regrettably, Washington—then on the verge of his second term as President—would not live to see the structure completed.

The next President, John Adams, moved into the partially completed mansion on November 1, 1800, only to lose his reelection bid less than a month later. Jefferson, his successor, spent the next eight years in the Presi-

dent's House (it was not called the White House until 1901), opening it to the public and establishing it as a national symbol. President James Madison enjoyed no such stability: The British burned the building to the ground in 1814, forcing Madison to abandon the President's House for temporary quarters nearby.

After Abraham Lincoln's assassination in 1865, some lobbied to move the President to a more secluded location, in Rock Creek Park. President Ulysses S. Grant, who had served as Lincoln's commanding officer, nixed that idea.

By the turn of the 20th century, it was clear that the White House—Theodore Roosevelt's designation for it—enshrined the American presidential legacy. Indeed, each President has left his stamp on the place: Rutherford B. Hayes put in the first telephone, Benjamin Harrison installed electric lights, and Theodore Roosevelt hung a moose head above the fireplace in the State Dining Room.

The presidential neighborhood grew in tandem with the White House. In the 1810s, St. John's Church, Decatur House, and a number of posh, federal-style residences were built around President's Park (renamed Lafayette Square in 1824). By 1900—when the Treasury Building, Old Executive Office Building, Corcoran Gallery, Renwick building, Blair House, the Octagon, and Willard Hotel had all gone up around 1600 Pennsylvania Avenue—the area was a thriving mix of government buildings, art galleries, hotels, and residences.

From west of 20th Street to the Potomac River, the Foggy Bottom neighborhood is a busy mix of 19th-century row houses, apartment buildings, and major institutions: the State Department, World Bank, Kennedy Center, and George Washington University. The breweries and gasworks that once filled this bottomland with foggy vapors were gone by the mid-20th century, when the area began to morph into a middle-class neighborhood.

From its tidy lawns and ornate facades to its clean sidewalks and crisply suited Secret Service agents, the White House area maintains and inspires a polished decorum. Until World War II, you could walk to the front door of the White House and leave your calling card. Security then moved outward to the fence line, and in 1995 Pennsylvania Avenue in front of the building was closed to traffic. ■

White House

White House

www.whitehouse.gov

🅼 Map p. 107

✉ 1600 Pennsyl-
vania Ave., N.W.

☎ 202-456-7041

🕐 Closed Sun.–Mon.

🚇 Metro: Federal
Triangle,
McPherson Square
or Metro Center;
Bus: 30-36, S2-4,
11Y, X2, 42, 68

**The dignified
north portico
basks in the glow
of early evening.**

THE OLDEST PUBLIC BUILDING IN THE DISTRICT OF
Columbia, the White House has been the home of every U.S. President except George Washington. In this most famous of residences,
the President signs bills into law, meets with national and international leaders, entertains guests, and does his best to lead a private
family life. Despite more than 200 years of expansions and renovations, the White House has kept its essential appearance and design.

Washington's designers intended
the executive mansion to be one of
two focal points of the new Federal
City (the Capitol would be the other). Nine blueprints were submitted
to a competitive design panel;
among those rejected was a plan
put forward anonymously by Thomas Jefferson.

The winning design—the work

of Irish-born architect James Hoban—honored the stately symmetries of Georgian manor houses in
the British Isles. Not that it lacked
detractors: Benjamin Henry Latrobe, who worked on the White
House in the early 1800s and is
considered the country's first professional architect, assailed Hoban's
concept as "a mutilated copy of a

House, muddy boots and all; while President Jackson slipped away to a nearby hotel, his aides filled tubs with juice and whiskey and set them on the lawn to coax the crowds outside. The Inaugural open houses continued until 1885, when Grover Cleveland replaced them with a parade, which he watched from the relative safety of a grandstand in front of the White House.

During the War of 1812, the British retaliated for the American burning of public buildings in Canada by burning down the President's House and other city landmarks in 1814. When British soldiers arrived at the hastily vacated executive mansion on the night of August 24, 1814, they found Dolley Madison's dinner still on the table (a few of them sat down and polished it off). Shortly after midnight, the soldiers threw flaming javelins into the mansion. By morning it was a smoldering shell. The house was rebuilt within its original walls over the next few years.

By the mid-20th century, the White House had reached a serious state of structural decline: The walls and floors could no longer support the alterations and additions of previous decades. From 1948 to 1952, Harry and Bess Truman lived in Blair House, across Pennsylvania Avenue, while the White House was gutted. Everything from furniture to paneling was taken out; a new basement was dug, new foundations were laid, and a steel framework was installed. The basic house was still there, but it was now much safer. Since then, each First Family has added its own decorative touch: The Kennedys redesigned the Rose Garden, while the Reagans contributed a new set of Lenox china.

VISITING

In the past, tours of the White House were so popular that as

badly designed original near Dublin."

Nonetheless, the cornerstone of the President's House (George Washington's preferred term for it) was laid in October 1792, a year before work began on the Capitol. The pale sandstone for the white-painted walls came from Aquia Creek, on the Virginia side of the Potomac. Eight years later, with President John Adams nearing the end of his term, the house was finally ready for occupation.

Jefferson, the third President, held the first Inaugural open house in 1805 and forged the tradition of throwing the house open to public tours. The custom got out of hand in 1829, when some 20,000 well-wishers tromped through the White

State Dining Room

West Wing

Red Room

South Portico

Inside:
Diplomatic
Reception
Room

Blue Room

Green Room

China Room

WHITE HOUSE

many as 6,000 visitors a day arrived— many before dawn—to wait in long lines for admission. However, individual self-guided tours were suspended after the events of September 11, 2001, for security reasons. Today, you can view the inside rooms only through reserved tours that can be arranged in advance for parties of 10 or more people, regardless of age or type of group; to schedule a tour up to six months in advance, call your congressperson (202-224-3121). The self-guided group tours will be scheduled about a month before the requested date, from 7:30 and 11:30 Tuesday through Saturday.

East Room

Library

East Wing

Visitor entrance

Vermeil Room

Another option is to forgo a tour of the interior altogether and, instead, stop by the White House Visitor Center in the lobby of the Commerce Department building (*SE corner of 15th & E Sts., 202-456-7041*). Open every day from 7:30 a.m. until 4:00 p.m., it features displays on many aspects of the White House, including its architecture, furnishings, First Families, and social events, as well as a 30-minute video. Allow yourself up to an hour to view the exhibits. The White House Historical Association sponsors a gift and souvenir area in the center, but no restrooms or food services are available.

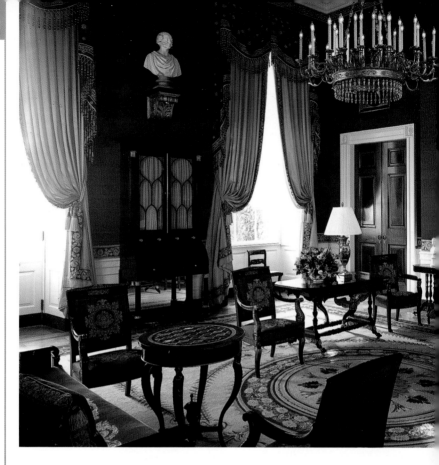

The Red Room's French Empire-style furniture dates back to the early 1800s.

If you do plan your visit to Washington well in advance and succeed in arranging to join a scheduled group tour, you will enter the grounds from a visitors entrance around the corner from Pennsylvania Avenue on 14th Street, next to the Treasury building and across the street from the Hotel Washington. When you arrive for your visit, look through the gate to see part of the mansion's lovely 18-acre grounds. Once you get inside, expect to spend 20 minutes to half an hour viewing the rooms.

After being cleared by security, you enter a corridor on the ground floor that has information panels on White House architecture and glass-walled views of the modern sculpture and well-groomed plant-ings in the **Jacqueline Kennedy Garden.** Next, peer into the roped-off **Library**, filled with federal-style furniture. Across the hall, the **Vermeil Room** has portraits of recent First Ladies and a collection of gilded silver known as vermeil.

The rooms you can actually walk through are up on the State Floor. The first one you enter—the expansive **East Room**—is also the largest in the house: It hosts press conferences, receptions, award ceremonies, and concerts. Among the weddings held here were those of Nellie Grant, Alice Roosevelt, and Lynda Bird Johnson. Imagine skid marks on this floor; the energetic children of Theodore Roosevelt are said to have roller-skated across it. The furnishings include a decorated entertain in the adjacent **Red Room,** furnished as an American Empire parlor of 1810 to 1830.

Some 130 guests can be seated in the gracious **State Dining Room,** which boasts painted oak paneling from a 1902 renovation. Out in the **Cross Halls,** the floors are of Tennessee marble (no skating here!). A carpeted marble staircase leads to the second and third floors, open only to the First Family and guests. Famous rooms up there include the Lincoln Bedroom and the Queen's Bedroom. The West Wing *(not open to public)* holds the Cabinet Room, numerous staff and reception rooms, and the President's Oval Office (built in 1909) and its adjoining Rose Garden. The White House also contains an indoor tennis court, jogging track, swimming pool, movie theater, bowling lane, and billiard room. The total number of rooms in the house: 132.

Your tour will exit the front door beneath a columned portico, then follow the walkway to the front gate. As photos are forbidden inside, many people pause here before leaving to get a shot. Through the viewfinder you may discover that the White House looks not at all palatial—a mansion, yes, but at heart just a home. ■

President and Mrs. Bush arrive at a State Dinner with Mexican president Vicente Fox and his wife, Martha Sahagun.

concert grand piano, a 1938 gift from the Steinway company.

Continue around to the **Green Room,** used by Jefferson as a dining room but now functioning as a reception parlor. The window affords a great view beyond the Ellipse (an open greensward just north of Constitution Avenue) to the Jefferson Memorial. Much of the Green Room's furniture came from the workshop of Duncan Phyfe in the early 1800s. The green watered-silk wall coverings were chosen by Mrs. Kennedy.

The elegant and oval **Blue Room** contains several pieces of furniture bought by James Monroe, who refurbished the room after the 1814 fire. Presidents still receive guests here. First Ladies frequently

A stroll around the White House

Walking in the area around the White House will give you a concentrated taste of Washington's core. Yet the knots of tourists, security officers, and limousines that buzz around the executive mansion like drones around a queen bee are only part of the picture. Because local laws bar skyscrapers, you can enjoy long, green views across the Ellipse and the Mall. The area is also dotted with house museums, art galleries, benches for idling, and restaurants for both tourists and power brokers.

Once you've viewed or visited the White House, you tend to forget it's there, as do the locals who go about their business in the area, regarding the structure mainly as an attractive backdrop. Since virtually no one sees the First Family come and go, it's easy to forget that the President of the United States is living in splendid isolation in that beautiful historic house. The isolation is heightened by the restricted areas and physical barriers added in recent years for greater security. The occasional presence of TV crews and reporters is a reminder that "presidential privacy" is something of an oxymoron.

The Old Executive Office Building's flamboyant style shocked the public upon its 1888 unveiling.

The section of Pennsylvania Avenue in front of the **White House** ❶ (see pp. 108–113) is closed to traffic, so it offers good photo opportunities if you aren't hampered at the time of your visit by security constraints and construction fences. The park just north of the White House, **Lafayette Square** ❷, is a perfect place to sit with a sandwich and people-watch. As a public park in full view of the

White House, the square has been strategically ideal for demonstrating for or against something. Activists for nuclear disarmament and other causes have mounted peaceful vigils here. In the middle of the square is Clark Mills's statue of Andrew Jackson on a rearing horse. Statues of foreign-born Revolutionary War heroes occupy the four corners: Marquis de Lafayette, Baron Friedrich von Steuben,

Thaddeus Kosciusko, and Comte de Rocham-
beau. Many of the federal-style row houses
along the square are White House offices,
saved from the wrecking ball by Jackie Kennedy's determination to preserve the historical
character of the square.

Across H Street from the square stands
the gold-domed **St. John's Church** ③
(see p. 128), known as the "church of the
Presidents." Diagonally across the corner from
here, at Jackson Place and H Street, is
Decatur House ④ (see p. 127), which was
built in 1818 for naval hero Stephen Decatur.

Next, head south and turn right on Pennsylvania Avenue to see the 1810 white brick
Blair House, where foreign dignitaries often
stay; Robert E. Lee was offered command of
the Federal Army here in 1861. On November
1, 1950—about midway through the Trumans'
four-year stay at Blair House while the White
House was being renovated—a policeman was
killed on the street defending the President
from an assassination attempt.

In that block, the **Renwick Gallery** ⑤
(see p. 117), a Smithsonian museum, shows off

⚑ See area map pp. 106–107
▶ White House Visitor Center
↔ 1.5 miles
⊕ 3 hours
▶ Corcoran Gallery of Art

NOT TO BE MISSED
- White House
- Lafayette Square
- Corcoran Gallery of Art
- Renwick Gallery

---

its mansard roof and redbrick-and-sandstone
exterior opposite the even more flamboyant
Eisenhower Executive Office Building.
A massive piece of architecture originally
named the Old Executive Office Building, the
EEOB is one of the country's finest Second
Empire-style structures. Built from 1871 to
1888 (just after the Renwick), the granite pile
shocked locals who had expected a neoclassic
temple to house the State, War, and Navy
departments. It now holds various presidential

agencies, including the National Security Council, the Office of Management and Budget, and the Office of the Vice President.

Head south on 17th Street and turn right on New York Avenue. The historic **Octagon** ❻ (see p. 122) stands on the corner of 18th Street. Go back to 17th and turn right; on your right is the **Corcoran Gallery of Art** ❼ (see pp. 118–19), housed in an attractive beaux arts building. From here, walk east on E Street, between the South Lawn of the White House and the Ellipse. *Marine One,* the President's helicopter, lands on the South Lawn, site of the annual Easter Egg Roll. The National Christmas Tree, planted during the Carter Administration, stands on the Ellipse near the

Zero Milestone, whence city distances are measured. On the corner of E and 15th Streets, a bronze William Tecumseh Sherman sits astride a horse, its tail raised toward the South, on the spot where he reviewed victorious Union troops. He faces the Greek Revival **Department of the Treasury** and its statue of Alexander Hamilton; sadly, the building blocks the view from the White House to the Capitol.

Cap the day with a drink in the rooftop Sky Terrace Restaurant of the 1918 Hotel Washington *(15th & F, May–Oct.).* On clear days, it offers a great panoramic view of the White House, Mall, and abundant treetops in parts of the city and neighboring Virginia. ■

The Willard

While you're in the vicinity of the White House, peek inside the Willard Hotel *(202-628-9100),* a Washington landmark since the 1850s at 1401 Pennsylvania Avenue. Nathaniel Hawthorne called the Willard the "center of Washington" for its role as the heart of political lobbying in the 19th century. The hotel has hosted Presidents, foreign heads of state, and a gaggle of celebrities from Mark Twain to Harry Houdini to Mae West.

In 1901 the venerable hostelry was rebuilt as a 12-story beaux arts hotel under the guid-

ance of Henry Hardenbergh, architect of New York's famous Plaza Hotel. Closed in 1968 when much of Pennsylvania Avenue hit the skids, the Willard reopened in grand style in 1986, a crowning achievement of the Congressionally created Pennsylvania Avenue Development Corporation.

The restored Willard boasts scagliola marble columns, polished wood paneling, glittering chandeliers, and other trappings of opulence. Shops, a bar, a café, and an elegant restaurant provide multiple opportunities to splurge. ■

Renwick Gallery

KNOWN AS MUCH FOR ITS ARCHITECTURE AS FOR ITS ART-
work, the Renwick occupies a building designed in 1859 by James
Renwick, architect of the Smithsonian Castle. Sandstone pilasters
and garlands embellish the redbrick facade, while decorative ironwork crowns the tripartite mansard roof. The Second Empire-style
building functioned as a military warehouse during the Civil War.

Upon its completion in 1874, the Renwick served as the original Corcoran Gallery until that collection moved to a new building nearby. The building then became the home of the U.S. Court of Claims from 1899 until 1964, when it was slated for demolition.

The Renwick came under the aegis of the Smithsonian Institution in 1965. Now a department of the Smithsonian American Art Museum, the Renwick offers changing exhibits of American crafts and decorative arts, as well as selections from its permanent collection of 20th-century American crafts.

Refurbished in 2000, the museum's sumptuous centerpiece, the **Grand Salon,** awaits you at the top of a red-carpeted staircase. Plush poufs (circular settees), brocade sofas, and dark red walls covered with 19th-century paintings confer the air of a Victorian picture gallery. Among the pieces on display here are several fine portraits of Native Americans by George Catlin. Masterpieces by John Singer Sargent, Winslow Homer, Childe Hassam, and others were moved here temporarily while the Renwick's sister museum, the Smithsonian American Art Museum, was closed for renovation. Lectures, concerts, and receptions are also held in the Grand Salon.

The smaller **Octagon Room,** opposite the Grand Salon, holds works by such iconic American painters as George P. A. Healy, Winslow Homer, and others. Additional rooms on this upper level contain fun, daring contemporary works in fiber, clay, wood, metal, glass, and mixed media. Exhibits from the permanent collection are rotated twice a year. The **first floor** holds short-term exhibits from the Renwick's own holdings or from those of other museums. ∎

Renwick Gallery
http://www.americanart.si.edu/renwick

⬛ Map pp. 106–107
✉ 17th St. & Pennsylvania Ave., N.W.
☎ 202-633-8998
🚇 Metro: Farragut West; Bus: 30-36, P17 & 19, W13, 42, 11Y, X2

**Grand indeed
is the Renwick's
90-foot-long
Grand Salon.**

Corcoran Gallery of Art

**Corcoran
Gallery of Art**

www.corcoran.org

- Map p. 106
- 500 17th St., N.W.
- 202-639-1700
- Closed Tues.
- $$ Wed., Fri., Sat., Sun.; donation Mon. (all day) & Thurs. after 5 p.m.
- Metro: Farragut West; Bus: 80, S1

WASHINGTON'S OLDEST ART MUSEUM (AND THE THIRD oldest in the country), the Corcoran Gallery holds a distinguished collection of American and European artworks. It is the largest non-federal art museum in Washington, D.C.

The Corcoran started out three blocks north, in the building that now houses the Smithsonian's Renwick Gallery (see p. 117). The stately mansion was built to hold the collection of banker-philanthropist William Wilson Corcoran (1798–1888).

When Corcoran's collection outgrew its available space, an architectural competition was held, which resulted in the hiring of New York architect Ernest Flagg. His stately beaux arts-style building, the first of its kind in the city, was completed in 1897. Bronze lions flank the entrance to the symmetrical white marble building; the green copper roof caps an architrave inscribed with the names of Rembrandt and other great artists.

Twin skylit atriums on the **first**

Philanthropist William Corcoran founded his art gallery "for the purpose of encouraging American genius."

floor draw the viewer in. A gift shop and auditorium lie off the north atrium, a café and numerous galleries off the south atrium.

Gallery 1 generally holds temporary exhibits of contemporary American art. The smaller galleries contain excellent examples of 19th- and 20th-century art, including works by Renoir, Corot, Eakins, Homer, Cassatt, and Whistler. John Singer Sargent's 1878 "Oyster Gatherers of Cancale" is an attention grabber.

The Corcoran is the place to learn that not everyone is cut out to be an artist—and that's a good thing. Samuel Morse's 1822 "Old House of Representatives," showing democracy in action as a routine business, was considered insufficiently dramatic for its time; discouraged, the painter went off and invented the telegraph.

Galleries 4-7 feature changing exhibitions.

Gallery 8 showcases the white-and-gold **Salon Doré,** an 18th-century room from Paris's St.-Germain quarter. Part of a sizable gift from industrialist and U.S. Senator William A. Clark (1839–1925) of Montana, the gilded room glitters with Corinthian pilasters, huge framed mirrors, and a ceiling mural.

Paintings on the **second floor** display a broad range of American styles, from the colonial period to the early 20th century. Among masterworks here are the magnificent "Washington Before Yorktown" (1824–25) by Rembrandt Peale and Frederic Church's "Niagara" (1857), described by a critic as the "finest oil picture ever painted on this side of the Atlantic."

Partly spurred by his rivalry with Church, Albert Bierstadt named his "Mount Corcoran" (1876–77) after the museum's benefactor in a bid to sell it to him (the plan worked; it's now part of the permanent collection). Also notable is his "Last of the Buffalo" (1889), which captures the essence of a

Art go boom!

With attendance exploding in the 1990s (from 100,000 visitors per year to nearly 900,000) and its collection expanding (from 12,000 to more than 16,000 pieces), the Corcoran needs to add a new wing. In 1999 the museum asked award-winning architect Frank O. Gehry, known for his innovative use of metals and indigenous stone, to design the addition. Construction is planned over the next several years. When the stunning new wing is complete, it will add 110,000 square feet of space, and is expected to draw thousands more visitors every year to this dynamic museum. ■

West that was coming to an end: It shows an Indian spearing a buffalo as it rams his horse.

Temporary and traveling exhibits of recent and current art often occupy much of the gallery space on the second floor. ■

Albert Bierstadt's "Last of the Buffalo" is one of the Corcoran's finest works.

It's a spooky little town

Intrigue. Mystery. Romance. Spies and spy catchers have captured the imagination of the moviegoing public for years, but in Washington—home of the CIA, the FBI, and the Pentagon—such cinematic proxies are redundant: The streets are alive with secret agents seeking or supplying classified information in nonstandard ways. Every now and then an agent is nabbed, exposing an underworld in which backyard barbecuers such as Aldrich Ames or Robert Hanssen turn out to have led lives of treachery and deceit.

"Rebel Rose" Greenhow and daughter

Spying caught on in Washington during the Civil War, when amateur agents on both sides of the Mason-Dixon Line scoured the capital city for war-related information. Thomas Nelson Conrad, a former Georgetown College headmaster, sat in Lafayette Park across from the White House for hours, meticulously noting President Lincoln's comings and goings. Conrad hoped to kidnap the President, then exchange him for prisoners of war. The Confederacy rejected his plan as infeasible.

The most romantic figure in Washington's espionage history may be the Rebel Rose. Intelligent, beautiful, and duplicitous, Rose O'Neal Greenhow (1815?–1864) haunted Washington's loftiest social circles before the Civil War, befriending Presidents, senators, and tycoons. When war broke out and men left for battle, spying became women's work.

None was more deft than Greenhow. Inside her modest house at 398 16th Street, N.W. (it's no longer standing), she plied unsuspecting targets with oysters, wild turkey, and champagne, pumping them for information all the while.

At one dinner party, Greenhow learned that the Federals were planning to move into Virginia. By quickly passing a coded message to Confederate Gen. Pierre G. T. Beauregard inside a woman's hair bun, she enabled him to reposition some of his troops—and, ultimately, to win the First Battle of Bull Run.

Soviet KGB colonel Vitaly Yurchenko made world headlines when he strolled into the U.S. Embassy in Rome in August 1985 and stated he wished to defect. Among the tidbits he had to share: NSA analyst Ronald Pelton had served as a double agent since 1980 and CIA officer Edward Lee Howard since 1984.

But Yurchenko was not a happy decamper. His ex-girlfriend, now the wife of a Russian diplomat stationed in Montreal, had no plans to leave her husband. Worse, the good colonel was relegated to a prisonlike existence in the United States, where his CIA case officers insisted on escorting him everywhere.

On November 2, 1985, Yurchenko and his CIA handler repaired to a popular neighborhood restaurant in Georgetown that is now defunct. At some point Yurchenko stepped out for a breath of fresh air—and grabbed a cab to the Soviet embassy, where he rescinded his defection. Four days later he was on a plane to the Soviet Union, leaving the intelligence community debating whether he had been a legitimate defector or a KGB plant.

Following in the forked footsteps of Greenhow and Yurchenko came career CIA officer Aldrich Ames, who in 1994 was accused of exposing U.S. intelligence assets inside the former Soviet Union. The info swap occurred at Chadwick's, at 3205 K Street in Georgetown; the blue mailbox that Ames chalkmarked to signal a "dead drop" still receives letters on R Street at 37th. For his tipoffs, Ames received more than 2.7 million dollars from the Soviets—and from the Americans, a lifelong prison sentence.

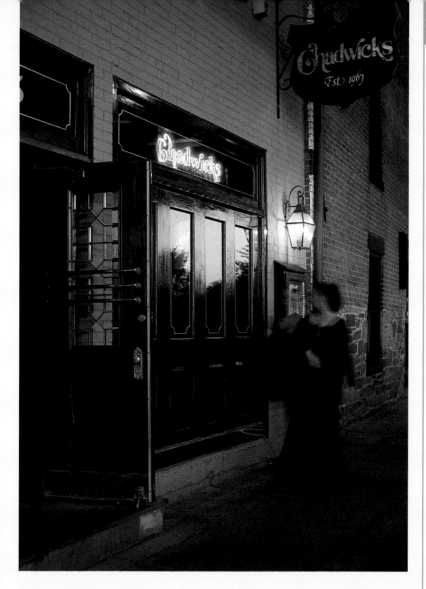

At this chummy beer-and-burger joint on Georgetown's K Street, the traitorous Aldrich Ames revealed to Russian agents the names of 20 CIA operatives working within the Soviet bloc; 10 were executed as spies.

TO WATCH A SPY

The Clandestine Capital emerges from the shadows in several formal ways. An unlikely team of former FBI, CIA, and KGB agents offers a popular **SpyDrive tour** of 30 espionage sites (866-779-8735, www.spytrek.com).

Another spy tour offered monthly in spring and fall is organized by the **Cold War Museum** (www.coldwar.org). Founded in 1996 to preserve Cold War history, this traveling exhibit is in search of a permanent home. The city's popular new **International Spy Museum** (see p. 138) houses one of the world's largest collections of espionage paraphernalia, plus interactive exhibits and a store. Or go to the source: The CIA's Langley HQ (www.cia.gov) has a museum and store.

—*Barbara A. Noe* ■

The Octagon

The Octagon
www.archfoundation.org/
octagon

🅰 Map p. 106

✉ 1799 New York
Ave., N.W.

☎ 202-638-3221

🕐 Closed Mon.

💲 $

🚇 Metro: Farragut West,
Farragut North; Bus:
80, H1, L1, S1

A gem of early Washington history, the redbrick Octagon stands bravely in the shadow of austere modern buildings. The neighborhood's first private residence, it was built about the same time as the White House. Its longevity owes much to its designer, William Thornton, also the first architect of the Capitol (see pp. 52–57).

The house was completed in 1801 for entrepreneur/political aspirant/urban pioneer John Tayloe III, who wanted to be near the power center of the new Republic. The location and stylish architecture paid off when the British burned the President's House in 1814 and the Madisons took shelter in the Octagon, just a five-minute walk from the executive mansion. Less than six months later, Madison signed the war-ending Treaty of Ghent in an upstairs parlor.

The Tayloes moved back in, grateful for the space; they raised 15 children. After Mrs. Tayloe's death in 1855, the Octagon was rented out as a girls' school, then a naval office, then a tenement house. The American Institute of Architects, whose modern headquarters looms just behind the Octagon, bought and restored the building in 1902.

Group tours (202-626-7387) cover the history and architecture of the Octagon, which, despite its name, has only six sides, plus a curved front pavilion. ∎

The Octagon was not named for the shape of its staircase.

DAR Headquarters

Daughters of the American Revolution
www.dar.org

🅰 Map p. 106

✉ 1776 D St., N.W.

☎ 202-628-1776

🕐 Closed Sun. & 2
weeks in June, July

🚇 Metro: Farragut
West; Bus: 80, H1,
L1, S1

This robust beaux arts building was built between 1905 and 1929 to serve as the headquarters of the Daughters of the American Revolution. Visitors may tour 33 **period rooms** that showcase early American decorative arts.

Highlights include an 18th-century Georgia tavern, an 1850s California whaling station, and a parlor furnished with pieces from the White House of James and Elizabeth Monroe. A museum displays exhibits drawn from the DAR's collection of 33,000 pieces of textile, ceramic, silver, glass, and furniture.

Built in the 1920s on the building's west side, **Constitution Hall** is a 3,800-seat horseshoe-shaped auditorium designed by John Russell Pope (the hand behind the National Gallery of Art, Jefferson Memorial, and National Archives). All kinds of concerts and lectures are held here, but Constitution Hall is best (or worst) known for the one that never took place: After the DAR's 1939 refusal to let black contralto Marian Anderson perform, Eleanor Roosevelt bravely stepped in, and Anderson sang at the Lincoln Memorial instead. ∎

Organization of American States

BLENDING CLASSICAL AND SPANISH COLONIAL ELEMENTS this striking white building is the headquarters of the Organization of American States, a regional alliance of 35 nations promoting peace and economic cooperation among its 35 member countries from the Americas and the Caribbean.

Dedicated in 1910, the building was the work of architects Paul Cret (also the designer of the Folger Shakespeare Library; see p. 64) and Albert Kelsey. Just inside the elaborate triple-arched entryway, a lush villa-like courtyard boasts an octagonal Aztec-style fountain and overflows with tropical plants. Upstairs, the large **Hall of the Americas** auditorium is graced by Tiffany stained-glass windows and a vaulted ceiling.

In the back, a walkway through an Aztec garden leads to the **Art Museum of the Americas,** roofed in red tile (the museum must be entered from 201 18th St.). In several attractive wood-floor galleries, the museum offers temporary exhibits from its permanent collection, plus traveling shows of Latin American and Caribbean art and photography.

After your visit, head for the triangular park across 18th Street to view the raised-sword equestrian statue of Simon Bolívar the Liberator. It was a gift to the United States in 1958 from Venezuela. ■

Organization of American States & Art Museum of the Americas

www.oas.org

www.museum.oas.org

⬛ Map p. 106

✉ 17th St. & Constitution Ave., N.W.

☎ 202-458-3000; museum, 202-458-6016

🕐 Closed Sat.–Sun., museum closed Mon.

🚇 Metro: Farragut West; Bus: 80, H1, L1, S1

The OAS courtyard offers a whiff of the tropics.

John F. Kennedy Center for the Performing Arts

John F. Kennedy Center for the Performing Arts

www.kennedy-center.org

🅼 Map p. 106

✉ 2700 F St., N.W.

☎ 202-416-8340

Ⓜ Metro: Foggy Bottom—GWU; Bus: 80

ONCE MALIGNED AS AN UNSIGHTLY PILLBOX BY THE Potomac, the Kennedy Center has since earned the affection of Washingtonians as the city's premier bastion of culture. The center was designed by architect Edward Durrell Stone as a living memorial to President Kennedy, and its 1971 opening elevated the city from a cultural backwater to a leader in the live arts. The world's foremost opera singers, pianists, jazz musicians, dancers, and actors have performed on the stages of the Kennedy Center. The National Symphony Orchestra and the Washington Opera, both based here, have achieved recognition. Among the many groups that have performed at the center are the Metropolitan Opera, La Scala opera company, the Bolshoi ballet, and the Berlin Philharmonic.

As a national memorial, the building and grounds of the Kennedy Center are maintained by the National Park Service. A presidentially appointed board of trustees oversees the operation of the center, which is supported both by ticket sales and by private donations.

VISITING

Free guided tours are offered daily; call for times. You may also wander about on your own, but some theaters are closed to the public during rehearsals. Tickets *(purchase at box office or call 202-467-4600 or 800-444-1324)* must be purchased for most performances. The Millennium Stage program, however, offers free daily performances at 6 p.m. in the Grand Foyer.

The Kennedy Center is at its best at night, when floodlights envelop its white Carrara marble in a vibrant glow. The north entrance opens into the **Hall of States,** its soaring ceiling lined with state flags; at the south entrance the **Hall of Nations** contains the flags of countries with diplomatic ties to the

2,450-seat **Concert Hall,** renovated in 1997, is home to the National Symphony; the 1,100-seat **Eisenhower Theater** is named for the President who signed legislation for a National Cultural Center; and the spectacular 2,300-seat **Opera House** completes the trio of big performance spaces. Just inside the north entrance, off the Hall of States, the 250-seat **Film Theater** presents classic films and live performances. On the Roof Terrace level, the 500-seat **Terrace Theater** is a delightful venue for jazz combos, solo recitals, chamber music, and dramatic performances. For a cozier setting, take in an experimental or family show at the 350-seat **Theater Lab.** An Education Resource Center on this level offers a list of seminars, workshops, and art displays.

Up on the **Roof Terrace,** walk out onto the patio for a view of the memorials, the Potomac, some Arlington high-rises across the river, and the distant form of the hilltop Washington National Cathedral. This promenade is always the place to be—especially on July 4th. ∎

The Kennedy Center (left) sits serenely beside the Potomac River. Inside (below), patrons hurry to a performance of the Washington Ballet.

United States. Both halls lead to the **Grand Foyer**—at 630 feet one of the longest rooms in the world. This royal, red-carpeted space is outfitted with floor-to-ceiling mirrors and 18 crystal chandeliers donated by Sweden. Halfway down the hall you'll find Robert Berks's big, emotive bronze bust of Kennedy.

Seeing a performance is the reason to come here—and the best way to take in the auditoriums. The

Robert Peary, Louis Leakey, Jacques Cousteau, and Jane Goodall are some of the explorers and scientists who have been supported by National Geographic, founded in Washington in 1888.

More places to visit around the White House

NATIONAL GEOGRAPHIC SOCIETY

The National Geographic Society's magazines, books and guidebooks (including this one), maps, TV programs, and classroom materials—all aimed at "the increase and diffusion of geographic knowledge"—are produced here at the organization's headquarters. Plenty of events, exhibits, and slide-illustrated lectures are also offered for visitors. Revamped in 2001, **Explorers Hall** often exhibits the work of National Geographic photographers, researchers, and explorers, including conservationist Mike Fay—whose grueling 2-year, 2,000-mile trek across the heart of Africa inspired the country of Gabon to set aside 10 percent of its land as national park—and paleontologist Paul Sereno with his newest dinosaur discoveries. Explorers Hall also houses a small permanent collection, as well as the National Geographic Store, which offers for sale much of the Society's product line of books, magazines, games, videos, and educational products.

🗺 Map p. 107 ✉ 17th & M Sts., N.W. ☎ 202-857-7588 Ⓜ Metro: Farragut North, Farragut West

B'NAI B'RITH KLUTZNICK NATIONAL JEWISH MUSEUM

This museum of Jewish art, history, and culture documents the life and festival cycles of Judaism. Named for the B'nai B'rith service organization and Chicago attorney Philip Klutznick, the collection includes 18th-century German and Italian berith knives, a silver phylactery (ca 1800) from Poland, 18th-century bronze Sabbath lamps, and a case of shining silver Torah finials and crowns. A 1790 letter from George Washington to Moses Seixas, a sexton of the Touro Synagogue in Newport, Rhode Island, promises that the U.S. government "gives to bigotry no sanction; to persecution no assistance."

✉ 2020 K St., N.W. (temporary location) ☎ 202-857-6583 🕐 Closed Sat., call other days for appointment Ⓜ Metro: Farragut West, Foggy Bottom-GWU

CATHEDRAL OF ST. MATTHEW THE APOSTLE

This redbrick 1890s cathedral, with its ribbed copper dome, is a commanding downtown presence. The funeral Mass of John F. Kennedy was held here in 1963; outside, three-year-old John Jr. bravely saluted his father's casket, creating an indelible image. A cavernous interior, embellished with mosaics, a skylit dome, flickering votive candles, and paintings and statues, forms a haven for prayer or meditation. Map p. 106 ✉ 1725 Rhode Island Ave., N.W. ☎ 202-347-3215 🚇 Metro: Dupont Circle

CHARLES SUMNER SCHOOL

Its handsome M Street exterior rivets the gaze on this redbrick building, opened in 1872 as a school for African American children (and named for the abolitionist senator from Massachusetts). Now an archive and museum of the District's public schools, the Sumner School also hosts concerts, lectures, films, and art exhibitions.
🗺 Map p. 107 ✉ 1201 17th St., N.W. ☎ 202-442-6060 🕐 Closed Sun. & July– Aug. 🚇 Metro: Farragut North, Dupont Circle

DECATUR HOUSE

For his triumphs in the War of 1812, Commodore Stephen Decatur earned enough to build this three-story federal-style house on Lafayette Square. Benjamin Henry Latrobe designed the redbrick town house, completed in 1818, but Decatur never really got to enjoy the place: He was killed in a duel with a fellow officer 14 months after moving in. His wife rented the house to the likes of Henry Clay and Martin Van Buren. Guided tours cover the period-furnished rooms of the first floor and

The Decatur House dining room contains period furnishings and table settings.

the lavish Victorian rooms of the second, which still seem to pulse with the vibrant presence of a later owner, Mrs. Truxtun Beale, who presided over a salon for ambassadors and politicians in these quarters.
🗺 Map p. 107 ✉ 748 Jackson Pl., N.W. ☎ 202-842-0920 🕐 Closed Mon. 💲 $ 🚇 Metro: Farragut West

DEPARTMENT OF STATE

What must foreign heads of state think when they arrive at the door of this drab 1961 building to meet with the Vice President or Secretary of State? Most of them aren't given the time to form a negative opinion; they are whisked to the eighth floor, where they step into a sparkling geode of elegance.

The designers of the **Diplomatic Reception Rooms** may have calculated this dismay-cum-delight effect on visiting dignitaries. Perhaps you'll experience a similar sensation when you visit the Department of State's suite of rooms decorated with one of the country's finest collections of early American furnishings. A 45-minute tour—which reveals such surprises as Paul Revere silver, George Washington's Chinese porcelain, and Francis Scott Key's side chairs—takes in eight of the reception rooms *(for reservations, call 202-647-3241)*. Elsewhere you'll come across portraits of George and Martha Washington by Rembrandt Peale, paintings by Gilbert Stuart and John Singleton Copley, and Chippendale furniture from Philadelphia, New York, and Boston. The rooms on the south side—among them the breathtakingly grand State Dining Room—give impressive views of the Mall and its monuments.
🗺 Map p. 106 ✉ 23rd and C Streets, N.W. ☎ 202-842-0920 🕐 Closed Sat.-Sun. 💲 $ 🚇 Metro: Farragut West

DEPARTMENT OF THE INTERIOR MUSEUM

Tucked inside the Department of the Interior, this small, quiet museum has a particularly good exhibit on Native Americans. Displays chronicle the Interior Department's 1930s origins, when it comprised the National Park Service, U.S. Fish and Wildlife Service, U.S. Geological Survey, and the Bureaus of Mines, Indian Affairs, Reclamation, and Land Man-

agement. Drawings, homestead claims, hand-made maps, exploration tools, and videos tell the story of the country's settlement.
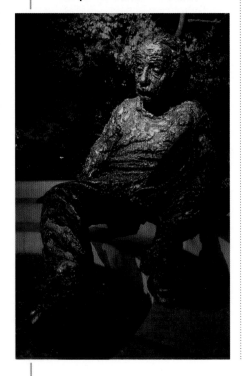 Map p. 106 1849 C St., N.W. 202-208-4743 Closed Sun., open third Sat. afternoon each month Metro: Farragut West, Foggy Bottom–GWU

HAY–ADAMS HOTEL
The elegant Italian Renaissance-style Hay–Adams, one of Washington's finest small hotels, fronts the north side of Lafayette Square, offering a good view of the White House. Built in the 1920s, the hotel occupies the site of residences owned by statesman John Hay and historian Henry Adams. Stop in for afternoon tea, fine dining, or the nighttime piano bar.
www.hayadams.com Map p. 107 16th & H Sts., N.W. 202-638-6600 Metro: Farragut West, McPherson Square

A bronze Albert Einstein at the National Academy of Sciences holds the three mathematical equations summarizing his most important scientific contributions.

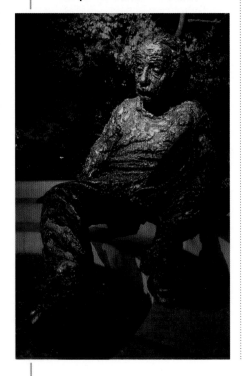

NATIONAL ACADEMY OF SCIENCES
Free concerts and art exhibits are often held in this think tank. Otherwise it is best known to visitors for its outdoor bronze of Albert Einstein, seated on white granite among a glade of elms and hollies. Robert Berks, who sculpted the similarly mudpie-style JFK bust in the Kennedy Center, uses proportion to emphasize his subject's amazing head. A 28-foot-wide sky map swirls at Einstein's feet.
Map p. 106 2101 Constitution Ave., N.W. 202-334-2000 Metro: Foggy Bottom–GWU

ST. JOHN'S CHURCH
Every U.S. President since James Madison has found some occasion to worship at St. John's Episcopal Church. The yellow stucco building, with its white wood bell tower and bright gold dome, was completed in 1816 after a design by Benjamin Henry Latrobe, who also helped conceptualize the Capitol, the White House, and neighboring Decatur House. A national historic landmark, the church is open weekdays from 9 a.m. to 3 p.m. for meditation and prayer. A skylit dome and memorial stained-glass windows brighten the interior, where a brass plate marks the President's Pew—No. 54.
Map p. 107 1525 H St., N.W. 202-347-8766 Metro: Farragut West, McPherson Square

ST. MARY'S EPISCOPAL CHURCH
Originally St. Mary's Church for Colored People, this handsome building was the city's first house of worship for black Episcopalians. The congregation pooled its money to hire famous architect James Renwick, only to learn that his design would break their budget. Around again went the collection plate. With the extra $3,000 thus raised, a simple yet lovely church was built; the first services were held in 1887. The altar triptych depicts two saints of African descent; the center window is Tiffany stained glass. A national historic landmark, the church boasts working gas lights and iron radiators.
Map p. 106 730 23rd St., N.W. 202-333-3985 Closed Sat. Metro: Foggy Bottom–GWU ■

With its eclectic mix of entertainment venues, hotels, historic structures, museums, retail establishments, and federal and private office buildings, downtown offers something for everyone.

Downtown

Detail at the entrance to the National Building Museum

Downtown

WASHINGTON'S DOWNTOWN HAS BEEN LOCATED JUST NORTH OF THE MALL since the city's founding in 1791. Sprung from the intersection of Pennsylvania Avenue and Seventh Street, where the city's main street met the main northern thoroughfare, the area has since sprawled to 14th Street and Louisiana and Massachusetts Avenues. Booming with new vitality, downtown buzzes with new restaurants, shops, theaters, and galleries, making all the more reason to come visit its clutch of long established museums.

Throughout the 1800s, boutiques, hotels, and theaters thrived downtown, catering to the area's residents. The turn of the 20th century, however, brought the exodus of affluent merchants and residents to the suburbs, thereby opening up the downtown area to successive groups of lower income citizens. Then came the assassination of Martin Luther King, Jr., in 1968, instigating riots and the large-scale abandonment of commercial ventures. As buildings fell into miserable disrepair and the crime rate exploded, the area became one to avoid.

The outlook soon changed. In 1972, Congress created the Pennsylvania Avenue Development Corporation to plan the revitalization of Pennsylvania Avenue—the neglected

Vendors and courting couples are often spotted on downtown sidewalks.

streetscape was unbefitting what many consider to be America's Main Street. Initially, the PADC focused on renovating Pennsylvania Avenue's historic buildings: the Old Post Office, the Willard Hotel, and the National and Warner Theatres. Each successful venture encouraged the next, as city planners and developers saw the possibility of returning downtown into a dynamic commercial district and residential neighborhood.

Coupled with renovation, new construction brought Market Square (1984, *N of the Archives*), with offices and apartments; the Lansburgh (1992, *8th & E Sts.*), a residential/retail/cultural arts venue complex; and in 2003 the splendid new convention center (*N of Mt. Vernon Sq.*). In the last few years, 3.5 billion dollars have been invested in the area's development, including 30 new restaurants.

The most important development, however, was the arrival of the MCI Center in 1997. This entertainment and sports arena showcases a year-round parade of basketball, hockey, concerts, and other special events; its presence alone has hugely increased annual downtown visitation.

All this new life complements several museums that often have been overshadowed by those on the nearby Mall, including the National Museum of Women in the Arts, the Smithsonian American Art Museum, the National Portrait Gallery, the National Building Museum, and the National Archives, several of which are also being renovated and revitalized.

Amid the modernization rush, tiny Chinatown clings to its heritage. Clustered on the north side of Pennsylvania Avenue in the 1880s, the enclave established its distinctive appearance after moving to the H Street area in the 1930s, where it remains today. The area features Cantonese, Szechuan, and Hunan restaurants, as well as Chinese pharmacies selling all kinds of traditional remedies. ■

Ford's Theatre National Historic Site

Ford's Theatre National Historic Site
www.nps.gov/foth
🗺 Map p. 130
✉ 511 10th St., N.W.
☎ 202-426-6924
🚇 Metro: Metro Center;
Bus: D1-6

Petersen House
✉ 516 10th St., N.W.

A WORKING THEATER AND A MUSEUM TO ONE OF THE nation's most tragic dramas, Ford's Theatre has a morbidly compelling quality. John Wilkes Booth shot President Abraham Lincoln here on April 14, 1865, five days after Lee's surrender at Appomattox. Lincoln's untimely death pushed to legendary heights the historical greatness he had achieved by keeping the Union from falling apart.

The theater closed shortly thereafter, serving as an office building and later as a storage facility. Acquired by the National Park Service in 1933, it was restored to

Scene of the crime: The Presidential Box is on permanent display at Ford's.

its original 1865 splendor and reopened to the public in 1968. The theater now hosts a full program of contemporary American plays.

The ornate interior boasts the authentically re-created **Presidential Box** with American flags, lace curtains, red velvet wallpaper, plush seats, and the original settee. You

can walk up to the balcony for a look. No one sits there anymore—which is just as well, since it's apparently the only bad seat in the house.

When the theater is not in use, Park Service officials offer short informative talks on the night's events. Booth, a disgruntled actor, shot Lincoln in the head and then jumped down to the stage, breaking a small leg bone; he supposedly shouted "*Sic semper tyrannis*" (thus always to tyrants) and hobbled off. He fled on horseback through the southern Maryland countryside, only to be caught 12 days later and shot dead.

The **museum** downstairs contains several noteworthy artifacts, including the .44-caliber derringer Booth used in the shooting, the hunting knife he used to stab one of Lincoln's box companions, and the clothes Lincoln was wearing (look for his custom-made black overcoat from Brooks Brothers).

Continue following the night's events across the street at the **Petersen House,** where Lincoln was taken. Never regaining consciousness, the President died the next day. Peek into the parlor where Mary Todd Lincoln waited through the night, the back parlor where Lincoln's secretary of war began investigating the murder, and the period-furnished bedroom in which Lincoln died. A weary sadness pervades these cramped quarters, the empty boots and jacket suggesting an owner that will never return. ■

National Museum of Women in the Arts

National Museum of Women in the Arts

www.nmwa.org

📍 Map p. 130

✉ 1250 New York Ave., N.W.

☎ 202-783-5000

💲 $

Ⓜ Metro: Metro Center; Bus: 80, S2 & 4, G8

THIS WELL-DESIGNED MUSEUM FOCUSES SOLELY ON THE work of women artists. Founder and art collector Wilhelmina Cole Holladay felt that women were often completely overlooked in standard art history texts. Determined to correct the imbalance, her resulting museum, which opened in 1987, showcases and promotes the talent of women artists from the Renaissance to the present.

Notable in itself, the Renaissance revival building began as a Masonic temple in 1907, served as a movie theater in the 1960s, and, after being threatened with demolition in the early 1980s, was purchased by Holladay in 1983. Restored to its former glory, the grand hall shines with polished marble floors and decorative plasterwork. On the mezzanine level's north side, added during the restoration, you can still see a Masonic cartouche with the letter *M* worked in.

Works in the permanent collection, on view in the **Great Hall, Mezzanine,** and **third floor** chronicle women's artistic achievements from the 16th century to modern times. Look for Lavinia Fontana's 1580 "Portrait of a Noblewoman"; Fontana was the first widely known woman to sustain a career as an artist. Other treasures include "Sheep by the Sea" (1869) and other works by Rosa Bonheur (1822–1899), famous for her straightforward depictions of animals, as well as "The Bath" (1891) and others by Impressionist Mary Cassatt (1844–1926). Georgia O'Keeffe (1887–1986) and Helen Frankenthaler (1928–) are among the 20th-century artists represented.

This musuem is the only place in Washington where you can see paintings by Frida Kahlo. Her "Self-Portrait –Dedicated to Leon

Trotsky" (1939), also known as "Between the Curtains," is now part of the museum's permanent collection; another of her works is on loan.

Special exhibits are found on the second floor, while the fourth floor has an 18,500-volume library and research center. ∎

"Self-Portrait– Dedicated to Leon Trotsky" (1939), by Frida Kahlo

Pennsylvania Quarter

THE SHINING STAR OF DOWNTOWN'S REVITALIZATION, the Pennsylvania Quarter neighborhood, also called the Seventh Street corridor, is quickly becoming Washington's hippest hangout. With an explosion of luxury apartment complexes, trendy restaurants, theaters, and galleries joining a panoply of established and future museums, the once neglected area teems with life both night and day.

The real success story of the Pennsylvania Quarter begins with the abandoned Lansburgh department store. In 1992 this imposing building was rehabilitated into a mixed-use complex housing 385 luxury residential units, retail space, and a cultural arts venue. The combination of location, amenities, and cultural flavor attracted people (former attorney general Janet Reno and actor Harry Hamlin have been among its residents); and new businesses moved into the commercial spaces.

The Lansburgh's reigning

Chinese influences along Seventh Street

tenant, the nationally renowned **Shakespeare Theatre** *(450 7th St., 202-547-1122)* moved to Seventh Street from its Capitol Hill quarters in 1992. Devoted to presenting the Bard's works— as well as those of his contemporaries and of the playwrights he influenced—the theater is considered one of the nation's most prestigious. Its noted company of classical actors has included Dixie Carter, Hal Holbrook, Stacy Keach, Kelly McGillis, Jean Stapleton, and Richard Thomas. The well-established repertory

Woolly Mammoth Theatre has moved in across the street.

A major contributor to revitalization is the colossal **MCI Center** *(7th & F Sts., 202-628-3200)*, which draws thousands of visitors on any given day. Opened in 1997, the 20,000-seat arena hosts circuses, ice skating performances, concerts, and other special events, such as the annual Washington International Horse Show. It's also home to the Washington Wizards and Mystics professional basketball teams (men and women, respectively), the Georgetown Hoyas college basketball team, and the Washington Capitals hockey team.

An even bigger addition to the downtown area is the new **Washington Convention Center** *(www.dcconvention.com)* at 801 Mount Vernon Place, which opened in 2003. With 2.3 million square feet of space—covering 6 city blocks on 17 acres—the behemoth is more than double the size of the old convention center just blocks away.

Keeping in step with the quarter's new face, many of its museums—including the **National Portrait Gallery** (see p. 137), the **Smithsonian American Art Museum** (see p. 136), and the **National Archives** (see pp. 140–41)—are being renovated.

And more museums are adding to the area's appeal. The highly popular **International Spy Museum** (see p. 138) opened in 2002 at 800 F Street. A year later the **City Museum of Washington, D.C.,** moved into the beautiful 1903 beaux arts-style former Carnegie Library on Mount Vernon Square at Eighth and K Streets (see p. 143). Formerly in Virginia, the **Newseum,** an interactive museum on newsmaking, plans to occupy a new home at Sixth Street and Pennsylvania Avenue beginning in 2007.

Sandwiched amid all this growth is Washington's small but distinctive **Chinatown** *(6th to 8th Sts. & G to H Sts.),* which has thrived since it was established here in the 1930s. Its shops cater to a heavily Chinese clientele, and the many restaurants offer a wide range of tasty Szechuan and Cantonese dishes. ∎

Top: The Friendship Arch recalls the quarter's Chinese legacy with stylized script and fiery dragons. Below: Shakespeare Theatre buzz

Smithsonian American Art Museum

Smithsonian American Art Museum

www.americanart.si.edu

⬛ Map p. 130

✉ 8th & G Sts., N.W.

☎ 202-275-1500

🕐 Closed for renovation until 2006

🚇 Metro: Gallery Place–Chinatown; Bus: 42

WITH SOME 39,000 PAINTINGS, SCULPTURES, PRINTS, DRAW-ings, photographs, and folk art, this museum holds the nation's premier collection of works by American artists. Dating from 1829, making it the nation's oldest federal art collection, the museum has renamed itself several times over the years in an effort to accurately reflect its character. Most recently known as the National Museum of American Art, in October 2000 it was rechristened the Smithsonian American Art Museum.

McKendree Robbins Long, Sr.'s "Vision from Book of Revelation" (1966) invites contemplation.

The museum's home—the stately, neoclassic Old Patent Office Building—is undergoing an extensive renovation that will significantly boost the number of works on display. When the building reopens in 2006, the art will be displayed on three levels, with a special "open storage" gallery that lets you browse through over 5,000 artworks densely packed in Plexiglas cases. In the interim, the collection remains a strong force in the world of American art: More than 500 of the museum's best paintings and sculptures have been exhibited in 70 cities.

The **19th-century collection** includes paintings by such notables as Albert Pinkham Ryder and Impressionist Mary Cassatt, and sculptures by Daniel Chester French and Augustus Saint-Gaudens. Among the favorites are the luminist scenes of the American West by Albert Bierstadt and Frederic Church, representing the flowering of grand landscape painting. The **20th-century collection** has such famous works as Edward Hopper's "Cape Cod Morning" (1950), Robert Rauschenberg's "Reservoir" (1961), and Georgia O'Keeffe's "Yellow Calla" (1926).

In the realm of folk art, you won't want to miss "The Throne of the Third Heaven of the Nations Millennium General Assembly." After he received a vision, local janitor James Hampton meticulously constructed this ecclesiastical piece for the Second Coming. Wrapping old furniture, jelly jars, and light bulbs in gold or silver tin foil, he is believed to have worked on the piece for 14 years; the throne was discovered in a rented garage upon his death in 1964.

Outside, looking as if about to leap from its pedestal, "Vaquero" (Luis Jimenez, 1980) jazzes up the building's columned front portico on G Street. The acrylic-urethane-fiber-glass-steel sculpture shows a shouting Mexican cowboy, pistol raised, hanging onto a bucking blue horse. ■

Jo Davidson's 1951 likeness of Franklin D. Roosevelt emerges from a block of marble.

National Portrait Gallery

CELEBRATING THE NATION'S HEROES, INTELLECTS, ROGUES, and famous personalities, the National Portrait Gallery offers a revealing look at America's history through portraiture and sculpture. An extensive renovation of the building began in January 2000, and the gallery is expected to reopen when the work is done in 2006.

The Old Patent Office Building in which the gallery is housed is a handsome Greek Revival edifice completed in the mid-19th century. During the Civil War it was a hospital; Walt Whitman was among those who attended the suffering. On the third floor is the spectacular Victorian-style **Great Hall,** with colorful skylight, fluted pilasters, and elaborate ceiling medallions.

The idea of a national portrait gallery dates back to 1857, when Congress commissioned George P.A. Healy to paint official portraits of all the Presidents for the White House. After World War I, a national portrait gallery was proposed as part of a general art collection being formed within the Smithsonian Institution. Yet not until 1968 did the National Portrait Gallery of the United States officially open to the public .

The gallery's collection consists of some 18,500 objects in media ranging from traditional oil-on-canvas and marble to photographs and drawings. Even caricatures by Al Hirschfeld and portrait covers from *Time* magazine are included. There's at least one formal portrait of every President since George Washington, along with the faces of writers, military leaders, inventors, captains of industry, entertainers, and others. A 1616 engraving of Pocahontas is one of the oldest portraits in the collection. Prominent Civil War figures are shown in a display that includes the "cracked plate" photograph of Abraham Lincoln taken in 1865, just two months before he was assassinated.

Among the rarest images in the gallery are David Geary's photographs of Marilyn Monroe singing to troops in Korea. One of the most striking portraits is Jo Davidson's large Buddha-like terra cotta bust of the avant-garde American writer Gertrude Stein. ■

National Portrait Gallery
www.npg.si.edu
Map p. 130
8th & F Sts., N.W.
202-275-1738
Closed for renovation until 2006
Metro: Gallery Place—Chinatown; Bus: 42

International Spy Museum

**International
Spy Museum**
www.spymuseum.org
🗺 Map p. 130
✉ 800 F St., N.W.
☎ 202-393-7798
$ $$$
🚇 Metro: Gallery
Place/Chinatown

ONE OF THE HOTTEST ATTRACTIONS IN WASHINGTON these days lies in the shadow of the city's grand monuments—fitting, perhaps, given the shadowy world it illuminates. The International Spy Museum takes you inside the world of espionage through engrossing exhibits and programs designed with the help of real agents and spy-catchers such as CIA masters of disguise.

The privately developed museum opened in 2002 in the shell of five historic buildings dating from 1875 to 1892. The American Communist Party had offices here during World War II. In the refurbished space, the museum's state-of-the-art exhibits highlight the people, tools, and techniques of espionage tradecraft

A not-so-secret entrance to the International Spy Museum

around the world.

The displays are built around a collection of more than 600 objects ranging from popular G-Man toys from the 1930s and 1940s ("G" for "Government") to spying devices such as a KGB pistol encased in a lipstick tube. Espionage from biblical times to the present is represented. One item on display is a 1777 letter by George Washington authorizing creation of a spy network.

Among the fascinating stories highlighted in the exhibits are those of women who traveled undercover as spies during the Civil War. In

fact, an entire room is devoted to women agents through the first decades of the 20th century.

VISITING

There is often a waiting line on weekends and holidays for same-day admission. To avoid long waits and disappointment, it's a good idea to reserve in advance (*800-551-7328, TicketMaster.com*). Inside, most visitors spend about two hours; add an hour to see the special exhibit, **The Enemy Within: Terror in America–1776 to Today.**

You begin the self-guided tour by adopting an alias. The role-playing continues through scenarios that test your skill at analyzing situations and maintaining your cover, as real agents must do. Find out in **School for Spies** whether you have what it takes for this risky business. The exhibits include 200 of the spying gadgets developed by agencies from the OSS to the KGB, some still in use today.

In **Secret History of History,** you'll learn how important secret intelligence has been to many notable leaders throughout history, from Elizabeth I to Joseph Stalin. **Spies Among Us** spotlights spy rings and intelligence gathering in the climate of World War II, such as the Allies' top-secret code-breaking success (named Ultra) and the brilliant work of Navajo code-talkers.

War of the Spies and **The 21st Century** bring espionage into the present, showing how spies from Kim Philby to Robert Hanssen have operated. ■

National Building Museum

THE GARGANTUAN REDBRICK PENSION BUILDING IS ONE of Washington's least known architectural treasures. Designed by civil engineer Gen. Montgomery C. Meigs, the 1887 Victorian building was referred to by critics, who thought it an eyesore, as Meigs's Old Red Barn. Though the building was badly deteriorated by the 1960s, a study highlighting its potential as a museum space saved it from proposed demolition. Congress called for its restoration in 1980 to house a museum about architecture, urban planning, engineering, and design.

National Building Museum
www.nbm.org
Map p. 130
401 F St., N.W.
202-272-2448
Metro: Judiciary Square; Bus: D1-6

Girdling the entire building, the most striking exterior feature is the 3-foot-high terra-cotta frieze designed by Bohemian-born sculptor Caspar Buberl (1834–1899). Depicting a procession of Civil War infantry, artillery, cavalry, and other units, it is emblematic of the building's original purpose: serving the needs of Union veterans.

The interior is just as impressive. The spectacular **Great Hall** will take your breath away. Standing in the middle of this immense, light-filled, open space, bordered on all sides with four tiers of arcades and high clerestory windows, you feel as if you've stepped into an Italian gallery. Eight Corinthian columns, made of brick but plastered and painted to resemble marble, rise 75 feet high on either side of a central fountain. Meigs modeled aspects of this room after several Roman palaces and churches, including the Palazzo Farnese.

The museum galleries, which feature a variety of changing exhibits on the building arts, ring the Great Hall's two levels. The museum's only permanent exhibition, **Washington: Symbol & City,** was reinstalled in late 2004. It presents a good overview of D.C.'s development. A push-button map of L'Enfant's original city plan, models of the evolving Mall, and a short video of citizens talking about Washington provide insight into the city. Artifacts include the five rejected designs for the U.S. Capitol and a copy of the 1792 letter signed by Jefferson dismissing city planner L'Enfant for refusing to take orders from the District Commissioners.

The museum offers lectures, films, and even outings to interesting architectural and construction sites in the area. Check the website for information. On the first floor is a café and a gift shop that *Washingtonian* magazine rated "best museum shop in Washington" for its interesting selection. ■

Elegant arcaded galleries and marbleized columns define the cavernous Great Hall, which measures 116 by 316 feet.

National Archives

National Archives

www.archives.gov

Map p. 130

700 Pennsylvania Ave., N.W.

202-501-5000

Metro: Archives—Navy Memorial; Bus: P1-2, 13A-B & F-G, X1, V8, 70-71

SERVING AS THE NATION'S MEMORY BANK, THE NATIONAL Archives contains several billion pages of documents, including the original parchment copies of the Declaration of Independence, the U.S. Constitution, and the Bill of Rights. John Russell Pope, architect of the Jefferson Memorial, designed the distinguished 1935 building expressly for the purpose of housing these all-important manifestos. In fact it was Jefferson, author of the Declaration, who first voiced concern about the deterioration of the national records.

The somber Rotunda room is where America's Charters of Freedom are displayed for all to see.

Ringed with 72 massive Corinthian columns, Pope's grand neoclassic edifice takes up a whole city block. Bas-reliefs decorate the pediments atop the north and south porticos. The 39 limestone steps that front the south portico on Constitution Avenue represent the 39 signers of the Constitution. The foot-thick bronze doors at the top of the stairs soar 40 feet high.

Inside, the echoing, semicircular **Rotunda** room, which recently underwent major renovation, rises to a 75-foot-high dome. New York artist Barry Faulkner painted the two large 1930s murals decorating the Rotunda. "The Constitution," on the right side, depicts James Madison presenting the document to George Washington. "The Declaration of Independence," on the left, shows Thomas Jefferson submitting the proclamation to John Hancock, presiding officer of the Continental Congress.

The low-lit, somber Rotunda room creates the right mood for viewing the United States' most important documents: the **Charters of Freedom.** Each sheet of the Declaration of

Independence, the U.S. Constitution, and the Bill of Rights lies in a new state-of-the-art case that fiercely protects the document against air and moisture. The cases allow all four pages of the Constitution to be shown at the same time. At night, and in the event of an emergency, the documents are retracted into a deep vault for safekeeping.

The upgraded Charters of Freedom display is the first component of a comprehensive redesign of public exhibits at the Archives aimed at helping visitors better understand how the documents stored here are a living instrument for directing the nation's future. **Public Vaults**, a new permanent exhibit opened in late 2004, shows what it's like to go "inside the stacks" to do research. Another display will examine how records are transformed through time and technological change, from the earliest Native American treaties to Presidential websites. A 290-seat theater will show a documentary explaining how important public records are to a democracy.

Other milestone documents related to the creation of the United States are also showcased in the Rotunda room. A large exhibit gallery encircling the room features rotating selected documents from the Archives, with interactive exhibits that enable visitors to piece together strands of history. Family, community, military, and other documents especially illustrate the way that ordinary people's lives are affected by government. Adjacent galleries to the east and west mount special exhibits drawn from the permanent collections.

OTHER TREASURES

The Archives preserve for posterity more than 18 million maps, aerial photographs, and charts; 9 million still photos; hundreds of thousands of films, videos, and sound recordings; and numerous other data files and artifacts. The National Archives and Records Administration, established in 1934 to oversee what to

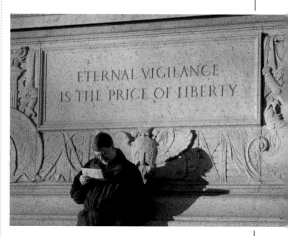

save, deems less than 2 percent of the federal records worthy of permanent storage.

Representing more than 200 years of history, the repository is creating a rich paper trail. Among the original treasures are the Louisiana Purchase Treaty, the Emancipation Proclamation, Mathew Brady's Civil War photographs, Robert Peary's polar expedition journals, Dust Bowl photographs, Indian treaties, recordings of FDR's fireside chats, captured German records and Japanese surrender documents from World War II, the check that paid for the territory of Alaska, and Nixon's letter of resignation.

The Archives are popular among scholars, students, historians, and researchers of all kinds, who are welcome to use the research facilities here and in College Park, Maryland. Alex Haley used slave ship manifests in researching his novel *Roots*. Opened in 1994, the Maryland branch is the largest archival facility in the world. ■

In search of guidance outside the National Archives

Federal Bureau of Investigation

Federal Bureau of Investigation
www.fbi.gov/aboutus/tour/tour.htm

- Map p. 130
- 9th & E Sts., N.W.
- 202-324-3447
- Metro: Archives–Navy Memorial; Bus: P1-6, 54, A3A-B & F-G

Note: As of press time tours were suspended until 2005. Call ahead or check the website for information.

A special agent shows the correct stance for shooting a firearm, the most popular part of the tour.

A HULKING CONCRETE STRUCTURE COMPLETED IN 1975, the J. Edgar Hoover Federal Bureau of Investigation Building houses the main investigative branch of the Department of Justice, which sits on the other side of Pennsylvania Avenue.

The investigation into federal crimes began with President Theodore Roosevelt's Secret Service agents, although specially trained operatives did not come under the Department of Justice until 1908. Over the years the concept of a premier law enforcement agency jelled, leading to the official Federal Bureau of Investigation in 1935.

The man most responsible for shaping the FBI was J. Edgar Hoover, under whose directorship between 1924 and 1972 it gained national importance and power. Hoover is known for engaging in controversial activities, including investigations into the lives of private and public citizens alike. In an effort to increase public awareness of the FBI, he established public tours in 1937.

The popular **one-hour tours** were temporarily suspended during renovations but are scheduled to resume in 2005, presumably in much the same format. They begin with a short film, followed by a walk through exhibits exploring the FBI's history. You will learn about the agency's fight against gangsters (don't miss the weapons used by Al Capone and other gangsters); its past and present ten most wanted fugitives; and its famous cases against organized and white-collar crime, counterintelligence, drug operations, and terrorism. The tour stops by analysis laboratories where scientific examinations of DNA, weapons, and crime-scene materials are done. At the end of each tour, an FBI agent gives a firearms demonstration. ∎

More places to visit downtown

FREEDOM PLAZA

The frequent venue of free concerts, popular rallies, and ethnic festivals, this granite plaza is anchored by an equestrian statue of Casimir Pulaski, the Polish nobleman who fought for America in the Revolution and was mortally wounded at the siege of Savannah. The plaza offers a sweeping view down Pennsylvania Avenue to the U.S. Capitol. Inlaid in bronze on the ground are L'Enfant's 1791 city plan, as are outlines for the Congress House and President's Palace.

 Map p. 130 ✉ Pennsylvania Ave. between 13th & 14th Sts., N.W. 🚇 Metro: Metro Center

MARY MCLEOD BETHUNE COUNCIL HOUSE

Now a national historic site, this former residence of educator Bethune (1875–1955), who founded Bethune-Cookman College in Daytona Beach, Florida, and the National Council of Negro Women, stores and displays artifacts pertaining to African American women's history. In addition, the house museum is decorated with Bethune's original furnishings and photographs.

www.nps.gov/mamc Map p. 130 ✉ 1318 Vermont Ave., N.W. ☎ 202-673-2402 Closed Sun. 🚇 Metro: McPherson Square

NATIONAL THEATRE

The sixth theater erected on this site since 1835, the National Theatre can claim to be Washington's oldest continuously operating theater. The current theater replaced an ornate five-story structure in 1922. The sumptuous decor includes dazzling chandeliers and the satin brocaded stage curtain. Unlike most large modern theaters, the mezzanine and balcony are close to the stage, giving the space an intimate feel for theatergoers. Lavish Broadway and pre-Broadway shows and other presentations are staged here, many starring well known actors of stage and screen.

www.nationaltheatre.org Map p. 130 ✉ 1321 Pennsylvania Ave., N.W. ☎ 202-628-6161 🚇 Metro: Federal Triangle, Metro Center

OLD POST OFFICE

This castlelike building was erected in the 1890s as headquarters for the U.S. Post Office. A group of preservationists prevented its demolition in the 1970s, and after several years of renovation it reopened as a spacious pavilion of government offices, retail stores, and eateries. For one of the best views in the downtown area, take the elevator to the ninth-floor exhibit room, then follow the signs to an elevator that takes you to the top of the tower.

www.nps.gov/opot Map p. 130 ✉ Pennsylvania Ave. & 12th St., N.W. ☎ 202-606-8691 🚇 Metro: Federal Triangle

CITY MUSEUM OF WASHINGTON

Housed in the 1903 beaux arts-style former Carnegie Library, this museum of the Historical Society of Washington, D.C., tells the 200-year-old story of the city and its many diverse communities. Multimedia presentations and changing exhibits are geared to all age groups. As of press time, financial pressures had forced the museum to close its doors to the public; check the website or

Performers entertain the lunchtime crowd at the Old Post Office Pavilion.

Around the world in more than 80 steps: A 100-foot-diameter map of the world graces the U. S. Navy Memorial plaza.

telephone to obtain current status.
http://www.citymuseumdc.org Map p. 130
✉ K St., N.W., between 7th & 9th Sts.
☎ 202-383-1800 💲 💲 🕐 Closed Mon.
🚇 Metro: Mt. Vernon Square/7th St., Gallery Place/Chinatown

MARIAN KOSHLAND SCIENCE MUSEUM OF THE NATIONAL ACADEMY OF SCIENCES

This 5,700 square-foot museum that opened in April 2004 provides insight into scientific issues at the core of many of the nation's public policy decisions. Interactive exhibits explore global warming, the wonders of science, and the use of DNA to detect diseases, improve crops, and catch criminals.
http://www.koshland-science-museum.org/
Map p. 130 ✉ 500 E St., N.W. ☎ 202-334-1201 💲 💲 🕐 Closed Tues. 🚇 Metro: Gallery Place/Chinatown, Judiciary Square

U.S. NAVY MEMORIAL & NAVAL HERITAGE CENTER

Situated directly behind the National Archives, this small center contains ship models, artifacts, photographs, a gift shop, and a selective computerized log of sea service personnel, including veterans of the Navy, Marine Corps, Coast Guard, and Merchant Marines. A 242-seat theater screens an exciting DVD film called *At Sea (fee)*. Outside, the circular memorial features a 7-foot bronze statue of "The Lone Sailor" and a correctly oriented granite map of the world. Bronze relief sculptures of famous events in naval history ring the perimeter of the memorial. Bands and choral groups perform here in spring and summer.
www.lonesailor.org/nmf.php Map p. 130
✉ 701 Pennsylvania Ave., N.W. ☎ 202-737-2300 🕐 Closed Sun. March–Oct., Sun.–Mon. Nov.–Feb. 🚇 Metro: Archives–Navy Memorial

WARNER THEATRE

A block east of the National Theatre, the Warner Theatre started life in 1924 as a silent-movie palace and vaudeville stage. From the mid-1940s to the late 1960s, it only presented movies. Thereafter it functioned mainly as a rock concert venue until shutting down completely. Reopened in 1992, the refurbished theater dazzles the eye with crystal, red velvet, and gold leaf; it now hosts a varied program of established dance and theater companies.
www.warnertheatre.com Map p. 130
✉ 13th St. between E & F Sts. ☎ 202-783-4000 🚇 Metro: Federal Triangle, Metro Center ■

Cobbled streets, red brick row houses, and mule-drawn canal boats elicit Georgetown's historic past. Come evening, the city's young and trendy flock to the neighborhood's buzzing bars, clubs, and restaurants.

Georgetown

Cobblestones of Georgetown

Georgetown

WASHINGTON'S POSHEST SQUARE MILE IS A HIGH-OCTANE COCKTAIL OF cultural refinement and giddy nightlife. While side streets exhibit elegant federal and Victorian architecture, Wisconsin Avenue and M Streets inject excitement with boutiques, bars, and restaurants.

Riggs Bank at the corner of Wisconsin and M marks Georgetown's center.

Georgetown began life as a tobacco inspection and shipment port at the confluence of Rock Creek and the Potomac, the highest navigable point on the river, on a 795-acre tract acquired by Scottish immigrant Ninian Beall in 1703. The Maryland Assembly established a town there in the 1750s and named it for George II. After independence, when the country was planning its federal city, Georgetown had become a thriving trade center, with lordly merchants' houses rising on the hill and artisans' houses and warehouses dotting the riverside. The new city proved a boon to Georgetown's silversmiths, cabinetmakers, and other craftspeople, who did a brisk business fitting the White House and other federal buildings. During the Civil War, Georgetown's significant black community made it an important Underground Railroad stop.

In 1871 the city of Washington annexed Georgetown. By then the little town needed the capital more than the reverse. The advent

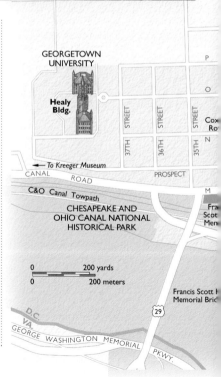

of the railroad and steam power had greatly diminished the importance of the C&O canal and thus Georgetown at its eastern end. In the first half of the 20th century, Georgetown lost the cachet of its early years; it functioned primarily as industrial muscle for Washington, its foundry and mills supplying iron, paper, and coal. During Roosevelt's administration, white-collar workers began moving back into Georgetown; then, in 1950, Congress declared it a national historic district, speeding its restoration and return to fashion.

Rock Creek and the Potomac River form Georgetown's eastern and southern borders; to the west lies Georgetown University and north the hill on which Dumbarton Oaks sits. In these blocks have lived members of such clans as the Washingtons, Lees, and Kennedys. Today diplomats, politicians, journalists, and socialites walk shady brick sidewalks and party in book- and art-filled houses, lubricating the wheels of government, business, and culture. ∎

The federal-style town houses of Cox's Row typify the neighborhood's elegant architecture.

Brick sidewalk tour

With its inviting brick sidewalks, tree-lined streets, and historic architecture, Georgetown was made for the leisurely stroller. You can try seeing the city's oldest neighborhood by car, but traffic moves slowly on the narrow streets, some of which are still cobbled and veined with trolley tracks. Better to leave the car behind.

If you drive in, you can find street parking, but it may take a while, especially on the weekends. The network of streets north of M Street is your best bet for parking, though you should pay attention to the signs—most streets are zoned for two-hour parking from 7 a.m. to 9 p.m. (except Sunday). There are several parking lots along M Street and below the canal. Metro buses service M Street and Wisconsin Avenue. You can also walk from the Foggy Bottom–GWU Metro—just over a half mile to the eastern edge of Georgetown.

If you do start from the Metro, you'll head west on Pennsylvania Avenue. Across the bridge, Pennsylvania feeds into M Street, Georgetown's main avenue for shopping, dining, and partying. Spring and summer evenings, the ten-block stretch from here to the Francis Scott Key Bridge is a steady parade of the chic, the casual, and the grungy. While the shops tend to be upscale, the bars, dance floors, and some restaurants cater to a young crowd, liberally supplied by Georgetown and George Washington Universities. One long-standing favorite restaurant on the east end of M, **La Chaumière** (2813 M St., 202-338-1784) features French provincial cuisine; hanging brass pans and a central fireplace give a rural ambience, nicely contrasting with the busyness outside.

Continue west on M to the **Old Stone House ❶** (3051 M St., 202-426-6851, closed Mon.–Tues.), one of the oldest structures in the city. A craftsman named Christopher Layman built the first floor of the three-story house of local fieldstones in 1765, probably as both home and shop. A legend, later disproved, that George Washington had a headquarters here helped preserve the house. In 1953 the National Park Service acquired the property, restored it, and opened it to the public in 1960. The ground floor has a shop with replicas of 18th-century tools and a kitchen with cast-iron stove. On the second floor, built

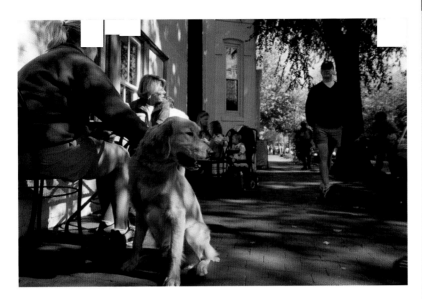

Casual posh: Georgetowners relax on shady sidewalks.

by the next owner, you'll find an oak-paneled dining room, a parlor, and bedrooms.

Cross M Street and head downhill on Thomas Jefferson Street to the eastern terminus of the **C&O Canal ➋,** a muddy-bottomed, shallow waterway, bordered by a towpath, that served as a key shipping link in the 19th century. Originally slated to stretch 460 miles to Pittsburgh and connect with the

> 🅜 See area map pp. 146–47
> ➤ M and 29th Sts. (Metro: Foggy Bottom–GWU)
> ↔ 2 miles
> ⏱ 2 hours
> ➤ St. John's Church

NOT TO BE MISSED
- Old Stone House
- Washington Harbour
- Cox's Row

66

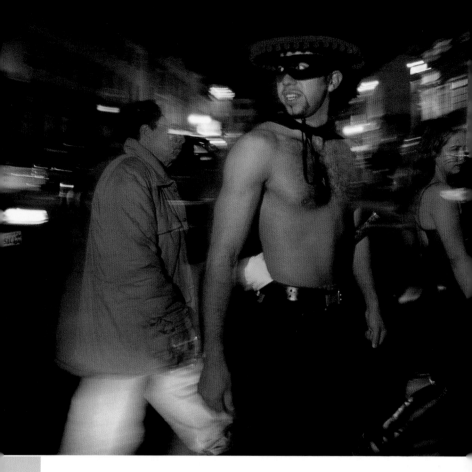

Ohio River, the Chesapeake and Ohio Canal, begun in 1828, made it only 185 miles up the Potomac to Cumberland, Maryland, where work stopped in 1850. From April through October you can take a scenic ride *(fee)* on a replica 19th-century canalboat, starting from the Georgetown Visitor Center *(1057 Thomas Jefferson St., 202-653-5190)*. A mule-drawn ride is a nice way to while away an hour.

Don't miss the small brick row houses that run along the canal just off Thomas Jefferson Street; they were built after the Civil War as homes for laborers. A few are now Asian take-out restaurants.

Go from the old to the new at the bottom of the hill by crossing K Street under the Whitehurst Freeway; in front of you spreads **Washington Harbour ❸,** a 1980s complex of offices, apartments, shops, and restaurants. At the entrance stands J. Seward Johnson's

realistic sculpture, *Let's Just Skip the Meeting.* You can see why they'd want to play hookey when you wander over to the central pool with its fountains, plantings, and views of the Potomac, Roosevelt Island, the Kennedy Center, Watergate, and the high rises of Rosslyn, Virginia, across the river.

Next head up 31st Street. On your right, just below M, **Cannon's Seafood** has supplied locals with fresh fish since 1937. The alleyway across the street from Cannon's leads to **Blues Alley** *(1073 Wisconsin Ave., 202-337-4141),* which may look like a dive outside but is actually Washington's swankiest jazz joint. On nights when a big name is in town, you might see 50 people lined up just hoping for no-shows on the reservation list. Definitely call ahead, and expect to pay a hefty cover charge—well worth it for the intimate setting.

Turn right from the alley onto Wisconsin

Zorro and other revelers make the streets of Georgetown the place to be and be seen on Halloween.

the new federal city. Gen. Uriah Forrest owned the house then; in 1800–1835 it belonged to William Marbury of the landmark *Marbury v. Madison* case, in which the Supreme Court established the doctrine of judicial review.

For a small detour into cinematic history, cross to the north side of M Street and walk west a short distance. Tucked away near a gas station, an eerily familiar 75-step stone stairway stretches upward. Known as the **Exorcist Steps,** the stairs played a prominent role in the 1973 horror classic *The Exorcist.*

Fortunately, nothing ominous awaits you at the top of the stairway on Prospect Street, which has some of Georgetown's oldest and most impressive houses. For an easier ascent to Prospect, go back east on M and turn left onto 34th Street. At the corner of 34th and Prospect stands the classic Georgian-style **Halcyon House** (1786). Built by Benjamin Stoddert, the first secretary of the Navy and an important Georgetown landowner, the house recently underwent a major restoration. A few buildings away is **Worthington House,** No. 3425, built in 1798 by prominent lawyer John Thomson Mason. Note the 24-paned windows lining both main floors. Just past 35th Street look for **Prospect House** (1788), No. 3508, another imposing Georgian, home of a 19th-century shipping merchant. Much of its structure and impressive gardens lie hidden behind a brick wall.

Prospect Street ends at 37th Street, the eastern edge of **Georgetown University** ❺, whose main entrance is at 37th and O. The Gothic-spired university is best known for its schools of medicine, law, and foreign service, and its basketball team.

From 37th, turn back east on N; across 34th on the north side runs a line of five stately brick town houses known as **Cox's Row** ❻, built in 1805 by Georgetown mayor John Cox. Down the block, in 1957–1961, Sen. John F. Kennedy and his wife, Jacqueline, lived at 3307 N Street, a three-story house with a fanlight and black shutters. On the corner of Potomac and O, Anglican services are still held at **St. John's Church** ❼, opened in 1804, and

Avenue and walk back up to M Street. This intersection is the area's busiest; the gold dome on the ornate old Farmers and Mechanics Branch of the Riggs National Bank serves as a landmark. Turn left heading west on M to the nearly block-long glitzy mall called **Georgetown Park** *(3222 M St.);* it has upmarket shops and restaurants on three levels, with skylit courtyards and chuckling fountains.

Continue west on M until you reach No. 3276, **Dean and Deluca,** a gourmet food shop where you can pick up lunch. Erected in 1865, the building sits on a site that also held markets in the 18th century.

A little farther down the street, just before Key Bridge, you'll come to the 1788 **Forrest-Marbury House** ❹ (now the Embassy of Ukraine). Here George Washington met with local landowners in 1791 to work out the agreement on the sale of their land to create designed by William Thornton, first architect of the Capitol.

East of Wisconsin Avenue lie several more blocks of elegant 19th-century houses. Bare brick alternates with stucco facades painted in muted shades of blue, gray, red, and yellow. Victorian bay windows and turrets are much in evidence. At the corner of Dumbarton and 31st Streets look for **Berry House,** built in 1810 when the street level was several feet higher. As a result, the front door stands unusually far above the street.

Walk one block south to N Street and turn left to see a noteworthy block. On your right is No. 3038, built in 1805, the longtime home of statesman Averell Harriman and his wife, Pamela. The large brick town house has a lovely arched doorway and odd, shingled dormers.

In No. 3017 across the street, Jackie Kennedy lived for several months after the assassination of President Kennedy. Almost directly facing it stands the 40-room **Laird-Dunlop House,** No. 3014, built in 1799. Robert Todd Lincoln, the only son of Abraham Lincoln to survive into adulthood, lived here from 1918 to 1926. Especially notable is the raised fanlight doorway.

If you stroll on to 28th and Olive Streets, you'll come upon one of Georgetown's oldest and smallest houses. The tiny wooden cottage at 1222 28th St. was built sometime before the Revolution, though the date is uncertain. Very little has changed in its basic structure. ■

Glitzy Washington Harbour, a splash both day and night.

Georgetown crawl

Before Adams Morgan and U Street became hip, anyone seeking nightlife went to Georgetown. Though club options have now spread to those and other locations in the city and suburbs, Georgetown still reigns supreme as party central. If you've a mind to join the fun, be aware that the revelry can be excessive at times, particularly on Halloween and the rare occasions the Redskins win the Superbowl. Traffic woes—Key Bridge, the main feeder from Virginia, is a solid jam on weekend evenings—and parking problems don't deter the crowds along M Street. Cabbing here makes the most sense; the fare for two from downtown costs about

as much as a single movie ticket.

There are many options to choose from. A sampler: The first thing you may notice when you enter **J. Paul's** (3128 M St., 202-333-3450) restaurant and tavern is the oyster shucking at the street-side raw bar. J. Paul's also features crab cakes and steaks and a 95-year-old mahogany bar. Down the street, **Clyde's of Georgetown** (3236 M St., 202-333-9180), with its interesting daily specials, old stone fireplace, vintage model planes, and gold record commemorating the 1976 hit song "Afternoon Delight"—inspired by Clyde's afternoon appetizers—offers a delicious dining experience. For simpler fare such as pizza, locals and students hit **The Tombs** (1226 36th St., 202-337-6668), a block from Georgetown University, beneath the upscale restaurant, **1789.**

If you're a sports fan, stop by **Champions** (1206 Wisconsin Ave., 202-965-4005) sports bar, where events are shown on multiple screens. Those who prefer music to sports will enjoy **Mr. Smith's** (3104 M St., 202-333-3104), which features a piano bar and an outdoor patio. Many people consider **Nathan's** (3150 M St., 202-338-2600) the place to go for weekend dancing.

If you want to find a table on the weekend at Georgetown's hot spots, arrive early. ■

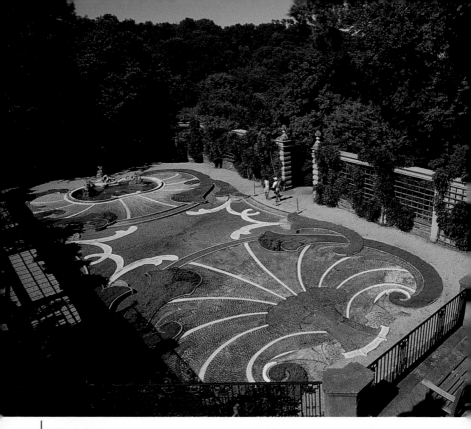

The Pebble Garden

Dumbarton Oaks

Dumbarton Oaks

www.Doaks.org

🅰 Map p. 147

✉ Garden entrance, 31st & R Sts., N.W.; museum, on 32nd bet. R & S

☎ 202-339-6401

🕐 Closed a.m.; museum Mon.

💲 Gardens: $$ March–Oct., free in winter; museum: donation

🚇 Metro: Dupont Circle, Foggy Bottom; Bus: D1-6, G2

AN ANTIQUE PROVENÇAL FOUNTAIN, A MINIATURE ROMAN amphitheater, and a 16th-century French-style arbor are among the many treasures awaiting you in Dumbarton Oaks's terraced gardens. Spring to fall, the gardens offer an ever changing display that includes early blooming dogwoods, magnolia blossoms, and cherries, peonies and roses, day lilies and chrysanthemums.

Presiding over the gardens is a federal-style house acquired in 1920 by Mildred and Robert Woods Bliss, stepsiblings and antiquities collectors who married and traveled widely in the Foreign Service. They hired the architectural firm McKim, Mead and White to renovate and enlarge the house for their extensive library and collection of Byzantine and pre-Columbian art. In 1940 they conveyed the property and museum to Harvard University, though they remained actively involved in Dumbarton Oaks until their deaths (Robert in 1962, Mildred in 1969). In 1944 a series of informal conferences held here laid the foundation for the establishment of the United Nations.

Today the main part of the house functions as Harvard's center for Byzantine studies and is not open to the public. Visitors are allowed only into the gardens, music room, and museum. A garden library, built in 1963, is open by appointment only.

Orangery; a pre-Civil War fig tree climbs its walls. Through here you access the main gardens. Outside, to the right, a tremendous beech presides over the **Beech Terrace.** Next, steps take you down to the **Rose Garden,** planted with nearly 1,000 varieties of roses. Just below are gardens with fountains and a wisteria-draped arbor based on a 16th-century French design. At the property's edge, a winding walkway skirts the reflecting pool of Lovers' Lane and its small amphitheater. Farther north the garden becomes less formal, with flowering cherry trees, a hillside of golden forsythia, and views of Dumbarton Oaks Park, given by the Blisses to the National Park Service and now part of Rock Creek Park.

Head back uphill to the **Ellipse,** an oval formed by a double ring of hornbeams, pruned to a uniform 16 feet, enclosing a Provençal fountain. Up the steps lies another landscaping masterpiece: **The Pebble Garden** is composed of rounded stones embedded on edge to create a terrace of varying textures; espaliered magnolias and wisteria vines bedeck the walls. Walk on past the pool to the grassy sweep of the **North Vista,** behind the main part of the house.

Visit the **music room** and the **museum** through the 32nd Street entrance. The Renaissance-style Music Room is a must-see for its antique European decorations. El Greco's "The Visitation" hangs with other paintings and tapestries. Concerts are held throughout the year.

Filled with natural light, the museum galleries display Byzantine and pre-Columbian art objects. The Byzantine collection includes 6th-century ecclesiastical silver and 13th-century mosaic icons. The circular galleries holding exquisite pre-Columbian works were designed by Philip Johnson. ■

VISITING

The 10-acre formal gardens, designed by landscape architect Beatrix Farrand, spread across a gentle hill and down to a wooded valley. Ornate ironwork and stonework—in the form of gates and balconies, fountains and urns, pillars and stairways—adorn the grounds. Brick paths lined by boxwoods and perennial borders lead from one garden to the next, and little trellised bowers offer places to sit and admire the sound of birdsong, scent of flowers, and garden aesthetics.

A self-guided tour brochure, available at the entrance, highlights the gardens and plantings. Inside the gates to the right stands an old Katsura tree, its limbs almost touching the ground. Head up the path to the early 19th-century

Tudor Place Historic House and Garden

Tudor Place
www.tudorplace.org
- Map p. 147
- Visitor entrance, 1644 31st St., N.W.
- 202-965-0400
- House closed Mon., garden closed Sun.
- House tour $$, garden tour $
- Metro: Dupont Circle, Foggy Bottom; Bus: D1-6, G2

SIX GENERATIONS OF THE PETER FAMILY, RELATIVES TO George Washington and Robert E. Lee, lived in this handsome neo-classic house. During those years (1805–1984), the country passed through many wars, two of them waged just outside the Peters' door.

Martha Custis, daughter of George Washington's stepdaughter, married Thomas Peter, son of Georgetown's first mayor. In 1805 the Peters purchased an 8.5-acre city block in Georgetown Heights; to design a home there, they hired William Thornton, architect of the Capitol—the building Martha would watch burn from a window of the house in 1814. The Peters' daughter Britannia inherited Tudor Place in 1854. A Southern sympathizer during the Civil War, she allowed Union officers to board at the house to prevent its becoming a hospital. In 1984 the house was transferred to the Tudor Place Foundation.

The one-hour guided tours of Tudor Place begin with a look at Thornton's design. On the south lawn, a domed "temple" portico projects from the two-story stuccoed main building, while one-story hyphens connect the two wings, lending a pleasing symmetry. The curving portico creates a convex wall of windows, which can be lifted to allow a breeze to circulate. All the furniture, silver, porcelain, and decorative objects are original, some pieces acquired from an auction at Mount Vernon in the early 19th century. Not limited to one period, the furnishings reflect 180 years of family continuity. The restored Pierce-Arrow automobile out in the garage, for example, was maintained by Armistead Peter III from 1919 until his death in 1983.

The 5.5 acres of gardens include a sweeping south lawn, woodlands, and a formal federal-style garden on the house's north side. Among highlights are trees and roses planted in the early 19th century, and an old-fashioned "flower knot" pattern of English boxwoods and pathways. ∎

The south-facing temple portico presides over a serene sweep of lawn, set apart from the hubbub of Georgetown.

Dumbarton House

Dumbarton House was built on a hill high above Rock Creek in the first years of the 19th century, when only a few large houses dotted the port of Georgetown. Originally called Cedar Hill, the federal-style brick house's second owner, Charles Carroll, changed its name in 1813 to Belle Vue; he sheltered Dolley Madison here the following year, after she fled the burning White House. In 1915, to make way for the extension of Q Street into Georgetown, the house had to be put on rollers and moved approximately 100 feet north, to its current location.

In 1928, the National Society of the Colonial Dames bought the house (which would become its headquarters), and renamed it Dumbarton House after the Rock of Dumbarton, the tract that originally encompassed much of present-day Georgetown. With great attention to detail, the Colonial Dames—one of the world's largest private historical preservation societies—restored the house to its early 1800s appearance.

The guided 45-minute tour here covers the parlor, dining room, library, music room, and three bedrooms, with furnishings primarily from the federal period, including furniture such as a mahogany sewing work table, silver, ceramics, textiles (including a carriage cloak belonging to Martha Washington's granddaughter), and paintings by artists such as Charles Willson Peale. Out back, the small formal courtyard and garden add a grace note to the estate. ■

Dumbarton House
www.dumbartonhouse.org
- Map p. 147
- 2715 Q St., N.W.
- 202-337-2288
- Closed. Sun.–Mon.; hourly tours at midday
- $
- Metro: Dupont Circle, Foggy Bottom; Bus: D1-6, G2

Oak Hill Cemetery

Occupying some of the city's finest real estate, this 1849 cemetery rambles over a hill above Rock Creek Park. William Wilson Corcoran, founder of the Corcoran Gallery and Riggs National Bank, bought 15 acres from George Corbin Washington, a great nephew of the first president. The following year he gave the parcel to the new congressionally established cemetery company, and James Renwick, architect of the Smithsonian Castle, designed the iron entrance gates and the English Gothic-style chapel.

At the attractive brick and sandstone gatehouse, you can buy a map showing the locations of 68 graves and mausoleums, including those of W. W. Corcoran, John Marbury, Edwin Stanton (Lincoln's secretary of war), Dean Acheson (Truman's secretary of state), and members of the Peter family from nearby Tudor Place. Also buried here is Philip Graham, publisher of the *Washington Post,* as is his widow Katharine, his successor at the *Post* until her death in 2001.

A murky overcast day makes a good time for wandering through this crowded village of the dead, with its elaborate Victorian monuments and obelisks. Winding paths circle knolls that offer views of adjoining Montrose Park, Rock Creek, and the parkway. Hiding behind trees and high walls, the property at the corner of 28th and R Streets is another Georgetown mansion with a long past: Evermay was built in the 1790s by Scotsman Samuel Davidson with funds acquired from selling some of his extensive property to the new federal city. Family members lie buried in Oak Hill. ■

Oak Hill Cemetery
- Map p. 147
- 3001 R St., N.W.
- 202-337-2835
- Closed holidays & during funerals
- Metro: Dupont Circle, Foggy Bottom; Bus: D1-6, G2

Famous denizens of Georgetown

By day, the power of national government is exercised in the monumental edifices clustered around Washington's Mall and at both ends of Pennsylvania Avenue. At night, some of the action moves to Georgetown, residence down the decades of political leaders, media heavies, diplomats, legal minds, writers, and society doyennes—names in the news past and present. In elegant 19th-century houses, the House or Senate bill that seemed doomed by day may be quietly revived over cocktails or at a formal dinner party, where fine wines and informed conversation are equally savored.

Even Hollywood celebrities have found their way to Georgetown, though at times reluctantly. Elizabeth Taylor, married briefly to Virginia Sen. John Warner, has said she thought the couple would live on his hunt country estate, near Middleburg, where the talk centered on horses. Instead, she found herself in Warner's Georgetown house at 3240 S Street, where dinnertime chat explored the ins and outs of arms control and tax bills.

As a bachelor, Sen. John F. Kennedy lived in a Victorian town house at 1528 31st Street. In fact, John and Jackie first met at a Georgetown dinner party in 1951. He later claimed that he made up his mind at that party that she was "the one," though they dated only sporadically over the next year. He finally proposed, and a year later, he and his bride moved to 3271 P Street. President-elect Kennedy purchased the three-story brick town house at 3307 N Street in 1960, while Jackie was in the hospital giving birth to their first child, Caroline. Tastefully austere, the 1811 house occupies an especially handsome street of classic federal-style homes.

After her husband's death, Jackie Kennedy and her children moved temporarily to 3038 N Street at the invitation of statesman W. Averell Harriman. (His widow, Pamela, a celebrated hostess and Democratic party activist, later became President Clinton's Ambassador to France.) The former First Lady soon bought the house across the street at 3017 N Street,

but departed for New York after only a few months to escape the busloads of gawkers.

Just up the street at 3014 N Street stands another grand federal-style mansion with a presidential link. Built in 1799, it was the home of Robert Todd Lincoln, the 16th President's oldest son, a railroad lawyer who served as secretary of war and minister to Great Britain. He lived here until his death in 1926. The current owners, a prominent newspaper couple, consider themselves "caretakers" of the 40-room property.

The top ranks of government have always been well represented in Georgetown. Dean Acheson, President Truman's secretary of state, lived in the Georgian town house at 2805 P Street. Here Acheson hosted a farewell luncheon for the president on his last day in office. A four-story town house at 3018 Dumbarton Street is the one-time home of Supreme Court Justice Felix Frankfurter. Later Henry Kissinger, secretary of state under Presidents Nixon and Ford, briefly rented it.

Washington Post owner Katharine Graham, once called "the most powerful woman in America," lived in the mansion at 2920 R Street. Set well back from the street, it is approached by a semi-circular gravel drive— a real Georgetown luxury—that gives it the look of a French country estate.

Writers, too, have found Georgetown's vibrant society congenial. In 1922 Sinclair Lewis moved to Washington from his Minnesota hometown, calling it the perfect place to write, "with neither the country nor lake tempting one out to play, as in Minnesota, nor the noise and phone calls of New York." As soon as he made his fortune with *Main Street,* which later won him the Nobel Prize for Literature, he moved to a stately Georgetown house, at 3028 Q Street. In the early 1960s, Katherine Anne Porter reportedly completed her acclaimed novel *Ship of Fools* while a boarder at 3106 P Street; with the money it made her she bought her dream house complete with lawns and a rose garden—outside of Georgetown. ∎

Washington Post owner Katharine Graham lived in the above house (R & 30th Sts., N.W.) from 1947 until her death in July 2001. Sen. John F. Kennedy bought a house (right and below) on N Street when he was elected president in 1960; from here he announced his Cabinet choices.

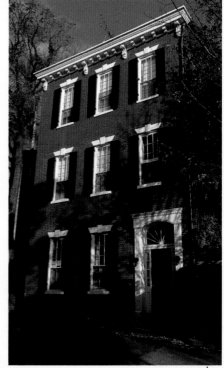

More places to visit in & around Georgetown

Tending bar at Martin's

BILLY MARTIN'S TAVERN

Opened by William G. Martin, a Georgetown University sports star who also played professional baseball in the early part of the 20th century, Billy Martin's Tavern has been operating at the southwest corner of N Street and Wisconsin Avenue since 1933. Four generations of Martins have managed the restaurant, and many of the staff have been here for years. Stop in for a draft or a meal and imbibe this Georgetown tradition.

Wood floors, dark paneling, and a friendly bar create the ambience of a European pub. Among menu offerings are crab cakes, bison steaks, linguine with clam sauce, and daily home specials such as meatloaf and corn beef with cabbage. The back of the menu lists some of the politicos and celebrities that have visited or been regulars, including former Secretary of State Madeleine Albright, actress Elizabeth Taylor, and the Kennedys. Martin's serves three meals a day, with a good brunch on weekends, at moderate prices.

✉ 1264 Wisconsin Ave., N.W. ☎ 202-333-7370 Ⓜ Metro: Foggy Bottom, Rosslyn, then bus

KREEGER MUSEUM

Designed by Philip Johnson and Richard Foster and completed in 1967, the modernist travertine house of late philanthropist David Lloyd Kreeger and his wife, Carmen, opened in 1994 as an art museum showcasing the Kreegers' collection of 19th- and 20th-century paintings and sculptures. A chairman of GEICO insurance company, Kreeger was famous for his contributions to the city's cultural life, at various times serving as president of the National Symphony, the Washington Opera, and the Corcoran Gallery of Art. The art collection, which the Kreegers began acquiring in 1959, includes more than 180 works by artists such as Monet, Cézanne, van Gogh, Rodin, Picasso, Miró, Munch, Kandinsky, and Chagall; among Washington artists represented are Gene Davis, Sam Gilliam, and Thomas Downing. Also on display are pieces of traditional African and Indian art. The building's spectacular **Great Hall,** with its 25-foot-high domed ceiling, was often the scene of concerts; an amateur violinist, Kreeger played his Stradivarius with such greats as Pablo Casals, Isaac Stern, and Pinchas Zukerman. www.kreegermuseum.org ✉ 2401 Foxhall Rd., N.W., 1.5 miles N of Georgetown ☎ 202-337-3050 🕐 Closed Sun.–Mon.; visit Tues,-Fri. by tours only, reservations required; Sat., open visits Ⓢ Donation suggested

MOUNT ZION CEMETERY

When Mount Zion Methodist Episcopal Church realized in 1879 that it needed a place to bury its members, it leased a parcel of land on the edge of the Dumbarton Cemetery. On this site had already been buried several generations of slaves and freed blacks. The resulting Mount Zion Cemetery, now showing its age with toppled and crumbling gravestones, is Washington's oldest black burial ground. The last burial occurred here in the 1950s, and in 1975 it was designated a national historic landmark. At the back is a brick vault where slaves escaping to the North via the Underground Railroad are said to have hid. Ⓜ Map p. 147 ✉ Q St., between 27th St. & the Buffalo Bridge ☎ 202-234-0148 Ⓜ Foggy Bottom, Dupont Circle, then bus ∎

A lively mix of cultures, cuisines, lifestyles, and music awaits in the neighborhoods beyond downtown, while stately mansions preserved as embassies and museums recall 20th-century glamour days.

Dupont Circle & Adams Morgan

A local artist at work in Dupont Circle

Dupont Circle & Adams Morgan

AT THE INTERSECTION OF THREE MAJOR THOROUGHFARES, DUPONT CIRCLE anchors the city's buzzing residential neighborhoods, replete with row houses, cafés, bookstores, restaurants, and galleries.

Chess match at Dupont Circle

Dupont Circle sits at the crossroads of New Hampshire, Massachusetts, and Connecticut Avenues, marking a key interface between business and residential Washington. The circle itself, centered on a marble fountain, is in constant motion, with pedestrians passing through and traffic circling around. Yet it is also a place for casual picnics, jackets-off meetings, people-watching, and general loafing. Bicycle messengers form little impromptu gatherings, chess players study their next moves, joggers pound through. In 15 minutes the scene has changed, and a new series of small dramas has begun to unfold.

Starting in the 1870s, the area, then called Pacific Circle, began developing into the most elite neighborhood in Washington. New millionaires with fortunes from mining, steel, railroads, and shipping started putting up ornate beaux arts mansions and attending receptions and musicals in one another's houses, every hostess seemingly intent on outdoing her neighbor. A newspaper reporter in the 1880s wrote that going to lavish parties at Senator William M. Stewart's "Castle" (torn down in 1901) made him feel like Marco Polo at the court of Kublai Khan. This belle epoque lasted only until the 1930s, when the stock market crash and Depression forced many of the wealthy to scale back.

Some mansions were razed, though many were sold to private clubs, organizations, and embassies; surrounding row houses became boarding establishments and apartments. In the 1960s, the area was a haven for hippies and other counterculturalists, and the circle became a focal point for marches and rallies. Development threatened many of the area's old "palaces" in the 1970s, but the efforts of preservation groups to save the neighborhood resulted in its designation as a historic district that stretches all the way to T Street.

Over the ensuing years Dupont Circle became the core of Washington's young gay community. Today the bars, restaurants, shops, and museums along the neighborhood streets attract a stimulating heterogeny of intellectuals, café-society devotees, and experimentalists of all stripes.

A residential zone of about ten blocks lies between the Dupont Circle neighborhood and the Latino enclave to the north—Adams Morgan, which centers on the intersection of Columbia Road and 18th Street, N.W. Adams Morgan has become a magnet for immigrants, artists, and young professionals, who now fill enormous apartment buildings or old brick houses and frequent the neighborhood's many restaurants and popular nightspots.

Running eastward from Adams Morgan into the Shaw neighborhood is the U Street corridor, where the black community was drawn beginning in the 1880s. This area possesses a rich legacy of music and culture— Pearl Bailey, Duke Ellington, and other greats once performed at its various theaters and clubs. Deteriorated after the 1968 riots, U Street has in recent years made a comeback, with restored theaters and new clubs, restaurants, and shops. ■

Washington, D.C.

NW | NE
Subject area
SW | SE

Md.

Virginia

Md.

Potomac

Anacostia

HARVARD ST.

MOUNT PLEASANT

Mexican Cultural Institute

ONTARIO PLACE

LANIER PLACE

ADAMS MILL RD.

COLUMBIA

ROAD

FULLER

MOZART PL.

15TH STREET

16TH STREET

ST.

CALVERT ST.

Duke Ellington Memorial Bridge

BILTMORE ST.

EUCLID ST.

18th Street

District of Columbia Arts Center

Rock Cr.

MINTWOOD PLACE

20TH STREET

19TH STREET

18TH STREET

CHAMPLAIN ST.

ONTARIO

17TH ST.

KALORAMA ROAD

CRESCENT PL.

Meridian Hill Park

CONNECTICUT

BELMONT

ASHMEAD PLACE

ROAD

BELMONT PL.

ROAD

ADAMS MORGAN

WYOMING AVE.

Meridian International Center

W ST.

KALORAMA

KALORAMA AVE.

WYOMING

AVENUE

ST.

CALIFORNIA ST.

VERNON ST.

FLORIDA AVENUE

V ST.

U STREET

SHAW →

To African American Civil War Memorial, Howard University, Lincoln Theatre, Mary Church Terrell House

23RD ST.

LEROY PL.

COLUMBIA ROAD

T STREET

WILLARD STREET

T STREET

BANCROFT PLACE

S STREET

AVENUE

19TH STREET

18TH STREET

SWANN ST.

S STREET

NEW HAMPSHIRE AVENUE

DECATUR PLACE

R STREET

FLORIDA

Conner Contemporary Art and Gallery

RIGGS PLACE

18TH

R STREET

CORCORAN STREET

Scottish Rite Headquarters

15TH STREET

Sheridan Circle

Cosmos Club

MASSACHUSETTS

The Phillips Collection

Q STREET

16TH STREET

CHURCH ST.

Anderson House

AVENUE

M Dupont Circle

CHURCH ST.

Washington Club

P STREET

Burton Marinkovich Fine Art

P STREET

Dupont Circle

Wadsworth House

17TH ST.

O STREET

Rock Creek

23RD STREET

22ND ST.

21ST ST.

Heurich House Museum

M Dupont Circle

MASSACHUSETTS AVENUE

Scott Circle

ISLAND AVE.

N ST.

NEW HAMPSHIRE AVE.

CONN. AVE.

RHODE

MASS. AVE.

0 | 200 yards
0 | 200 meters

To Metropolitan Club

M STREET

M STREET

Thomas Circle

The Phillips Collection

The Phillips Collection

www.phillipscollection.org

🅰 Map p. 163

✉ 1600 21st St., N.W. (corner of 21st & Q Sts.)

☎ 202-387-2151

🕐 Closed Mon.

💲 $$

🚇 Metro: Dupont Circle; Bus: D1-6, N2-6, L4

WHEN ASKED WHAT THEIR FAVORITE LOCAL ART MUSEUM is, many Washingtonians name the Phillips. There are many reasons for this choice, and one of them is the location. Just two blocks from Dupont Circle, the Phillips Collection lies in the heart of an art-loving community. It's also far from the crowded Mall, close to a Metro station, and reasonably handy enough for many office workers to stop by during a long lunch break. Then there's the fact that the publicly supported, nongovernment museum is staffed with students, artists, and others who seem less like guards than friendly docents. Of course, the art itself is a big attraction.

Begun in the 1920s by founder Duncan Phillips (1886–1966), the Phillips Collection ranks as the first modern art museum in the United States. Its permanent holdings currently include more than 2,400 pieces of carefully chosen late 19th- and early 20th-century art.

Perhaps more than anything, the charm of the Phillips is its setting. You feel as though you have walked into a rich friend's comfortable old house and were free to wander, or were encouraged to plop down in a museum holds one of the largest collections of works by this artist. Phillips also acquired art by such 18th-century masters as El Greco, Francisco Goya, and Jean-Baptiste-Siméon Chardin to show the influence of earlier painters on modern art. Currently, the permanent collection includes works by Paul Cézanne, Pierre-Auguste Renoir, Pablo Picasso, Thomas Eakins, Edgar Degas, Paul Gauguin, Vincent van Gogh, Claude Monet, Édouard Manet, Georges Braque, Winslow Homer, James Whistler, Georgia O'Keeffe, and Mark Rothko.

In 1930, Phillips and his family moved to a new home on Foxhall Road, opening up their entire former home, an 1896 brick-and-brownstone house, to the expanding collection. A new wing was added to the north side in 1960, and in the late 1980s it was renovated and renamed the Goh Annex—after Yasuhiro Goh, a donor of the Phillips. A skywalk connects the annex to the main building.

The growth of the museum in the 1980s was guided by Phillips's son, Laughlin, a founder of *Washingtonian* magazine. Now chairman emeritus of the museum's board of trustees, Laughlin Phillips delights in the realization of his early vision to make the museum a "joy-giving, life-enhancing influence, assisting people to see beautifully as true artists see."

A patron admires "The Luncheon of the Boating Party." This delightful painting by Renoir remains a highlight of the Phillips Collection.

plush chair and admire his taste in art. Indeed, that informal effect is what Duncan Phillips had in mind when, as a memorial to his recently deceased brother, James Laughlin Phillips, and their father, Maj. D. Clinch Phillips, he opened up two rooms of his home in 1921 so that other art lovers could enjoy the works that he and his brother had collected.

An heir to the Jones and Laughlin steel fortune, Duncan Phillips married artist Marjorie Acker, also in 1921. Soon after, the couple began assembling an outstanding group of Impressionist, Postimpressionist, and Cubist art. To Phillips, a key link between Impressionism and Expressionism was Pierre Bonnard, and today the

VISITING

In response to its popularity the museum has been expanding to provide additional space for exhibitions, administrative offices, and a new Center for Studies on Modern Art. The recently renovated **Goh Annex**, which displays works in the rotating art collection as well as special exhibitions, now also features a sculpture garden.

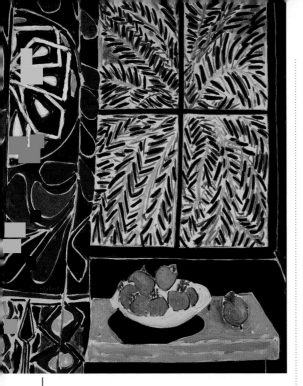

of the museum's European master-works, for example, were on world tour through mid-2005, including the centerpiece of the Phillips's collection: Renoir's "The Luncheon of the Boating Party" (1880-81). When Phillips purchased this delightful painting—a scene of Renoir and his friends picnicking along the Seine—for $125,000 in 1923, it was the highest price that had ever been paid for an Impressionist work.

Among other famous pieces included in the remarkable breadth of talent represented on these walls are Pierre Bonnard's "The Open Window" (1921) and paintings from The Migration Series by Jacob Lawrence.

On the first floor, take time to visit the **Music Room,** a perennial favorite, with its dark oak paneling, decorative ceiling, and elaborately carved stone and wood mantelpiece. Since 1941, Sunday afternoon concerts *(May–Sept., free with admission)* have showcased the talents of many musical artists, including Jessye Norman.

Besides its concerts, the Phillips Collection hosts traveling exhibitions and maintains a busy schedule of classes, lectures, workshops, and films. ■

Masters of color and light: Henri Matisse's "Interior with Egyptian Curtain" (1948, above) and Pierre Bonnard's "Woman with Dog" (1922, opposite)

Housed in the main building are exhibits from the museum's permanent collection. The selection of paintings is rotated and their locations are often rearranged, so it's a good idea to check in advance before you plan your visit to find out whether your favorite piece will be on display when you arrive. Fifty-five

Collect your own

If the Phillips stirs your desire for an original Picasso of your own, Dupont Circle, with more than two dozen galleries, is the place to shop. In recent years one gallery offered a Toulouse-Lautrec lithograph for $70,000, a Picasso painting for a mere $16,000, and a piece by Miró for under $5,000. Stop in Burton Marinkovich Fine Art (1506 21st St.), for example, and you can purchase prints and works on paper by the likes of Frankenthaler, Hockney, Motherwell, and Diebenkorn. Or

check out Conner Contemporary Art (1730 Connecticut Ave.), which has had works by Annie Leibovitz, Claes Oldenburg, Roy Lichtenstein, Robert Indiana, and Andy Warhol. Some of the galleries specialize in African art, Inuit sculpture, and English and American crafts. To find your way around, pick up a free guide, available in any of the galleries. A consortium of galleries in the area coordinates opening receptions the first Friday of every month from 6 to 8 p.m. ■

The Indonesian Embassy boasts 60 rooms and four stories behind its beaux arts facade.

A walk down Embassy Row

Walking west from Dupont Circle along Massachusetts Avenue takes you past the affluence and glamour of the early 1900s, when this was the fashionable neighborhood for Washington tycoons. After the Great Depression, many of the grand residences were sold to foreign delegations. Today the triangle formed by Massachusetts and Connecticut Avenues and Rock Creek holds more than 50 embassies, or about one-third of the city's total. It's about a mile from Dupont Circle to the Islamic Center, at the end of the walk, but you'll probably spend at least a good half day here if you stop for the museums. For a coffee or lunch break, you need to return to the circle; Connecticut Avenue on either side of Dupont has several good cafés and restaurants.

Start your walk a block east of Dupont Circle and take a look at the kind of structure wealthy people had in mind when they thought of the term "apartment building." On the northeast corner of 18th Street and Massachusetts Avenue stands the **National Trust for Historic Preservation ❶**, a beaux arts palace originally built in 1915 as the McCormick apartment building. The first floor contained two apartments, while five floors above each held an 11,000-square-foot apartment with six bedrooms and 14.5-foot ceilings. The most famous tenant, Andrew W. Mellon, founder of the National Gallery of Art and a U.S. secretary of the treasury, lived on the top floor from 1921 to 1937. In 1936 he paid 21 million dollars for paintings and sculptures owned by Sir Joseph Duveen, an art dealer leasing the apartment below; at the time, it was the largest art transaction on record. Robert Woods Bliss, owner of Dumbarton Oaks, also lived here in the 1920s.

Head west to the circle, where you can see more fine examples of turn-of-the-20th-century mansions that never became embassies. Now housing the Sulgrave Club *(private)*, a stalwart sorority of socially prominent Washington ladies, the circa 1900 **Wadsworth House** *(1801 Massachusetts Ave., N.W.)* was the winter residence of landowners Herbert and Martha Wadsworth of upstate New York. With a bow window facing the circle like the prow of a ship, the house is an early illustration of how a large building could be designed to fit the triangular lots around the circle.

Taking a different approach to the same problem, the Wadsworth's neighbor to the north, the ornate **Washington Club** *(private)*, fits into its wedge at 15 Dupont Circle with symmetrical wings and a concave front. Now a women's social club, the 1903 house was designed by Stanford White for Robert W. Patterson, publisher of the *Chicago Tribune*.

Standing in **Dupont Circle ❷,** you can see a striking example of how L'Enfant's city plan works, with grand avenues vectoring out from the central green. In the middle of the circle is a marble fountain designed in 1921 by Daniel Chester French, who is also known for the giant statue of Lincoln in the memorial. Spilling into a large pool, an upper basin is supported by a central column surrounded by three allegorical figures representing the sea, wind, and stars—elements that Civil War naval hero Samuel Francis du Pont would have known well. Benches around the circle and grassy plots under trees are constantly in use for lounging and informal lunching. Tables with built-in chessboards draw an egalitarian cross section of suits, uniforms, jeans, and cutoffs for serious games.

A block southwest, at 1307 New Hampshire Avenue, the **Heurich House Museum ❸** (see p. 176) preserves a piece of the 1890s and now houses the Historical Society of Washington, D.C.

Now head north 1.5 blocks to 2000 Massachusetts Avenue. This brick Victorian mansion was built in 1881 for Republican presidential candidate James Blaine, who lost in 1884 to Grover Cleveland. Shops occupy its first floor, with offices above.

On the same side of the street, the curving sweep of the **Indonesian Embassy ❹** (*2020 Massachusetts Ave.*) makes an impressive sight. Featuring marble columns, arched windows, and a red-tiled mansard roof, the mansion was built at the turn of the 20th century by Irishman Tom Walsh, who struck gold in a Colorado mine. He moved to Washington, built

- See area map p. 163
- National Trust
- 1 mile
- 3–4 hours
- Islamic Center

NOT TO BE MISSED
- Heurich House Museum
- The Phillips Collection
- Islamic Center

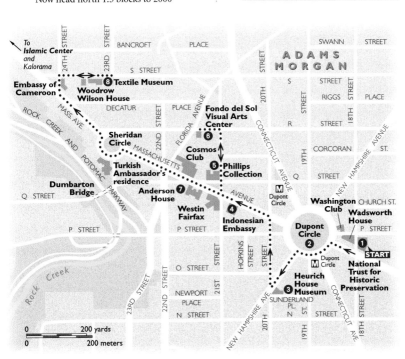

his dream house, and became part of the new moneyed class. His daughter, prominent hostess Evalyn Walsh McLean, was the last private owner of the Hope Diamond (now in the National Museum of Natural History; see p. 94); in 1951 she sold the mansion to the Republic of Indonesia.

At 2100 Massachusetts Avenue, the building housing the **Westin Fairfax,** dating from 1927, gives Embassy Row a European-style hotel flair. Al Gore lived here when his father was a U. S. senator. Across Massachusetts, a statue of Mahatma Gandhi stands in front of the Embassy of India. A block north on 21st Street, the **Phillips Collection ❺** (see pp. 164–67) is one of Washington's most cherished museums.

If Latin American art interests you, continue north another block to **Fondo del Sol Visual Arts Center ❻** *(2112 R St., 202-265-9235, closed Sun.–Mon., $),* which helps preserve and promote the cultural heritage of the Americas with exhibits, concerts, poetry readings, and lectures. A permanent collection of pre-Columbian and folk art is on display.

Back on Massachusetts, the double-winged mansion at 2118 Massachusetts Avenue is the **Anderson House ❼** (see p. 176), headquarters of the Society of the Cincinnati. Across the avenue, at 2121 Massachusetts, stands the exclusive **Cosmos Club** *(private),* completed in 1902 as the home of Richard Townsend, president of the Erie & Pittsburgh Railroad. The fabulous limestone mansion was sold in 1950 to the club, whose members have earned recognition in the arts and sciences.

A number of embassies edge **Sheridan Circle,** named for Union general Philip H. Sheridan; the 1908 equestrian bronze in the center is by Gutzon Borglum, sculptor of Mount Rushmore. Among the impressive buildings nearby are the **Turkish Ambassador's residence** *(1606 23rd St.),* built in the 1910s for industrialist Edward Everett. A block south, the 1914 **Dumbarton Bridge**—often called the Buffalo Bridge for its bronze bison—carries Q Street over Rock Creek into Georgetown.

Back on Massachusetts, at the corner of Massachusetts and 24th, is the château-style **Embassy of Cameroon.** It was built in 1907 to house Norway's ambassador and legation, but it was never used as such because the ambassador died.

The Islamic Center's lofty minaret

Turn up 24th Street, then go east on S Street. Compared to many area houses, the **Woodrow Wilson House** *(2340 S St., 202-387-4062, closed Mon., $),* designed in 1915 by Waddy B. Wood, has a modest appearance. The president spent the last three years of his life in this Georgian Revival brick town house after leaving the White House in 1921; his wife stayed until her death in 1961.

Next door, the **Textile Museum ❽** *(2320 S St., 202-667-0441, donation)* was founded in 1925 by President Wilson's neighbor, George Hewitt Myers, to house a collection of rugs and other textiles. The museum incorporates Myers's residence and the adjoining house he bought as his collection grew; John Russell Pope designed the latter house in 1913. The collection numbers over 17,000 carpets and textiles, dating from 3000 B.C. to the present.

About four blocks away is the **Islamic Center** *(2551 Massachusetts Ave., 202-332-8343),* a mosque richly embellished with tilework, arches, and pillars; in the carpeted sanctuary, shoes and shorts are not allowed, and women must cover their heads. The network of streets to the east is the prestigious Kalorama neighborhood, which holds several embassies and large houses. ■

Adams Morgan

THE CITY'S TRADITIONALLY HISPANIC NEIGHBORHOOD, Adams Morgan became in the 1980s and '90s the top apartment-and-nightlife nexus for artists and hip young professionals alike. With its international restaurants, funky shops, and rocking nightclubs, the little neighborhood sprang to life with a personality all its own, an enclave of bohemian flair in the center of staid Washington. Never mind that all this popularity meant there was no longer any place to park—especially on weekend evenings.

Adams Morgan

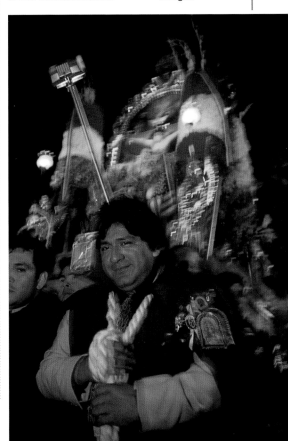

Map p. 163

Between Columbia Rd., 16th St., & Florida Ave., N.W.

Metro: Dupont Circle (1.5 miles S) or Woodley Park–Zoo/Adams Morgan (0.75 mile NW); Bus: 90-93, L1-4

The name itself alludes to the neighborhood's cultural mix: By combining the names of two schools—the mostly white Adams School and the predominantly black Morgan School—local citizens coined the term Adams Morgan in the 1950s for an area that had been part of four neighborhoods. In that same decade, the Spanish-speaking population swelled as an influx of students from Latin America and Mexican professionals added to the existing community of embassy workers. The early 1960s saw an increase in Cuban immigration, followed by large numbers from South and Central America through the next few decades. The ethnic influence still tends toward Latin—Spanish is heard on the streets as often as English; but in the smorgasbord of restaurants and shops, you'll find many other cultures, including Ethiopian, Chinese, Thai, Indian, and Vietnamese.

The heart of Adams Morgan is the intersection of **Columbia Road** and **18th Street.** On the northeast corner a kiosk provides lists of upcoming cultural events. At the intersection's southwest corner is a plaza where vendors set up shop on weekends and sell fresh produce and breads. Most of the area's action—eating, drinking, and dancing—takes place south of the intersection on 18th Street between Columbia Road and Florida Avenue, and along

a little branch west on Columbia Road to Belmont Road. That's pretty much it. Although the few attractions are worth seeing, they do not draw crowds.

VISITING

The three-story, brightly painted brick buildings lining the blocks of 18th Street south of the

Local Peruvians celebrate Our Lord of Miracles Day in Adams Morgan.

Shoppers examine local wares at a street fair on 18th Street—the heart of Adams Morgan.

Columbia Road–18th Street intersection hold most of the ethnic restaurants, bohemian bars, and boutiques. On sultry summer evenings, the sidewalks buzz with people strolling, walking dogs, or sipping cool drinks at sidewalk cafés and bars. Ethiopian seems to be the most sought-after cuisine here; among a number of places to give it a try is Meskerem *(2434 18th St., 202-462-4100)*, where diners scoop up communal stews with pieces of spongy sourdough bread.

If you're looking for some off-beat culture, try the **District of Columbia Arts Center** *(2438 18th St., 202-462-7833)*, which features the work of emerging artists and holds live performances in a 50-seat theater.

Columbia Road on either side of 18th also has several good restaurants—including Perry's, *the* place to be and be seen *(1811 Columbia Rd., 202-234-6218)*; its rooftop dining is one of the city's most pleasant experiences. Along

Columbia you'll also find Latino grocery stores, outdoor jewelry stands, and vintage clothing and sundries shops.

Daytime Adams Morgan offers different sights to see. For grand interiors, walk down **16th Street.** Just below Columbia, the **Mexican Cultural Institute** *(2829 16th St., 202-728-1628, closed Sun.–Mon.)*, in a 1911 Italianate house, holds a huge tile-covered solarium, a lively stairwell mural, and ornately furnished salons; rotating exhibits are presented on two floors.

A few blocks farther, opposite Meridian Hill Park, **Meridian International Center** *(1624 & 1630 Crescent Pl., 202-667-6800, closed Mon.–Tues.)* promotes international understanding through cultural exchanges. The adjoining houses, with free art exhibits, were designed by John Russell Pope in 1911 and 1921; the 1630 address boasts antique French furnishings and a courtyard with 40 linden trees.

Pope also designed the glorious 1911 **Scottish Rite Headquarters** *(1733 16th St., 202-232-3579, closed weekends),* just beyond Adams Morgan at S Street; he modeled the building after the Mausoleum at Halicarnassus in Turkey.

The northwest portion of Adams Morgan, up 18th and onto Adams Mill Road and Calvert Street, is quieter, more residential, with tightly packed town houses. Just off Adams Mill, on the right, you can see one of the neighborhood's many colorful wall murals, this one dating from the 1970s and depicting life in Washington's barrio. If you follow Calvert, you'll come to the **Duke Ellington Memorial Bridge** over Rock Creek *(toward Woodley Park–Zoo/Adams Morgan Metro station).* ■

Chuck Brown

Since its birth some 25 years ago, go-go music appeared to be an indigenous creation that was not exportable beyond the Beltway. It's finally beginning to gain national attention. The "godfather" of go-go, Chuck Brown (1934–) cobbled the style by combining Latin and soul rhythms, jazz progressions, and gospel-style call-and-response lyrics. The result is a very funky sound that is more melodic and less aggressive than its rap and hip-hop cousins. Distinguishing features include long songs, heavy use of horns, cowbells, and congos, and undeniably danceable rhythms. For an introduction, try his *Greatest Hits* release, with "Bustin' Loose," "Back It On Up (Sho' Ya Right)," and "It Don't Mean a Thing (If It Don't Have the Go Go Swing)." Brown's latest album, *Your Game... Live at the 9:30 Club, Washington, D.C.,* was recorded in January 2001. ■

U Street

During the first half of the 20th century, the U Street corridor in the Shaw neighborhood—named for Robert Gould Shaw, the white colonel of the first African American regiment in the Civil War—was the center of black D.C. social and cultural life. It was often referred to as the "Black Broadway." People would dress in their finest outfits to frequent the restaurants, movie theaters, pool halls, and dance halls lining the street.

The baroque 1910 Howard Theatre *(624 T St.)* was the country's first legitimate theater built for black audiences and entertainers. Hosting vaudeville acts, musicals,

road shows, and concerts, the Howard commanded center stage: All the big names in entertainment played its boards. In 1922 the opulent Lincoln Theatre opened at 13th and U Streets. Both a movie palace and live-performance venue, it was designed to have the look and feel of a great opera house. Big bands played at the Colonnade, the dance hall in the basement.

At both theaters, the level of performance was so great that racial segregation was often ignored. Many white people also would come to see luminary performances by Duke Ellington, Cab Calloway, Ella Fitzgerald, Sarah Vaughan, and many more.

Ironically, desegregation in the 1950s led to the eventual decline of U Street's venues. The 1968 riots (which fanned out from 14th and U) led to further deterioration, and by the early '70s, both the Howard and the Lincoln had closed. In recent years, however, U Street has been revitalizing, though it is no longer the center of African American nightlife. Many nightclubs cater to crowds from all walks of life, and the eclectic mix of restaurants, cafés, and shops attracts a diverse group.

The Lincoln Theatre has been restored, and Bohemian Caverns *(11th & U Sts., 202-299-0800),* formerly known as Crystal Caverns, has returned; closed down in 1968, the Caverns was a haunt of Pearl Bailey, Miles Davis, John Coltrane, and others. You can catch live jazz every night except Tuesday. Other hot clubs include Republic Gardens, State of the Union, and the 9:30 Club.

Opposite: Edward Kennedy "Duke" Ellington (1899–1974) returned to his native Washington many times as a preeminent jazz bandleader and composer. Right: Another Washingtonian, singer and film star Pearl Bailey (1918–1990) strikes a seductive pose. Above: A chanteuse performs at Utopia on U Street.

At 1816 12th St., the Shaw Heritage Trust offers exhibits on the neighborhood in a 1912 building designed by W. Sidney Pittman, one of the country's first black architects. Another way to get to know this area's legacy is to take the U Street Heritage Trail, a self-guided, 90-minute walk past historical buildings relating to the once thriving black community. Pick up information from merchants along the trail.

For a taste of yesterday, stop by Ben's Chili Bowl (1213 U St.). Opened in 1958, it still serves up half smokes and burgers beneath a pressed-tin ceiling and overhead fans. ■

More places to visit in Dupont Circle & beyond

ANDERSON HOUSE

This spectacular 1905 mansion serves as the headquarters and museum of the **Society of the Cincinnati,** a patriotic organization whose first president general was George Washington. The house was once the winter residence of diplomat Larz Anderson III, whose wife, Isabel Weld Perkins, inherited $17,000,000 from her grandfather's shipping fortune. After Anderson died in 1937, his widow turned the mansion over to the society, of which Anderson was a member.

A bulwark of fraternal tradition dating from 1783, the society's 3,500 members descend from officers in the Continental Army or Navy. Its name comes from the Roman senator Cincinnatus, who, like Washington, gave up farming to defend his country.

Among the first-floor treasures are walnut choir stalls from 16th-century Italy, decorative Japanese screens, and a ballroom with Verona marble columns. Off the ballroom, a sun-drenched winter garden room opens onto a Japanese garden. A billiard room holds society members' portraits by Gilbert Stuart and John Trumbull. On the second floor are English furniture, Belgian tapestries, Italian paintings, and Chinese jades and porcelains. A 42,000-title research library focuses on the military history of the American Revolution.

🅜 Map p. 163 ✉ 2118 Massachusetts Ave., N.W. ☎ 202-785-2040 🕒 Closed Sun.–Mon. 🚇 Metro: Dupont Circle

HEURICH HOUSE MUSEUM

Built in 1895 for brewer Christian Heurich, this Romanesque castle is now a landmark building on the National Register of Historic Places. Until 2003 it housed the Historical Society of Washington, D.C., which moved to a new city museum in the old Carnegie Library (see p. 134).

Heurich, a poor German immigrant, came to the U.S. in 1872. Within seven years he had gotten married and purchased this property just off Dupont Circle. His first two wives died, but his third wife—the 33-year-old niece and namesake of his first wife, Amelia—survived him by 11 years. After her death in

1956, their house was deeded to the Columbia Historical Society (as it was then called). A self-guided tour takes you through 11 rooms on three levels. Sumptuous decorations include a marble mosaic floor in the main hall and elaborately carved furniture in the dining room.

🅜 Map p. 163 ✉ 1307 New Hampshire Ave., N.W. ☎ 202-785-2068 🕒 Walk-in tours Wed. only, 12:15 & 1:15 💲 $ (suggested donation) 🚇 Metro: Dupont Circle

MARY CHURCH TERRELL HOUSE

The LeDroit Park neighborhood *(S of Howard University)* has been the home of many prominent African Americans since the 1890s. Civic leader Mary Church Terrell, wife of the city's first black municipal judge, lived a long, active life but is mostly remembered now for the work she did in her late 80s. In 1950, at age 86, she spearheaded a campaign to reinstate antidiscrimination laws that had been written in the 1870s. Her three-story brick house *(not open to the public)* is located at 326 T Street, N.W. Other blacks who have lived in this area include poet Paul Laurence Dunbar and Mayor Walter Washington. ■

Oliver O. Howard

Gen. Oliver Otis Howard (1830–1909) came to Washington after the Civil War and took charge of the new Bureau of Refugees, Freedmen, and Abandoned Lands (better known as the Freedmen's Bureau). Under Howard's leadership, the bureau bought the Barry Farm near what would become the Anacostia neighborhood, in southeast Washington, and sold off parcels to black families. The Freedmen's Bureau also helped fund and establish educational programs for freed people. In 1867 Howard University was founded (named for the general against his wishes) on land that was purchased by the bureau. The institution, located at Seventh and Bryant Streets, N.W., is now the country's leading black university, with an enrollment of more than 10,000. ■

With inducements ranging from the bucolic (Rock Creek Park) to the divine (Washington National Cathedral), this city-center enclave is a pleasing paradox: a tourist destination that provides a respite from touring.

Cleveland Park & beyond

Soaring arches inside National Cathedral

Noodleheads spill onto the sidewalk of a Thai restaurant on Connecticut Avenue.

Cleveland Park & beyond

BY FOOT, METRO, OR BICYCLE, THE LEAFY NEIGHBORHOOD OF CLEVELAND
Park offers a pleasant afternoon of relaxed sight-seeing or lounging in cafés. Higher elevations and the nearness of Rock Creek Park provide relief from the heat of downtown.

Tourists who venture this far from the Mall generally come for the zoo. That's a great reason for a visit, made easy by the Metro's Red Line to Cleveland Park or Woodley Park–Zoo/ Adams Morgan stations. And any of the outstanding sites nearby may land on your list of D.C. favorites.

The tony neighborhood of Cleveland Park is named for President Grover Cleveland, who spent the summers of his second administration (1893–97) at Woodley, a Georgian mansion built about 1800 at 3000 Cathedral Avenue. President Cleveland preferred the cool breezes that buffeted Woodley to the miasmas of the marshy lowlands around the White House about 2.5 miles away. Woodley is now part of the private Maret School.

When the city's trolley tracks were extended across Rock Creek valley at Calvert Street in the 1890s and thence up Connecticut Avenue, the area took on a fashionable cachet. Today Connecticut Avenue is still lined with big apartment buildings (the more ornate ones from the 1920s and '30s), behind which stand fine old houses with wide front porches and trim gardens. Indeed, the city's largest hotel, the Marriott Wardman Park (*Woodley Rd. & Conn. Ave.*), got its start in 1928 as a luxury apartment building called the Wardman Tower. The tower's residents have included Herbert Hoover, Earl Warren, and Clare Booth Luce. Across Calvert Street, the 1930 Omni Shoreham has hosted inaugural balls since Franklin Delano Roosevelt took office in 1933.

Farther up Connecticut Avenue is one of the city's top attractions: the almost pastoral, 163-acre National Zoological Park. It abuts Rock Creek Park, a delightful preserve of trees, meadows, and cycling paths.

A mile west of the zoo, Washington National Cathedral towers gloriously on its high hill. Scores of stonemasons labored 83 years to complete this national architectural masterpiece. Unknown to many locals, the Hillwood estate to the north is a jewel box of Russian and French antiques. Afterward, reward yourself with a Frappuccino or some Thai food at one of the many establishments clustered near the Metro stops along Connecticut Avenue. ■

National Zoological Park

National Zoological Park

www.si.edu/natzoo

 Map p. 179

✉ 3001 Connecticut Ave., N.W.

☎ 202-673-4800

$ Parking up to $11 per day

🚇 Metro: Cleveland Park, Woodley Park–Zoo/Adams Morgan; Bus: L1-4, H5 & 7

THE NATIONAL ZOO WAS CONCEIVED AS "A HOME AND A city of refuge for the vanishing races of the continent." In 1887, Smithsonian taxidermist William T. Hornaday corralled some of North America's vanishing bison and a few other animals in a small zoo on the Mall. Two years later, Congress set aside acreage along a bend in Rock Creek to create the National Zoo "for the advancement of science and the instruction and recreation of the people."

Part of the Smithsonian Institution, the 163-acre biological park opened in 1891 and is now home to more than 2,700 animals representing 435 species. Nearly a third of the species—including Asian elephants,

F Food   **G** Gifts   **🚻** Restrooms   **♿** Handicapped accessible   **✳** Seasonal

Valley Trail, the steeper of the two zoo paths, includes major aquatic exhibits, birds, and Amazonia.

1. Wetlands
2. Bird House
3. Great Flight Exhibit
4. Free-ranging Golden Lion Tamarins ✳
5. Beavers, Otters
6. Mexican Wolves
7. Bald Eagles
8. Seals, Sea Lions
9. Spectacled Bears, Sloth Bears
10. Amazonia, Amazonia Science Gallery

Olmsted Walk passes most indoor exhibits.

1. Visitor Center, Bookstore, Gifts, Wheelchairs, ATM
2. Cheetah Conservation Station, Zebras
3. Information, Panda Pavilion, Strollers, Wheelchairs
4. Giant Panda Habitat
5. Elephants, Giraffes
6. Hippos
7. Camels
8. American Indian Heritage Garden
9. Small Mammal House
10. Great Ape House
11. Gibbon Ridge
12. Reptile Discovery Center
13. Invertebrate Exhibit
14. Think Tank
15. Lions
16. Tigers
17. Lemur Island
18. African American Heritage Garden
19. Police
20. Bat Cave
21. Mane Restaurant
22. Information, Strollers, Wheelchairs
23. Kids Farm

cheetahs, Sumatran tigers, giant pandas, western lowland gorillas, and Komodo dragons—are endangered. The animal enclosures aim to re-create natural habitats. Meanwhile, at the zoo's 3,000-acre Conservation

14

16

20

22

Rock Creek

Parking Lot E

To Harvard Street

Picnic Area

Olmsted Walk

To Rock Creek and Potomac Parkway

3

Parking Lot D

and Research Center near Front Royal, Virginia, zookeepers have bred golden lion tamarins, red wolves, and black-footed ferrets for reintroduction to the wild.

VISITING

Given the zoo's 5 miles of hilly paths, it's hard to avoid at least some uphill walking. To minimize your efforts, pick up a map at one of the information stations at either end of the zoo's main east-west thoroughfare, the Olmsted Walk (landscape architect Frederick Law Olmsted designed the zoo's original layout). With more than 30 exhibit areas to choose from, you may want to hit a few highlights and save the rest for another day. Fall and winter are the least crowded seasons, but the buildings close early from November 1 to April 2.

If you begin at the visitor center inside the Connecticut Avenue entrance, the **Olmsted Walk** will lead you past the cheetahs, zebras, and other enclosures to the **Giant Panda Exhibit.** This indoor-outdoor area features Tian Tian and Mei Xiang, a pair of pandas on long-term loan from China. Within days of arriving in December 2000,

Pandas at play: Tian Tian ("more and more") and Mei Xiang ("beautiful fragrance"), born in Wolong, China, are star attractions at the zoo.

the pandas had adapted so well that they were literally chewing up the scenery, devouring the decorative plantings of ornamental bamboo. The exhibit outlines efforts to save the panda, whose numbers had dwindled to about 1,000 in the wild and 140 in captivity.

Continue downhill and east past the Elephant House to reach the **Small Mammal House,** where the challenge is to spot the golden lion tamarins, pygmy marmosets, two-toed sloths, and three-banded armadillos that occupy the glassed-in jungle. The **Great Ape House** next door is home to gorillas and orangutans. The latter can climb over an aerial pathway called the O Line to Think Tank, swinging on vinelike cables attached to a set of towers. A popular stop nearby, the **Reptile Discovery Center** features Komodo dragons, huge Aldabra tortoises, spiky matamata turtles, and hands-on exhibits.

Behind the center lies the fascinating **Invertebrate Exhibit.** Here you'll find giant octopuses, anemones, and spiders; an adjoining greenhouse thrums with pollinators such as butterflies, hummingbirds, and honeybees. Beyond you'll find the Bat Cave, the Great Cats, and Monkey Island.

Recently added to this area, near Parking Lot D, is a 2-acre **Kids' Farm** that was designed to introduce young children to farm animals and the basics of animal care.

Head back to Connecticut Avenue on the **Valley Trail,** south of the Olmsted Walk. Your first stop will be the warm, humid **Amazonia** exhibit, which simulates a journey through a rain forest; here parrots and other tropical birds flit through kapok and mahogany trees beneath a domed 50-foot-high ceiling.

Next on the Valley Trail is a delightful outdoor exhibit housing seals and sea lions, followed by enclosures for red wolves, beavers, otters, and free-ranging golden lion tamarins. Farther up the trail, the raucous **Bird House and Flight Exhibit** offers a walk-through aviary and a boardwalk spanning a wetland. ∎

Feeding time for the sea lions is one of the zoo's most popular spectacles.

Rock Creek Park

WHEN YOU NEED TO GET AWAY FROM THE HURLY-BURLY OF urban living (or touring, for that matter), a peaceful Washington park awaits nearby. Rock Creek Park runs in a long strand of hilly woods and meadows from the National Zoo to the Maryland border 4 miles north, with tendrils of green branching off the main park into other parts of the city. At 1,739 acres—more than twice the size of New York's Central Park—Rock Creek is one of the nation's largest urban parks. Visitors and residents seek solace and rejuvenation in the park's 18-hole golf course, tennis courts, picnic areas, playing fields, nature center and planetarium, and more than 35 miles of trails for jogging, hiking, biking, and horseback riding.

Rock Creek Park
www.nps.gov/rocr
🅰 Map p. 179
Rock Creek Nature Center & Planetarium
✉ 5200 Glover Rd., S of Military Rd.
☎ 202-895-6070

For some 5,000 years, Algonquin Indians camped in the woods around Rock Creek above its run-in with the Potomac. There they gathered fruits and nuts and hunted deer, bear, and elk. They also quarried the Rock Creek valley, extracting quartz for tools and soapstone for bowls and other implements.

By the early 1700s, however, the Indians were gone, displaced by white settlers who cleared out more of the forest and built mills along Rock Creek. The only one remaining—restored 19th-century **Peirce Mill** *(Tilden St. & Beach Dr.)*—has a museum where you can view the millworks and a historical film.

During the Civil War, Washington erected a ring of 68 forts to protect itself from Confederate attack. You can see some earthworks remaining from **Fort DeRussy,** half a mile north of the nature center. Other nearby fort sites—most of them long since reduced to fields for picnicking or playing ball—include **Fort Bayard Park** *(River Rd. & Western Ave.);* **Fort Reno Park** *(Chesapeake St. & Belt Rd.),* occupying the highest point of land in Washington; and partially recon-

Bridges, trails, and autumn glory are among the enticements of this sprawling urban sanctuary.

structed **Fort Stevens Park** *(13th St., N of Military Rd.)*, the only Washington-area battlement that came under enemy fire.

Set aside in 1890, Rock Creek Park is today the city's playground, administered by the National Park Service. About 85 percent of the park is forested; the remainder is wildflower-dotted meadows and fields. Over the years, Theodore Roosevelt, Ronald Reagan, and other Presidents have availed themselves of the park's walking and bridle trails. Unlike them, the average citizen will need no bodyguards; the park is generally safe by day.

Just spin 'em: Rock Creek Park's 10 miles of bike paths link to a Washington-wide web of other trails.

VISITING

Start your visit at the **Rock Creek Nature Center** *(closed Mon.–Tues.)*. Here you can learn about the park's flora and fauna that fill this urban wildlife mecca, scope out its cycling and running paths, and pick up a trail map describing each route. The center's excellent displays include a bee colony, dioramas, and several hands-on exhibits; astronomy programs are staged in a planetarium.

Outside, two short nature loops—the **Woodlands Trail** and the wheelchair-accessible **Edge of the Woods Trail**—help you identify local trees and plants. Towering oaks, hickories, and beeches are much in evidence; come spring the dogwoods, redbuds, and azaleas emerge in a gaudy show of blossoms.

From the nature center, you can also access the park's larger trail network. Some pathways are open to bikes and horses; others allow only foot traffic. One bike trail heads north from the nature center to the Maryland border and 14 miles beyond that to Lake Needwood. You can return the same way and pick up **Beach Drive;** normally a pulsing commuter artery, it closes on weekends, allowing cyclists a traffic-free ride from the Maryland border all the way to its intersection with Broad Branch Road. From there, a paved **bike trail** extends south beyond the park boundary, running alongside the Rock Creek and Potomac Parkway until it hits Memorial Bridge. About halfway along this trail, near Calvert Street and Connecticut Avenue, you'll come across a 1.5-mile **exercise course** with fitness-apparatus stations.

Hikers should seek out the moderate, blue-blazed, 5.6-mile **Valley Trail,** which winds along the east side of Rock Creek all the way from Boundary Bridge on the Maryland line down to Bluff Bridge at the park's southern end. Its analogue on the park's western edge is the strenuous, green-blazed, 4.6-mile **Western Ridge Trail.**

Just south of the nature center, sign up for a trail ride or lesson at the **Rock Creek Horse Center** *(202-362-0117)*, an NPS concessioner amid a 13-mile web of bridle trails. Much farther south, where Rock Creek joins the Potomac, **Thompson Boat Center** *(202-333-9543)* rents canoes and kayaks for exploring the river and Theodore Roosevelt Island (see p. 209); it also rents bicycles. ∎

Frank O. Salis-
bury painted
Marjorie Merri-
weather Post in
1934, when she
was 47.

Hillwood Museum & Gardens

A HIDDEN GEM, THE HILLWOOD MUSEUM WAS THE FINAL
home of cereal heiress Marjorie Merriweather Post (1887–1973).
With her fabulous collection of Russian and 18th-century French
decorative arts, she furnished the house with the idea that it would
become a museum after her death. The site opened to the public in
1977, and Hillwood is now one of the top art collector's house museums in the country. Objects on display include Romanov family treasures, Fabergé eggs and other objets d'art, Russian religious icons,
French tapestries, and Sèvres porcelain. The 25 acres of formal and
natural gardens enhance the museum experience, while family photos and memorabilia remind visitors that Hillwood was once a home.

**Hillwood
Museum &
Gardens**
www.hillwoodmuseum.org
🅰 Map p. 179
✉ 4155 Linnean Ave.,
N.W.
☎ 202-686-5807
🕐 Closed Sun.–Mon. &
all Jan.
💲 $$ (reservation
deposit per person
refunded by mail on
request)
🚇 Metro: Van Ness–
UDC; Bus: L1-4

As the only child of cereal magnate
C. W. Post, Marjorie inherited a for-
tune at age 27 when her father died
(just two years after her mother).
She and her husband bought a
mansion on Fifth Avenue in New
York and began furnishing it with
the help of flamboyant art dealer
Sir Joseph Duveen, who became
Post's mentor. She also educated
herself by taking classes on tap-

estries, porcelain, and furniture at
the Metropolitan Museum of Art.
   In the course of a long and busy
life, Post married and divorced four
times and amassed a tremendous
collection of European artwork.
An astute businesswoman, she also
donated millions of dollars to char-
ities and other organizations, in-
cluding $100,000 to help build the
Kennedy Center (see pp. 124–25).

It was after her third divorce, in 1955, that Post purchased Hillwood—a 1926 Georgian house on the woodsy edge of Rock Creek Park. She spent two years renovating and enlarging the house, transforming it into a residence where she could entertain in legendary style. Hillwood parties routinely exceeded 200 guests, the politicians mixing with celebrities in the gardens. At formal dinners, guests ate off Post's antique porcelain and silver; informal dinners sometimes ended with square dancing in the Pavilion.

In the interstices between soirées, Post expanded her art collection, eventually turning Hillwood into a stunning showcase of decorative and fine arts. Today the museum is best known for its collection of 18th- and 19th-century Russian imperial art—the most comprehensive outside Russia—and for its distinctive array of French decorative art.

Post's treasures include the French Drawing Room (top) and Russian imperial Easter eggs created by Fabergé.

VISITING

Get oriented to the museum and gardens with a 15-minute film at the visitor center. You can take a one-hour **guided tour** of the house, usually offered several times a day, or a self-guided audio tour, and you can stroll the gardens. There's a café on site; reservations for lunch are recommended (*202-243-3920*).

By contrast with the unremarkable exterior of the brick house, the inside customarily prompts a chorus of oohs and aahs. One highlight, the **Russian Porcelain Room,** contains Imperial Glassworks pieces from the 1730s.

More tsarist treasures are on display in the outstanding **Icon Room,** where you can feast your eyes on the diamond wedding crown worn in 1894 by Russia's last empress, Alexandra Fyodorovna; two Fabergé Easter eggs (one dates from 1914 and is studded with gold, diamonds, and pearls); and Russian Orthodox icons from the 16th century. Post discovered her love of Russian art while living in the Soviet Union from 1937 to 1938 with her third husband, American ambassador Joseph E. Davies.

The elegant **French Drawing Room** is furnished in the style of Louis XVI, with 18th-century tapestries designed by painter François Boucher and furniture by David Roentgen. Upstairs, Post's bedroom is likewise decorated in Louis XVI style; a display of her ball gowns, hats, and jewelry adds life and personality to the collection.

Almost as impressive as the house, the lovely **gardens** include 12 acres of lawns and formal plantings and 13 acres of native woodlands. A French parterre with a fountain, a circular rose garden, a crescent-shaped lawn, a Japanese-style garden, and an orchid-filled greenhouse round out the gardens. The trees and flowers bloom year round, making a stroll through Hillwood a delight in any season. ∎

Washington National Cathedral

DOMINATING THE CITYSCAPE, WASHINGTON NATIONAL Cathedral is visible from points all over the district. Conversely, its lofty perch on Mount St. Alban gives cathedral visitors a commanding vista of the urban skyline. Officially known as the Cathedral Church of St. Peter and St. Paul, this towering Gothic church is one of Washington's most magnificent architectural achievements.

Washington National Cathedral
www.cathedral.org/cathedral
🅰 Map p. 179
✉ Massachusetts & Wisconsin Aves., N.W.
☎ 202-537-6200
🚌 Bus: N2-8, 30-36

The idea of a national church occurred as early as Pierre Charles L'Enfant's design for the Federal City, which envisioned a "church… to serve as a moral lighthouse for the nation." But the constitutional separation of church and state scotched the idea until the 1890s, when it was revived by a group of Episcopalians and endorsed by President Benjamin Harrison.

In 1893, Congress chartered the Protestant Episcopal Cathedral Foundation. The church would be a house of prayer for all people, built and supported by private donations from people of many faiths. As contributions flowed in from every state, a 57-acre site was set aside atop Mount St. Alban.

After the cathedral's initial two designers died in 1917 with their plan still incomplete, up stepped Philip Hubert Frohman, an unknown whose dream it was to become the cathedral's architect. Frohman spent the next 50 years building the church. Obsessed with detail and scornful of expense, he once ordered all the molding on the central tower shifted by one-eighth inch because of its effect on the tower's shadow. He toiled away until 1972, when at age 85 he was hit by a truck on the cathedral close.

Others who dedicated their lives to the cathedral were the many masons, stonecarvers, and stained-glass artisans who conveyed 14th-century skills to the 20th. The 215 stained-glass windows, 3,000 stone sculptures, and other works of art were crafted to perfect the nation's "moral lighthouse." From the day Theodore Roosevelt laid the cornerstone in 1907 until the day President George H. W. Bush attended the dedication of the Tower of St. Paul in 1990, the cathedral took 83 years to construct. The building's 150,000 tons of Indiana limestone, says the U.S. Bureau of Standards, should stand without major restoration or reinforcement for 2,000 years.

VISITING

Guided tours *(donation)* are offered several times daily; you can also wander about on your own. There are daily services and prayer sessions. As an Episcopal institution, the church hosts many interfaith services; the building's main sanctuary and its other chapels are routinely used for weddings of cathedral-school alumni. Weekly **musical events** include organ demonstrations *(Wed. & Sun.)*, carillon recitals *(Sat.)*, and ten-bell peals *(Sun. after a.m. service);* all take place around noon or 1 p.m.

Stroll outside to admire the flying buttresses, the arches, and some of the 112 **gargoyles** whose expressions range from silly to fiendish. In addition to warding off evil, the gargoyles repel rainwater; in storms they spout water well away from the building. The figures are carved in various shapes: wild

A stained-glass window shows Jesus urging followers to evangelize.

boars, mythical beasts, cats, dogs, even caricatures of people (such as master carver Roger Morigi) central to the construction or life of the cathedral. Binoculars are handy for inspecting the higher ones.

Outside is also the best place to drink in the immensity of the sixth largest cathedral in the world, and the second largest in the U.S. (only New York's St. John the Divine is bigger). The central Gloria in Excelsis Deo tower rises 300 feet, while the nave runs one-tenth of a mile.

The west-entrance central portal features Frederick Hart's spellbinding tympanum sculpture, "The Creation," in which half-formed men and women swirl about in a chaos of clouds and waves.

Walk inside and let the huge space swallow you up. Faithful to its Gothic style, the church was built in a cruciform shape. Stand at the crossing and look up; the massive piers rise 98 feet to the vaulting overhead. Instead of steel, the arches are held in place by a keystone and supported by buttresses.

The intricate pulpit, from which Dr. Martin Luther King, Jr., delivered his final sermon on March 31, 1968, was carved from stone donated by England's Canterbury Cathedral. The 10,500 pieces of glass in the spectacular **West Rose Window** cast a rich late-afternoon rainbow on the floor.

Running along the nave are memorial alcoves, or bays. The **Woodrow Wilson Bay** symbolizes the life of the 28th President, the only U.S. President whose final resting place is Washington, D.C. The floor of the **Lincoln Bay** is inset with 33 Lincoln-head pennies —one for each state in the Union at the time of the Great Emancipator's assassination. About halfway down on the right (south) side, the modernistic **Space Window** is captivatingly 3-D; a moon rock is embedded in the center lancet.

Scattered throughout, nine chapels vary from the tiny **Good Shepherd Chapel** to the church-size **Bethlehem Chapel** on the crypt level. Especially appealing is the intimate **Children's Chapel,** where every item has been scaled to the size of a six-year-old. Also on the crypt level is a store offering books, tapes, cards, and snacks.

For a closer look at the cathedral's towers and gargoyles (and a terrific view of the city), take an elevator to the **Pilgrim Observation Gallery** on the seventh floor of the St. Peter and St. Paul towers. ■

Bell appeal

National Cathedral's central tower holds ten peal bells and a 53-bell carillon. It is the world's only cathedral blessed with both kinds of bells in one tower.

Each peal bell is mounted on a wheel, from which a rope hangs down to the ringers' chamber. The pull must be smooth and even, so one ringer is assigned to each bell. Weighing 600 to nearly 3,600 pounds apiece, the bells cannot be rung fast enough to play a melody; instead, sequences of notes called "changes" are played.

Change ringing is difficult and dangerous: Lose your concentration and you not only sabotage the change but risk injury when the bell's momentum jerks you high off the floor. Peals (Sun. after a.m. service) can last from several minutes to the rare "full peal," a three-hour extravaganza of 5,000 changes. The joyous noise can be heard at the White House, 3 miles distant. ■

Opposite: The St. Peter and St. Paul towers on the west facade of Washington National Cathedral bask in the golden sunrays of late afternoon.

More places to visit in Cleveland Park & beyond

NATIONAL MUSEUM OF HEALTH & MEDICINE

Though it now stresses science over spectacle, this museum is not for the squeamish: Exhibits range from preserved human fetuses and a stomach-shaped hairball to a leg swollen by elephantiasis and a hands-on brain. The collection was begun during the Civil War as a research tool for military medicine and surgery. Included are photos of war wounds, fragments of Lincoln's skull, and microscopes from the crude to the complex. Check the website for tours on permanent and changing exhibitions. http://nmhm.washingtondc.museum/
✉ Walter Reed Army Medical Center, 6900 Georgia Ave., N.W. ☎ 202-782-2200
💲 Donation 🚇 Metro: Takoma Park

Upton Sinclair, Cabinet members, Supreme Court justices, and National Geographic Society founder Gilbert H. Grosvenor. The cemetery also houses one of the finest works by one of America's greatest sculptors: The Adams Memorial (1890) by Augustus Saint-Gaudens was commissioned by historian Henry Adams to honor his wife, Clover. It depicts a seated figure wearing a heavy cloak, the face obscured by shadows. Mark Twain remarked that the sculpture embodied all of human grief, while Saint-Gaudens himself called his work "The Mystery of the Hereafter" and "The Peace of God that Passeth Understanding." Magnifying the work's mystery, it bears no inscription.
🅰 Map p. 179 ✉ Rock Creek Church Rd. & Webster St., N.W. ☎ 202-829-0585

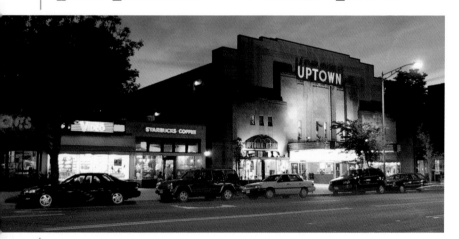

The last picture palace: The Uptown theater anchors upper Connecticut Avenue.

ROCK CREEK CEMETERY

A mile and a half east of Rock Creek Park in the Petworth neighborhood, this 86-acre site exudes the feel of an old country parish. Set amid this pastoral glebe, St. Paul's (or "Rock Creek") Church is the city's sole surviving colonial church. The church was founded in 1712, long before Washington was a city; the current building dates from 1775, though only the walls are original.

Some of the city's finest cemetery memorials reside here. They honor crusading novelist

UPTOWN THEATER

Opened in 1936, the art deco Uptown is Washington's premier movie palace. Its 830 seats, including a balcony, make it the city's largest remaining cinema theater. A curved screen, 72 feet long and 32 feet high, wraps viewers in movie magic, while a Dolby digital sound system keeps the illusion up-to-date. Though the Uptown offers only one film at a time, almost anything looks great in a house this big.
🅰 Map p. 179 ✉ 3426 Connecticut Ave., N.W. ☎ 202-966-5400 🚇 Metro: Cleveland Park ∎

A lesser known niche away from the tourist center, the land east of the Capitol holds a few charms of its own, including a museum honoring African Americans, a dazzling basilica, and gardens galore.

East of the Capitol

Stokes' aster at the National Arboretum

Rev. Willie Wilson plays washboard at Union Temple Baptist Church in Anacostia.

East of the Capitol

MORE THAN HALF THE CITY LIES EAST OF THE CAPITOL, AN AREA RICH IN AFRICAN American and military history, as well as gardens, marshes, and woods. Architecture lovers will find one of the city's most awe-inspiring buildings here, the nation's largest Catholic church.

The history of the eastern part of the city is tied to its river, the Anacostia, first seen by a European, explorer John Smith, nearly 400 years ago. Back then the Nacotchtank Indians (whose corrupted name, Anacostan, would be given to this East Branch of the Potomac) lived here, harvesting shad, catfish, and yellow perch. The arrival of white settlers meant the Indians' demise and the spread of tobacco plantations. In 1790 the lower Anacostia became part of the new capital. Soon developments arose on the northwest riverfront—the Washington Navy Yard (1799) and the U.S. Arsenal (1803).

Across the river from the Navy Yard, the city laid out its first planned, whites-only suburb, Uniontown, in 1854. During the Civil War, the military erected several forts east of the river. After the war, the Freedman's Bureau bought nearby, 375-acre Barry farm and sold

lots to 500 black families. Still the community, renamed Anacostia in 1886, remained mostly white until the 1950s. That changed with the migration of whites to the suburbs, and by 1970, Anacostia had become 86 percent black.

While the area along Martin Luther King Jr. Avenue (formerly Asylum Avenue) supports take-out restaurants, auto shops, and several other small businesses, the neighborhoods on U, V, and W Streets possess many early working-class row houses. The District government and private corporations have recently committed nearly a billion dollars to this area, hoping to improve neglected neighborhoods and enhance the waterfront. In the past decade, a rise in new housing and the arrival of the Metro have brought new residents, tourists, and life.

On the other side of the river, one of the last areas of the city to develop, the Northeast quadrant is anchored by the glorious grounds

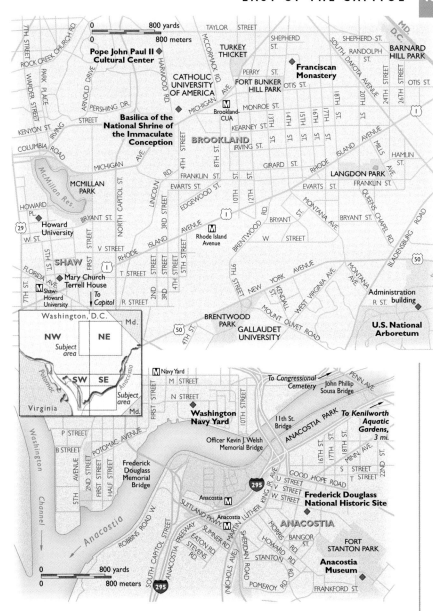

of the U.S. National Arboretum and by the Catholic University of America, home of the Shrine of the Immaculate Conception. Also in this area is Gallaudet University, the country's premier school for the deaf.

Sports fans know Northeast for the Langston Golf Course and RFK Stadium. The government built Langston in 1938 at the urging of black male and females golfers, who were barred from all but one of the District's courses. RFK Stadium, which opened in 1961, was once home to the Washington Redskins football team and the now defunct Washington Senators baseball team. Today the stadium draws crowds for its world-class soccer and music concerts. ∎

Frederick
Douglass NHS
www.nps.gov/frdo

🅰 Map p. 193

✉ 1411 W St., S.E.

☎ 202-426-5961 or
800-967-2283
(reservations)

🚇 Metro: Anacostia,
then Bus B2, U2,
W6-8 & transfer

Frederick Douglass National Historic Site

SITUATED AMONG THE ROW HOUSES OF ANACOSTIA, Cedar Hill—former home of abolitionist Frederick Douglass—harks back to a time when this area was a quiet country suburb. Built in the 1850s atop a grassy knoll, the 21-room white brick house offers a commanding view of the Washington skyline from its gracious front porch. A visit to this National Park Service site provides a fascinating glimpse into the life and work of the "sage of Anacostia," the most prominent African American orator of the 19th century.

Douglass was born a slave in Maryland's Talbot County in 1818, son of a black mother and a white father, possibly his owner.

Sent to Baltimore as a servant, he taught himself to read; at 20 he escaped to New York, then Massachussetts, where he lectured for the Massachusetts Anti-Slavery Society. To elude slave hunters after publishing his autobiography, in 1845, he fled to Europe. The purchase of his freedom by friends allowed him to return two years later. He began the *North Star* newspaper and kept working for the rights of blacks and women.

After the Civil War, he moved to Washington, D.C. Appointed U.S. marshal of the District in 1877, he bought 9-acre Cedar Hill. He expanded it to 15 acres and enlarged the house by seven rooms. After his 1895 death, his widow, Helen, preserved Cedar Hill and organized the Frederick Douglass Memorial and Historical Association; the restored house opened to the public in 1972.

The guided one-hour tour begins in the **visitor center** with a 17-minute orientation film. Among items on display is a Lincoln cane given to Douglass by the President's widow. After the video, you climb the steps to the **Victorian house.** Inside, the tastefully appointed parlors, library, and dining room look much as they did in Douglass's time—some 90 percent of the furnishings are original. The kitchen, with its coal and wood-burning stove, and the adjoining washroom are reminders of the days before electricity and indoor plumbing. Upstairs, Douglass's bedroom has a 19th-century bootjack and pair of shoes tucked by the bed. To see the different styles of his two wives, peek into their separate bedrooms.

Outside, you'll find the **Growlery** (a reconstruction), the private study to which Douglass often escaped. Cedar Hill was originally a farm estate with chicken coops, barn, and carriage house; Hurricane Hazel destroyed all but two of the outbuildings in 1967. ■

The home of Frederick Douglass still offers a commanding view of the city.

Kenilworth Aquatic Gardens

A cool feast of water lilies and lotuses floats on the waters of the Kenilworth Aquatic Gardens, on the east bank of the Anacostia. Started in 1880 by Civil War veteran Walter B. Shaw, this lovely 14-acre sanctuary, now managed by the National Park Service, is in full bloom in midsummer.

A **visitor center** near the gardens' parking lot has exhibits on the area. From here, stroll onto the dikes around the 40 ponds to see willows and post oaks, geese and red-winged blackbirds. At the gardens' end, a 335-yard **boardwalk** extends into the marshes, where great blue herons and egrets stalk prey amid wild rice and duck potato. Other denizens include osprey, mallard, snapping turtles, and muskrat.

The 0.7-mile (one way) **River Walk** offers a closer look at 77-acre Kenilworth Marsh, which borders the gardens. A city dump in the 1950s and '60s, the fill area is now

rich in bird and plant life. Here American bittern, long billed marsh wrens, and spotted salamanders live in a cattail-fringed wetland.

The best time for seeing wildlife and catching night-blooming lilies is early morning. The gardens open at 7 a.m. ■

Kenilworth Aquatic Gardens
www.nps.gov/nace/keaq
⚑ Map p. 193
✉ 1550 Anacostia Ave., N.E.
☎ 202-426-6905
🚌 Bus: V7 & 8

An aquatic perennial indigenous to Asia, the sacred lotus flower opens in the early morning.

Anacostia Museum & Center for African American History and Culture

Located in Fort Stanton Park, site of a Civil War fortification, the Anacostia Museum opened in 1967 as a neighborhood museum devoted to the interpretation of the African American experience, particularly in Washington, D.C.

Now part of the Smithsonian Institution, the museum greatly expanded its mission and resources not long ago. After an extensive renovation, it reopened in 2002 with expanded exhibition, archives, and library space. The center now offers a changing program of music, art, dance, storytelling, and poetry

as part of its documention of black culture.

Exhibits have included retrospectives on black photographers, such as New Orleans's Jules Lion, who began producing daguerreotypes in 1840, and inventors such as Benjamin Banneker, who helped plan the capital city. Other exhibits have explored topics as diverse as African American quilts, black churches, the antebellum South, the Civil Rights movement, Malcolm X, the 1920s Renaissance, and the meaning of the Kwanzaa and Juneteenth holidays. ■

Anacostia Museum & Center for African American History and Culture
www.si.edu/anacostia
⚑ Map p. 193
✉ 1901 Fort Pl., S.E.
☎ 202-287-3306
🚌 Metro: Anacostia, then Bus W2-3, W2-3 & 6-8, 93

U.S. National Arboretum

U.S. National Arboretum

www.usna.usda.gov

◮ Map p. 193

✉ 24th & R Sts., N.E., or 3501 New York Ave.

☎ 202-245-2726

🚍 Bus: X6, B2

A BIT OFF THE BEATEN TOURIST TRACK, THIS WHOLLY delightful oasis of fields, ponds, fountains, gardens, and flowering trees is just the tonic for those in need of some outdoor beauty. Established by an act of Congress in 1927, the National Arboretum is run by the Department of Agriculture as a living museum and a research and education facility. The arboretum's 446 acres include 9.5 miles of gentle roadways that wind past a dozen garden areas.

A pleasure any time, the arboretum is especially beautiful in spring, with 15,000 multicolored azaleas and blossoming dogwoods, cherries, and crabapples blushing on the hillsides. The sweet fragrances of magnolias and roses blend with those of woodland wildflowers.

In summer, the delicate flowers of high grasses stipple meadows, while daylilies and crape myrtles take to the heat with ease, and water lilies bloom in the koi pool that surrounds one wing of the administration building. Fall enriches the color palette with the vivid yellows of hickory and tulip poplar and the wine reds of sweet gum and dogwood. The late flowers of witch hazel and spider lilies fan the flames.

In the cold quiet days of winter, the bright red berries of holly glisten like little beads, and dwarf conifers and other evergreens are often rimed with ice. Ornamental grasses and dry leaves chatter in the winds that sweep through the open fields.

VISITING

On the way to the administration building from the New York Avenue entrance, you'll notice beehive-shaped **brick kilns.** When the brickyard, dating from 1909, shut down in 1972, the acreage and buildings were sold to the arboretum.

At the administration building, you'll find maps and a list of gardens currently in bloom. Next to

Children create their own floral tableaus beneath a flowering "Tonto" crape myrtle at the arboretum.

this building, the recently redone **National Bonsai and Penjing Museum** has an outstanding collection of miniature trees from Japan, China, and America. Breezes lilt through feathery Japanese maples and gravel paths meander among bonsai pavilions.

Across the drive, the 2.5-acre **National Herb Garden** features some 800 varieties of herbs in ten themed gardens. Standing like ruins in a nearby field are 22 sandstone Corinthian columns, removed from the Capitol's east central portico in 1958 when the Senate side of the Capitol building was enlarged. To see other gardens, take the guided 40-minute open-air tram tour *(weekends mid-April–mid-Oct., $)* starting near the R Street entrance. Or drive or bike to most by looping the outer roads.

Heading southwest from the administration building, you come first to the **National Boxwood Collection**—more than a hundred species on 5 acres. Adjoining perennials include irises, peonies, and daylilies. Continue to the **azalea collections**, which peak in late April. To the east, on Crabtree Road, pull over for **Fern Valley** and its native plants of the eastern United States; a half-mile wooded path traipses past wildflowers, a meadow, prairie, and a stream. Plants are grouped by geographical origin—piedmont, southern mountains, coastal plain, and prairie. Along here is a specimen of Franklinia, a small tree with white flowers, discovered in 1765 in Georgia by naturalist William Bartram; by 1790 it was extinct in the wild, perhaps the victim of flooding or rampant collecting.

At the arboretum's far eastern end, the **Asian collections** are one of the city's highlights. Flora from Japan, Korea, and China have been planted on a hillside so that from strategically placed benches you have glimpses of a pagoda through the trees and views down to the Anacostia River. Ginkgos and bamboo bend in gentle breezes, and in spring Japanese wisteria and other flowers scent the air. To the north, the **Gotelli Collection of dwarf and slow-growing conifer** is considered to be among the world's best. The 1,500 specimens include juniper, cedar, spruce, fir, hemlock, and arborvitae. ■

Anacostia River

Since the arrival of Europeans nearly 400 years ago, the Anacostia watershed has been used, overused, and abused. Runoffs from big farms in the 18th century silted the river, and urban growth has troubled the waters ever since. In the early 20th century, efforts to re-shape the waterway and "re-claim" the adjoining swamps for development nearly killed the Anacostia.

Fortunately, the tide is turning. Government agencies as well as citizen groups, such as the Anacostia Watershed Society, are working to protect this valuable ecosystem, a vital part of the country's largest estuary—the Chesapeake Bay. Over the past decade, hundreds of tons of debris have been cleaned up, and some 12,000 trees have been planted. In the city, the river's watershed is essentially sidewalk and street drains, which means that unfiltered trash too often finds its way into the river. With an eye on the future, the Anacostia Watershed Society has enlisted the help of thousands of city youths to help clean up this river. ■

Basilica of the National Shrine of the Immaculate Conception

THE BLUE DOME AND 329-FOOT-TALL CAMPANILE OF THE National Shrine preside over the skyline of Northeast Washington. Built along Byzantine and Romanesque lines, the National Shrine is the country's largest—and the world's eighth largest—Catholic church and one of the most beautiful and impressive pieces of architecture in a city renowned for its monuments.

Basilica of the National Shrine of the Immaculate Conception
www.nationalshrine.com
- Map p. 193
- Michigan Ave. & 4th St., N.E.
- 202-526-8300
- Metro: Brookland-CUA; Bus: 80, H1-4

In 1913, while rector of the Catholic University of America, Bishop Thomas J. Shahan (1857–1932) presented Pope Pius X with plans for building a shrine to the Blessed Virgin Mary on the campus. With the Pope's support, work began in 1920; the building was dedicated four decades later, in 1959. In 1990, John Paul II designated the shrine a basilica because of its significance as a national center of worship.

You can arrange a free tour on the website, or pick up a floor plan near the entrance and wander on your own. Sixty-five chapels and oratories, many funded by American ethnic groups, circle the perimeter of the crypt level and upper church. You should enter on the upstairs level, where the grandiose **Great Upper Church,** its vaulted ceilings soaring to a height of 100 feet, takes your breath away. Natural light floods the vast interior, stained glass casts color on walls and floors, and mosaics and candles sparkle in almost every niche and dome. Notice the swirling cosmos and the Garden of Eden depicted above the east transept and, in the west transept, the people rising toward a cloud-enthroned Jesus. The chancel dome holds a huge mosaic titled "Christ in Majesty," a hallmark of Byzantine art. A soothing contrast can be see in the green marble walls and trickling fountain of the **Mary**

Queen of Ireland chapel.
Stairs lead downstairs to the **crypt level,** where inscribed black and white marble walls and pillars adorn **Memorial Hall,** as a remembrance to those who donated to the construction. Also noteworthy here is the **Crypt Church,** modeled on the Roman catacombs. It holds services six times a day during the week. In **Our Mother of Africa Chapel,** sculpture groups depict African American

Pope John Paul II Cultural Center

Up the street from the Romanesque National Shrine is this modernistic limestone and granite multimedia museum (3900 Harewood Rd., N.E., 202-635-5400, closed Mon., $). Visitors watch a short orientation video about the center, then take a self-guided tour through galleries exploring such themes as church and papal history, community, and the Virgin Mary. Computer terminals offer background information and activities such as designing a stained-glass window. One room is filled with memorabilia of Pope John Paul II, while another—equipped with bell ropes and headsets—offers an opportunity for "virtual" change ringing. ■

Opposite: The National Shrine's tiled dome and soaring bell tower punctuate the city's skyline.

More places to visit east of the Capitol

CONGRESSIONAL CEMETERY

Originally intended to contain the graves of congressmen and officials who died in office, the Congressional Cemetery, established in 1807, is the oldest national cemetery and the final resting place of many Washington notables. Beginning in 1839, sandstone monuments were created for every member of Congress, though only 80 are actually occupied (the others are empty memorials to people buried elsewhere). Congress stopped the practice in 1877 after a furious debate, in which Senator George Hoar of Massachusetts argued that being buried under one of the massive monuments added "a new terror to death." Among its famous residents are Capitol architect William Thornton (1828), Civil War photographer Mathew Brady (1916), Marine Corps bandmaster John Philip Sousa (1932), and J. Edgar Hoover (1972), director of the FBI. Visitors can stroll the grounds; a map is located at the entrance. www.congressionalcemetery.org 🗺 Map p. 193 ✉ 1801 E St., S.E. ☎ 202-543-0539 🚇 Metro: Stadium Armory

FRANCISCAN MONASTERY

If you can't afford a trip to the Holy Land, this working monastery near the National Shrine of the Immaculate Conception offers a good

A monk leads a tour down into the catacombs of the Franciscan Monastery.

facsimile. Tours are offered hourly. Built in 1899 to educate missionaries, it contains full-scale reproductions of such sacred places as the Grotto of Lourdes, the Grotto of Gethsemane, the Tomb of the Virgin Mary, and the Holy Sepulcher of Christ. The Byzantine-style church is laid out in the shape of a five-fold Jerusalem or Crusader's Cross, with chapels at each end. Especially memorable are the Roman-style catacombs downstairs and the gruesome tales of Christian martyrs. In spring the gardens grace the monastery with flowering rosebushes, dogwoods, and cherry trees. You'll almost forget you're in the middle of a 21st-century city. 🗺 Map p. 193 ✉ 14th & Quincy Sts., N.E. ☎ 202-526-6800 🚇 Metro: Brookland–CUA

WASHINGTON NAVY YARD

On a plot of land set aside by George Washington is this ceremonial "Quarterdeck of the Navy." Kids enjoy clambering through the passages and up and down the ladders of the decommissioned destroyer **U.S.S. *Barry*,** permanently moored here. The 424-foot-long ship took part in the 1962 Cuban missile crisis and in the Vietnam War. You can walk through the wardroom, bunk room, sick bay, galley and mess deck, and pilothouse. Just across the parking lot from the ship stands the **Navy Museum,** whose highlights include working periscopes with views to Virginia, a fighter plane, more than a hundred model ships, and hands-on antiaircraft guns. The **art gallery** and the **Marine Corps Historical Center,** in Building 58, are a bit more static, but you might want to look at **Willard Park,** a parade ground surrounded by 33 cannon captured as trophies from the 17th to 19th centuries, and the museum grounds. To the north are the Greek Revival arched gate and guardhouses designed in 1804 by Benjamin Henry Latrobe, one of the Capitol's architects. www.history.navy.mil 🗺 Map p. 193 ✉ 9th & M Sts., S.E. ☎ 202-433-6897 (Navy Museum), 202-433-3377 (U.S.S. *Barry*), 202-433-3534 (Marine museum) 🕐 Hours for branches vary; reservations required to visit Navy Museum on weekends 🚇 Metro: Eastern Market, Navy Yard ∎

Only on the Virginia side of the Potomac can you complete the story of the country's past, including colonial Alexandria and its early associations with the Revolutionary War, and Arlington, famous for its national cemetery.

Across the Potomac

Pineapple door knocker, symbolizing hospitality

Across the Potomac

GRACEFULLY ARCHING ACROSS THE POTOMAC RIVER, CONNECTING Washington to Virginia, Arlington Memorial Bridge makes a powerful visual statement by linking memorials dedicated to Union Commander in Chief Abraham Lincoln and Confederate Gen. Robert E. Lee—a symbolic joining of North and South. Overlooking Lincoln's templelike memorial on the Mall is Lee's Arlington House, high on a hill in what is now Arlington National Cemetery, surrounded by the somber white graves of Civil War veterans from both North and South, as well as servicepeople from all succeeding wars.

The Northern Virginia region just outside Washington proper is a suburban mix of historic sites, residential neighborhoods, and shopping malls. Arlington and Alexandria especially have much to offer. Separated by the Crystal City high-rises around Ronald Reagan Washington National Airport, the two heavily populated and developed communities are connected by the Metro system and highly scenic George Washington Memorial Parkway.

Both of these suburban areas originally belonged to the District of Columbia, then a diamond-shaped city straddling the river. But in 1846, Virginia took back its part, the returned land equaling about one-third of the entire city. The fortunes of the two areas have been tied to Washington ever since.

Already a tobacco port, Alexandria got its official start in 1749 as a 60-acre townsite. George Washington, who lived 9 miles south at Mount Vernon, and Robert E. Lee, both considered Alexandria their hometown.

Falling on hard times after the Civil War, the town has prospered in recent years with the sprucing up of its waterfront and the restoration of 18th-century town houses. Now a fashionable residential area, the town draws a steady stream of tourists to its bars, boutiques, restaurants, and riverside craft shops. Historical sites give insight into the lives of Washington, Lee, and other prominent locals.

One of the nation's smallest counties, and containing no incorporated cities or towns within its boundaries, Arlington did not exist as its own separate entity until after 1846, when the land was returned from Washington to Virginia. Today it is home to Arlington National Cemetery and the Pentagon. The moving Marine Corps War Memorial, Theodore Roosevelt Island and its tribute to the 26th President, and the string of Potomac River parks along the parkway are other good reasons for venturing to the Virginia side of the river. ■

Theodore Roosevelt Memorial Bridge connects Washington with the burbs.

Arlington National Cemetery

Arlington National Cemetery
www.arlingtoncemetery.org
🅰 Map p. 203
✉ Virginia side of Arlington Memorial Bridge, off Va. 110
☎ 703-607-8000
🕐 Changing of the Guard, every hour Oct.–March, every half hour April–Sept.
💲 $ (parking fee)
Ⓜ Metro: Arlington Cemetery; Bus: 5A & B, 13A-B & F-G

Hundreds of thousands of servicemen and women lie buried beneath Arlington's green expanses.

ROWS OF WHITE HEADSTONES ON ROLLING HILLS, THE Changing of the Guard at the Tomb of the Unknowns, the eternal flame at John F. Kennedy's grave: These enduring images immediately bring to mind the nation's most famous national cemetery.

Another image, visible from the Washington side of the river, is the stately hilltop mansion called Arlington House (see p. 206). Once the beloved home of Robert E. Lee and his wife, Mary, it was on their surrounding plantation that the cemetery was established.

Shortly after Lee left to fight for the Confederacy in 1861, the federal government confiscated the property and put up fortifications. Union Quartermaster Gen. Montgomery Meigs recommended in 1864 that acreage on the Lee estate be set aside for a national cemetery. Later that year, Meigs's son was killed in the war; the high-relief tomb effigy of him lying slain in his uniform by the side of the road is one of Arlington's more unusual memorials.

Over Meigs's objection, Confederate soldiers were allowed burial in Arlington, though official decorations or observances were not permitted. Meigs's bitterness largely kept Confederate widows outside the gates until the late 1800s. In a show of reconciliation, Congress in 1900 allowed a Confederate section of the cemetery to be set aside, and in 1914 the **Confederate Memorial** was dedicated by President Woodrow Wilson, with 3,000 veterans from both sides in attendance. As for the Lee family's fate, Lee's son, G. W. C. Lee, sued the government after the Civil War for confiscating their land. The Supreme Court ruled that he should be paid the market value, $150,000.

The 612-acre cemetery is now the final resting place for more than 290,000 servicepeople. With 25 to 30 funerals conducted every weekday, the cemetery is expected to be filled by 2025, at which time it may be expanded onto other nearby government-owned land. To qualify for burial here, a serviceperson must have died on active duty, or be entitled to retirement pay, or have been awarded a high military decoration. Any veteran with an honorable discharge may have his or her cremated remains entombed in the Columbarium. For a funeral with full military honors, a flag-draped coffin is accompanied by an honor guard and a steady drum beat. After three rifle volleys, the coffin is lowered, while "Taps" is played. The guards then fold the flag and present it to the next of kin.

VISITING

As you approach the cemetery via the Ceremonial Entrance on Memorial Drive, you'll see the large, semicircular building of the **Women in Military Service for America Memorial.** Dedicated in 1997, it honors the nearly two million women who have served since 1776.

A guard will direct you to a left turn into the parking area for the cemetery's **visitor center.** Stop by for exhibits and a 12-minute film, as well as a good cemetery map. From here, quiet, tree-shaded streets and pathways meander to the main sites, making for a lovely stroll. Since the cemetery covers of lot of hilly ground, many people hop aboard the tourmobile ($), which stops at major points of interest.

Leaving the back of the visitor center, head up the pathway to reach the **gravesite of President John F. Kennedy.** At his funeral in 1963, his widow, Jacqueline, lit an eternal flame that continues to flicker even in the rain. She and their two infant children are also interred here. From this site, you have a grand view of the Lincoln Memorial, Washington Monument, and U.S. Capitol. Nearby, a white wooden cross marks the **grave of Senator Robert F. Kennedy.**

The best view of Washington

from the cemetery, however, awaits farther up the hill at **Arlington House.** Appropriately, the grave of city designer Pierre Charles L'Enfant is situated here, in front of the mansion, facing Washington.

About a half-mile walk south from the house, adjacent to the amphitheater, the **Tomb of the Unknowns** holds the remains of unidentified servicemen, one each from the World Wars and Korea (the Vietnam veteran's remains were removed in 1998 when they

were identified). A 24-hour guard patrols this symbolic site, carrying an M-14 rifle with a ceremonial bayonet. The sentinel takes 21 steps on the plaza (symbolic of a 21-gun salute), then turns to face the tomb for 21 seconds. A dignified ritual, the Changing of the Guard always draws a crowd.

Others buried at Arlington include polar explorer Richard Byrd, boxer Joe Louis, 229 sailors from the U.S.S. *Maine* (sunk in Havana harbor in 1898), and Gen. John J. Pershing, the cemetery's highest ranking officer. Commander in chief of the American Expeditionary Forces in World War I, Pershing lies buried among the men with whom he served. ∎

A horse-drawn caisson and flag-draped coffin are standard at a full military funeral.

Arlington House

Arlington House
www.nps.gov/arho

🗺 Map p. 203

✉ Arlington National
Cemetery

☎ 703-235-1530

🚇 Metro: Arlington
Cemetery

BEFORE ARLINGTON CEMETERY, THERE WAS ARLINGTON House, the buff-hued Greek Revival mansion on a prominent hill above the Potomac. Built by Robert E. Lee's father-in-law in 1802–1817 and once anchoring a 1,100-acre plantation, it's now surrounded by the graves of servicepeople from many wars.

The Lees lived here off and on for 30 years while traveling between U.S. Army posts. Then, on April 18, 1861, when Virginia succeeded from the Union, Lincoln offered the 54-year-old Lee command of a Union Army that would invade the South. After a long and agonizing night Lee declined, deciding instead to accept command of Virginia's forces. His 32 years of distinguished service to the U.S. Army were over, and the country spiraled toward a long and bloody civil war.

"I can anticipate no greater calamity for the country than a dissolution of the Union," Lee later wrote. "I am willing to sacrifice everything but honor for its preservation." Loyal to his native state, home of his family for six generations, Lee left his home on April 22 to accept command of Virginia's forces, never to return. "I did only what my duty demanded," he said.

The Union Army soon moved in, using the house as a defense post headquarters. After the war, the cemetery superintendent lived and worked here for many years. In 1955 it officially was designated the Robert E. Lee Memorial.

Restored to its antebellum appearance, the gracious, high-ceilinged house looks much as it did during the Lee years. Though many heirlooms were looted, about one-third of the furnishings are original. A genuine touch is the original china, glassware, and silver in the Family Dining Room. After walking through the mansion's 15 rooms, you can take in some interesting exhibits on the Lee and Custis families in the slaves' quarters and museum out back. Vegetable gardens add to the authenticity of the site. From in front you can see the Lincoln Memorial, directly and symbolically connected by Memorial Bridge to Arlington House. ■

Overlooking Arlington National Cemetery, Arlington House honors Robert E. Lee and his family.

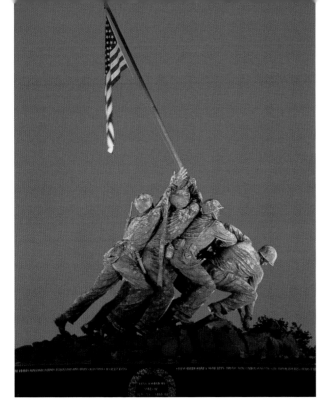

Marine Corps War Memorial

KNOWN AS THE IWO JIMA MEMORIAL, ONE OF THE NATION'S most famous war monuments sits in a grassy park adjacent to Arlington Cemetery. Its larger-than-life realism rests on the fact that the figures are nearly six times life size, and the event they depict really happened.

There were, however, actually two flag raisings. On Feb. 23, 1945, four days into a vicious struggle for control of Iwo Jima, a detachment of U.S. Marines made it to the top of Mount Suribachi, the island's highest point, and raised a small American flag. Later that afternoon, after the slopes had been cleared of enemy resistance, five Marines and a Navy hospital corpsmen raised a larger flag. It was this second flag raising that news photographer Joseph Rosenthal captured in the famous image that won him a Pulitzer Prize. The Marines' capture of the island three weeks later was a crucial victory in the Pacific campaign.

Sculptor Felix de Weldon, then on duty with the U.S. Navy, was so moved by the image that he cast it in bronze. Dedicated in 1954, the 78-foot-high sculpture depicts the soldiers standing atop a chunk of jagged black granite that resembles the island's volcanic rock, their cloth flag flying 24 hours a day. On Tuesday evenings in summer, the Marine Corps presents a spirited parade here.

Nearby rises the **Netherlands Carillon,** with 49 bells, presented by the Dutch in 1960 in thanks for American aid during the war. ■

Marine Corps War Memorial
www.nps.gov/gwmp/usmc.htm

🅰 Map p. 203

✉ N. Meade St., just N of Arlington Cemetery

☎ 703-289-2500 or 703-289-2530 (concert & parade information)

Ⓜ Metro: Arlington Cemetery or Rosslyn; Bus: 4A

Only three of the six men depicted in the memorial survived the war.

George Washington Memorial Parkway

George Washington Memorial Parkway

www.nps.gov/gwmp

 Map p. 203

☎ 703-289-2500

The parkway in springtime splendor

OFFERING PEERLESS VIEWS OF THE CAPITAL CITY, THIS stunning roadway lends the perfect excuse for a leisurely drive. Ambling along the Potomac River between Mount Vernon and the American Legion Bridge, it links historic sites, riverside parks, and overlooks.

Beginning south of Alexandria at **Mount Vernon** (see pp. 222–224), the parkway winds north through maples, oaks, beeches, and tulip polars, chosen when the parkway was designed in the 1930s to give it the look of the Virginia countryside. Two miles beyond Mount Vernon sprawls **Fort Hunt Park,** preserving batteries that guarded the river approach to the city from 1898 to 1918. Look across the river to see its mate, **Fort Washington** (1824).

Ahead, a right turnoff leads to **River Farm** *(703-768-5700, closed weekends),* once part of George Washington's estate. Beyond **Belle**

Haven Marina spreads a wide-sweeping upriver view—birders congregate along here to scan the water and sky for migrating geese and songbirds. For a closer look, take a stroll at **Dyke Marsh** *(Belle Haven Marina),* a 240-acre bird haven.

Within **Old Town Alexandria** (see pp. 212–214), the parkway becomes Washington Street. Two blocks beyond King Street rises **Christ Church** (see p. 211), on the left. Beyond town you'll spot **Daingerfield Island,** site of a small marina and restaurant with a view.

Just north of Reagan Washington National Airport comes the most breathtaking stretch—the **Washington skyline** and its parade of monuments: the Capitol, Jefferson Memorial, Washington Monument, and Lincoln Memorial. The grassy riverbank here is ideal for picnicking. Beyond the 14th Street Bridges rises the **Navy and Marine Memorial.** Farther, you'll pass through the **LBJ Memorial Grove** and **Lady Bird Johnson Park,** abundant with flowers.

About a quarter mile beyond Roosevelt Bridge, you'll spy the turnout for **Theodore Roosevelt Island** (see opposite). The road passes beneath Key Bridge, with **Georgetown University's** spire looming across the river. The drive then climbs above the Potomac, offering overlooks of the increasingly wild and rocky river. About 1.5 miles beyond Turkey Run Park, the parkway ends at I-495 and the American Legion Bridge. ■

Theodore Roosevelt Island

An arcadia of wooded paths and bird-filled marshes, this 91-acre island opposite the Kennedy Center is a favorite lunchtime retreat for office workers. Some 2.5 miles of trails are just right for walking, running, bird-watching, and general relaxing from city life stresses.

In 1967 the island was turned into a memorial to the charismatic, conservation-minded U.S. President. Many people heading over the footbridge for a walk are surprised to find, tucked in the middle of the woods, a rather grandiose **memorial** featuring a 17-foot-high bronze of Roosevelt, fountains, and several enormous granite tablets inscribed with his words. About the outdoors, he remarked: "There are no words that can tell the hidden spirit of the wilderness, that can reveal its mystery, its melancholy, and its charm."

After a look at the memorial, you can choose between wooded or river-edged paths. One of the most delightful areas is the **boardwalk** through the swamp and marsh on the island's east side. Along here, herons stalk prey among cattails and pickerelweed, while bald cypresses and gnarled oaks suggest a pre-Washington landscape. ∎

Finding peace and quiet near the city's bustle

Theodore Roosevelt Island
www.nps.gov/gwmp/tri.htm
Map p. 203
Potomac River, 0.25 mile N of Theodore Roosevelt Bridge via George Washington Memorial Pkwy. north (no vehicle access southbound)
703-289-2550
Metro: Rosslyn

The Pentagon

It's certain that no one will look at this massive fortress quite the same way again following the tragic Sept. 11, 2001, crash of a hijacked jetliner into its south side, now rebuilt. One of the world's largest office buildings, the 6.5-million-square-foot Pentagon was built in 16 months during World War II to combine the offices of the War Department under one roof. The number five has no particular significance here—the building originally conformed to a five-sided site, and since President Franklin Roosevelt liked the unique shape, it was kept.

Today, the Pentagon is a city unto itself, housing 26,000 military, civilian, and support personnel working to protect national interests. On weekdays, volunteers from the military services conduct tours of 30 to 90 minutes along more than a mile of corridors where military art, model planes, and portraits of military leaders are on view. Out of sight are the top-secret War Room and other situation rooms. Walk-in tours begin every hour; call ahead for groups of 10 or more. The tour registration window is at the Pentagon Metro entrance. ∎

The Pentagon
www.defenselink.mil/pubs/pentagon/#tour
Map p. 203
I-395 and Jefferson Davis Hwy. (Va. 110)
703-697-1776
Closed Sat.-Sun.
$ for parking at Pentagon City
Metro: Pentagon; Bus: 5A & B, 16, 13A-B & F-G, Art73SH 4

Alexandria

With its brick sidewalks, federal town houses, and quaint shops and restaurants, Alexandria's Old Town reminds many people of Georgetown. No coincidence here, since both arose as tobacco ports in the mid-1700s a mere 8 river miles from one another.

Scotsman John Alexander, for whom Alexandria is named, purchased much of present-day Alexandria in 1669 from an English ship captain for 6,000 pounds of tobacco. Incorporated in 1749, the town blossomed as a foreign port of entry. Strolling along Old

plies—hundreds of thousands of soldiers tramped through on their way to postings and battles, and train after train rolled in with the wounded. Warehouses, churches, hotels, even large houses were requisitioned for use as military stations and hospitals.

King Street's panoply of shops and restaurants is housed in centuries'-old row houses.

Town's beautifully preserved wharf today, it's easy to visualize how Alexandria must have looked, when tall-masted brigs and schooners docked at the piers, mariners bustled between brick warehouses, and captains strutted cobbled lanes. Slaves and grain as well as tobacco added to the early prosperity of this genteel Southern town.

The Civil War, however, changed all that. As a buffer for Washington, only 100 miles north of the Confederate capital of Richmond, Alexandria was immediately occupied and soon overrun with Union forces. The fortified town became a crossroads for men and sup-

After the war, the small-town atmosphere was all but gone, and as Washington grew Alexandria sprawled and deteriorated. In 1946 the City Council stepped in to protect the splendid 18th- and 19th-century row houses, making Old Town the nation's third officially designated historic district.

Today, Old Town is a delightful place to spend a sunny afternoon, poking into shops, eating ice cream, watching boats glide by on the river. Especially on weekend evenings, crowds pack a spate of restaurants and pubs, enjoying the vibrant nightlife against its historical backdrop. ∎

Christ Church

Historic Christ Church has sat behind its iron-gated fence on Washington Street since before Alexandria was established. Completed in 1773 in simple Georgian country style, it features a typical brick exterior and white-washed interior. The fine Palladian chancel window is unusual ornamentation for a church of its time.

George Washington was one of the first to buy a pew here, now marked by a silver plaque (No. 60). Tradition says that on the lawn he first declared to friends his intent to fight the war of American independence. Robert E. Lee was confirmed here on July 17, 1853 (a fact marked by another silver plaque, on the chancel), and he worshiped here with his family.

The tree-shaded **burying ground** was used for Alexandrians until 1808; the earliest tombstone is dated March 20, 1791. Look for one of the latest tombstones, for Anne Warren, a popular actress in her day. Her 1808 epitaph reads in part: "The unrivaled excellence of theatrical talents was surpassed by the mighty virtues…which adorned her private life. In her were contained the affectionate wife and mother and the sincere friend."

Docents lead **tours** daily; meet at the church's front door. ■

Christ Church
www.historicchristchurch.org
🗺 Map p. 203
✉ 118 N. Washington St.
☎ 703-549-1450
🚇 Metro: King St.; Bus: 10A

Gadsby's Tavern Museum

Consisting of a 1770s tavern, 1792 hotel, and three outbuildings, Gadsby's Tavern was colonial Alexandria's center of social, political, and business life. Festive balls, patriotic meetings, and presidential receptions once enlivened its rooms, earning it praise as the finest public house in America. Restored as a museum and operating restaurant, the tavern appears just as George Washington (a frequent visitor) might have seen it, complete with colonial decor and fare served on candlelit tables.

A 30-minute **guided tour** of the museum shows the taproom where patrons dined on whatever the tavern happened to be serving that night—perhaps ham and cheese "pye" or cream of County Surrey peanut soup. You learn that the drink of choice was rum, sometimes mixed with fruit juice and imported sugar to make a punch. You also see the dining room; ballroom; assembly room, where the Masonic Orders, the Alexandria Dragoons, and other local groups convened; and the third-floor communal bedchambers—the beds and floors were shared by as many travelers as could fit the space. ■

Gadsby's Tavern Museum
www.gadsbystavern.org
🗺 Map p. 203
✉ 134 N. Royal St.
☎ 703-838-4242
💲 $
🕐 Closed Mon.–Tues. Nov.–March
🚇 Metro: King St.; Bus: AT2-7

Setting up for lunch

Old Town by foot

Strolling is the best way to enjoy Old Town's colonial ambience, allowing you plenty of time to study the architectural details of historical row houses, admire postage-stamp gardens filled with peonies and begonias, visit the many historic buildings once frequented by Thomas Jefferson, George Washington, and Robert E. Lee, poke into specialty shops, and simply see what there is to see. The walk outlined here can be done in a couple of hours, but, depending on how many sites you stop by, you could easily spend a day.

Begin in the heart of the historic core at the two-story, yellow-frame **Ramsay House Visitors Center** ❶ *(221 King St., 703-838-4200)*, a reconstruction of the 1724 home of town founder William Ramsay. Across Fairfax

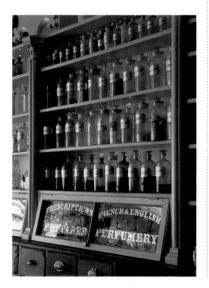

Street, **Market Square** holds a Saturday morning market that dates from 1749, making it one of the country's oldest.

From the visitor center, walk south on Fairfax Street. About half a block down on the right, the **Stabler-Leadbeater Apothecary Museum** ❷ *(105–107 S. Fairfax St., 703-836-3713, $)* operated from 1792 to 1933. George Washington, James Monroe, and Robert E. Lee all knew these walls, stocked with all kinds of goods including medical supplies, house paint, and garden seeds. Preserved intact, the shop contains original potions, herbs, mortars, and journals.

Now go back to King Street and turn right. Situated along the river, the **Torpedo Factory Art Center** ❸ *(105 N. Union St., 703-838-4565, www.torpedofactory.org)* holds 80-odd studios where you can watch artisans sculpt, paint, weave, and make stained glass. A museum of local archaeological artifacts is on

The wharf (above) offers pleasant waterfront views. Dating from 1792, the Stabler–Leadbeater Apothecary Museum (left) was George Washington's pharmacy.

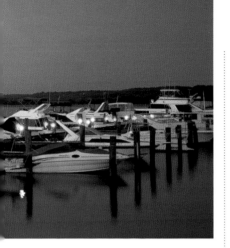

stroll along the boat docks, or park yourself on a bench and enjoy the fresh air.

Walk south on Union and make a right on Prince Street. Known as **Captain's Row**, this cobblestoned block is lined with sturdy federal town houses, many of which were owned by ship captains in the 18th century. Cross Lee Street, and on the right stands the 1851 pink stucco Greek Revival **Athenaeum** (*201 Prince St., 703-548-0035),* which once functioned as a bank; with the onset of the Civil War, the bank closed and documents were hidden until after the war, when customers were reimbursed. Now owned by the Northern Virginia Fine Arts Association, the Athenaeum features a contemporary art gallery. A little farther up the block, William Fairfax, an original trustee of Alexandria, lived at **207 Prince**

the third floor. Built in 1918, the factory turned out torpedo shell casings and other weaponry for both World Wars (look for the torpedo on view on the ground floor); the federal government used the spacious building for storage until the city of Alexandria bought it in 1969. The art center opened in 1974, and it was incorporated into a major waterfront development a decade later. Out back, you can

See area map p. 203
Ramsay House visitor center
2 miles
3 hours, without stops
Carlyle House

NOT TO BE MISSED
- Torpedo Factory Art Center
- Christ Church
- Gadsby's Tavern Museum

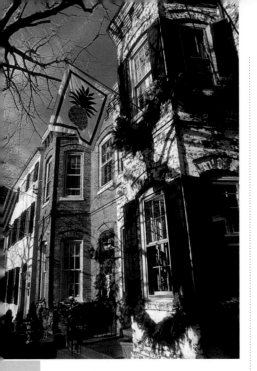

Green Christmas boughs adorn town houses on historic Queen Street.

Street, and next door at **209 Prince** lived Dr. James Craik, the surgeon-general who was with George Washington throughout the Revolutionary War, and who attended him at his death at nearby Mount Vernon.

At Fairfax Street, turn left and head south across Duke Street to the **Old Presbyterian Meeting House** *(321 S. Fairfax St., 703-549-6670, www.opmh.org)*. Built in 1774, the church has a large unadorned interior with wood floors and clear windows; in the churchyard lies the Tomb of the Unknown Soldier of the American Revolution.

Proceed back up Duke Street to Washington Street, the main north-south thoroughfare, and head north. On the street's west side, the Greek Revival-style **Lyceum** *(201 S. Washington St., 703-838-4994)* was built in 1839 as a cultural center and library. It now maintains permanent and temporary exhibits on Alexandria's history.

At the intersection of Washington and Prince stands the bronze **Confederate Statue,** a memorial to the town's Confederate dead. Created by Casper Buberl and erected in

1889, the defeated-looking veteran faces south, head bowed, arms folded. A block north you're back at **King Street,** Old Town's main commercial avenue. Along here you can find a busy assortment of restaurants, bars, and boutiques. Antique shops pack the stretch to the west.

The monument rising on the hill a mile or so west is the grandiose **George Washington Masonic National Memorial** *(King St. & Callahan Dr., 703-683-2007, www.gwmemorial.org)*, with sprawling views of Alexandria and Washington from the ninth-floor observation deck. The free one-hour tour lingers a bit much on Masonic history, but it is worthwhile for the good collection of Washington memorabilia, including his family Bible and leather field trunk. If you don't want to walk from Washington Street, it's an easy drive and there's plenty of parking.

Back at Washington and King Streets, the next block north holds historic **Christ Church** ❹ (see p. 211). Three blocks farther north on Washington, the **Lee-Fendall House** ❺ *(614 Oronoco St., 703-548-1789, closed Mon., $, www.leefendallhouse.org)* was built in 1785 by lawyer Philip Fendall, who married an aunt of Robert E. Lee. Family heirlooms are on display, including portraits, letters, and books. Across Oronoco Street, at No. 607, the **Boyhood Home of Robert E. Lee** was recently bought by private owners; although locals complained that the house would be closed to the public, no one came forth with the several million dollars needed for renovations and upkeep.

Head back down Washington and make a left on Cameron. To get a feel for how early Alexandrians dined out, stop by the **Gadsby's Tavern Museum** ❻ (see p. 211). Then walk east to Cameron and Fairfax Streets and end your stroll at the Georgian Palladian-style **Carlyle House** *(121 N. Fairfax St., 703-549-2997, closed Mon., $, www.carlylehouse.org)*, built in 1753 by Scottish merchant John Carlyle. British Gen. Edward Braddock convened a meeting here in 1755 with five colonial governors to discuss the financing of the French and Indian War. Interesting tours showcase the lifestyle of an 18th-century Virginia family and their servants and slaves. ■

Buzzing with life before Washington, D.C., was there, the land beyond the Beltway is laced with a wealth of historic sites that would be worth a peek even without the capital city nearby.

Excursions

Standing in formation at the U.S. Naval Academy, Annapolis

Excursions

WITH RIVERSIDE PARKLANDS AND COBBLE-LANED VILLAGES, COLONIAL plantations and busy harborfronts, Washington is blessed with an abundance of easy escapes within an hour's drive away.

Among the most accessible is the Chesapeake & Ohio National Historical Park, which preserves the ruins of a 19th-century canal and its towpath. Beginning in Georgetown and paralleling the Potomac River for more than 180 miles north, it's especially popular with walkers, bikers, and campers. Great Falls—its most distinctive feature and probably the most spectacular natural attraction anywhere between the Blue Ridge and the Chesapeake Bay—is only 5 miles beyond the Beltway (I-495). Great Falls Park on the Virginia side of the river is also a popular place to view the falls.

One of the area's newest additions is the National Air and Space Museum annex, near Washington Dulles International Airport in northern Virginia. The hangarlike facility houses notable aircraft too large to fit in the downtown museum, including the *Enola Gay* and a supersonic Concord.

You'll find history that goes even further back on the Potomac River south of Washington. More than 250 years ago, Virginia colonists established vast plantations and manor houses, including Washington's Mount Vernon and Gunston Hall. Built by the slaves of early citizens, these historic houses, and the younger Woodlawn, stand today as tributes to the quality workmanship and to the tireless efforts of preservationists.

Annapolis, poised some 30 miles east of Washington at the point where the Severn River spills into the Chesapeake Bay, is equally well preserved. You couldn't ask for a more charming, history-saturated, seafood-proud water town. It's easy to fill a day—or two, if you're lucky—exploring the town's lively colonial historic center and admiring the sailboats.

To the north, Baltimore, with its vibrant Inner Harbor, sits on the Patapsco River off the Chesapeake Bay. Boasting a world-class aquarium, stellar museums, and the only Civil War-era vessel still afloat today, this popular, newly revitalized city makes for another good waterside excursion. ■

Randolph Hills
185
97
586
WHEATON
WHEATON REGIONAL PARK
650
29
CALVERTON
95
1
To **Baltimore**
295
PATUXENT RESEARCH REFUGE
◁ **6**

355
Garrett Park
WHEATON
WHITE OAK
212
BELTSVILLE
To **Baltimore** and Baltimore Washington Intl. Airport (BWI)

7
185
Chevy Chase View
97
193
495
OAKVIEW
650
ADELPHI
95
495
201
Greenbelt
564

ETHESDA
410
410
Chevy Chase
SILVER SPRING
Takoma Park
LANGLEY PARK
193
Berwyn Heights
College Park
295
GLENN DALE
193
◁ **5**

90
ROCK CREEK PARK
212
LEWISDALE
University Park
201
GREENBELT PARK
SEABROOK
450

96
Chillum
410
Riverdale
New Carrollton

410
450
Hyattsville
704

Mount Rainier
29
Bladensburg
450
202
50

MASS. AVE.
RHODE ISLAND AVE.
Colmar Manor
Cheverly
KENTLAND
Glenarden
To **Annapolis** and Sandy Point SP

GEORGETOWN
White House
50
U.S. NATIONAL ARBORETUM
202
PALMER PARK
704
WOODMORE
202
193
◁ **4**

ROSSLYN
50
Lincoln Mem.
U.S. Capitol
Seat Pleasant
LARGO
214
KETTERING

ARLINGTON
395
E. CAPITOL ST.
FORT DUPONT PARK
214
95
202

Arlington Nat. Cem.
Pentagon
Capitol Heights
495

120
CRYSTAL CITY
Ronald Reagan Washington Nat. Airport
4
District Heights
CAPITAL BELTWAY
RITCHIE MARLBORO ROAD
WESTPHALIA
◁ **3**

1
295
SUITLAND
SUITLAND
PKWY.

LEXANDRIA
400
HILLCREST HEIGHTS
5
MARLOW HEIGHTS

OLD TOWN
7
Forest Heights
414
TEMPLE HILLS
5
337
4
To Chesapeake Bay

4
241
Huntington
OXON HILL PARK
295
95
495
223

611
Camp Springs

RGINIA HILLS
Groveton
210
223
WOODYARD
◁ **2**

FORT FOOTE VILLAGE
CLINTON
E

TANTALLON
△ **1**

Mount Vernon

3 miles
3 kilometers

PA.
Philadelphia
MD.
Baltimore
N.J.
WASHINGTON, D.C.
Annapolis
DEL.
VA.
Richmond
ATLANTIC OCEAN
Norfolk

△ C
△ D

Chesapeake and Ohio Canal & Great Falls

C&O Canal NHP

www.nps.gov/choh

🅰 216 A5

✉ Georgetown Visitor Center, 1057 Thomas Jefferson St., N.W.

☎ 202-653-5190

✉ Great Falls Tavern Visitor Center, 11710 MacArthur Blvd., Potomac, MD

☎ 301-767-3714

$ $

SNAKING 184.5 MILES NORTHWEST FROM GEORGETOWN to Cumberland, Maryland, the Chesapeake and Ohio Canal National Historical Park has to be one of the longest, skinniest parks in the system. The most dramatic section is certainly the Great Falls area, just north of Washington, where the Potomac River hurls over steep, ragged rocks in a spectacular series of thundering falls before flowing through narrow Mather Gorge.

President John Quincy Adams broke ground for the C&O Canal on July 4, 1828. At that time, it was considered a Great National Project that would link Georgetown in Washington with Pittsburgh on the Ohio River, thus connecting the Atlantic Ocean with the Mississippi River. Plagued with problems from the start, however, including stiff competition by the new Baltimore & Ohio Railroad, the canal only made it as far as Cumberland.

Thousands of laborers—using hand tools, mule scoops, and black powder—toiled for 22 years to carve the trench, sometimes out of pure rock. A feat of engineering, its 74 lift locks raise it 605 feet in elevation from beginning to end.

The mule-drawn canal barges hauled coal, hay, fertilizer, and cement from the Appalachian Mountains to the city until 1924. Today, you can hop aboard a mule-powered canal boat in Georgetown for a ride through a working lock (*April-Sept., $$*).

In the early 1950s, Supreme Court Justice William O. Douglas led a movement to preserve the abandoned canal. The C&O was designated a national historical park in 1971.

A kayaker hones his technique in the holes and waves below Great Falls.

VISITING

If you have the stamina, bike or hike the 14-mile towpath stretch from Georgetown to Great Falls, a lovely trek offering pretty river views; otherwise, you can drive, via MacArthur Boulevard, to the Great Falls Tavern section of the national historical park.

The big white stucco building overlooking the canal houses the **visitor center.** Built in 1831, the structure served as a lodge for travelers and boatmen for nearly a century. Exhibits tell about the area and the canal's history.

To see the falls, and perhaps bald eagles, head a short distance downstream on the towpath to the quarter-mile trail leading to **Great Falls Overlook.** A combination of boardwalk and bridges, the trail links the two sections of Olmsted Island, ending at a close-up look at frothing, roaring Great Falls as it narrows and tumbles 76 vertical feet over craggy boulders into swirling eddies.

Back on the towpath, continue downstream a little way. Before the stop-lock bridge, pick up the **Billy Goat Trail,** a wild, 2-mile romp over jagged rocks high on the river's edge and along Mather Gorge. In spring, trout lilies, jack-in-the-pulpits, and bluebells sprinkle the forest floor, and goose honks and songbird trills fill the air. On nice days kayakers play in the rapids below the falls and rock climbers scale the opposite gorge wall. The blue-blazed trail ends farther down on the towpath, allowing an easy 1.25-mile walk back to the visitor center.

Away from the water, the 4.2-mile **Gold Mine Loop** behind the visitor center winds through post oaks and river birches to the Maryland Mine. This little known outfit, now in ruins, operated from 1867 to 1939.

On the Virginia side of the falls, a short distance as the crow flies but about 12 miles by car, lies 800-acre **Great Falls Park.** Learn about local flora and fauna, kayaking and rock climbing at the **visitor center.** Nearby overlooks provide splendid views of the wide river. The popular, blue-blazed **River Trail** ambles downstream from here for about a mile and a half, edging the bluff high above Mather Gorge.

Here, too, you'll find the ruins of the **Patowmack Canal,** started by George Washington in 1786 and closed in 1830 after work on the C&O had begun; five locks raised or lowered boats the height of the falls. A 2.2-mile trail runs alongside the canal's shallow ditch, taking you past the ruins of **Matildaville,** a town that served the needs of the canal industry. ■

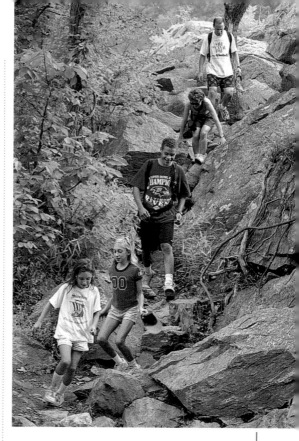

Great Falls Park
www.nps.gov/grfa

🗺 216 A5

✉ 9200 Old Dominion Dr., McLean, VA

☎ 703-285-2966

💲 $

Clambering along the Billy Goat Trail provides a chance to exercise and commune with nature.

Aircraft is displayed high and low at the Smithsonian National Air and Space Museum's new facility.

Steven F. Udvar-Hazy Center

www.nasm.si.edu/museum/udvarhazy

✉ 14390 Air & Space Museum Parkway, Chantilly, Va. (S. of main terminal at Dulles Airport, near Rtes. 28 & 50)

☎ 202-357-2700

💲 Parking, $$$; RT shuttle from downtown Air & Space musuem, $$

Steven F. Udvar-Hazy Center

THIS ANNEX OF THE NATIONAL AIR AND SPACE MUSEUM (see pp. 75–81), located near Washington Dulles International Airport in northern Virginia, was built to house additional aircraft and space artifacts too large and numerous to fit into the downtown building. But the splendid hangarlike facility, named the Steven F. Udvar-Hazy Center for its major donor, hardly plays second string to the more established museum when it comes to attractions.

The aviation hangar alone here is as long as three football fields and 10 stories high. Among the giant objects currently on display are the B-29 Superfortress *Enola Gay*, which dropped the first atomic bomb; a sleek, black SR-71 Blackbird reconnaissance aircraft, the fastest airplane in the world; and a supersonic Concord. The newly restored space shuttle Enterprise is a highlight of the adjacent space hangar.

Planning for the annex began in the early 1980s. In 1998, the Smithsonian and the Metropolitan Washington Airports Authority signed a long-term lease for the center's 176.5-acre site, which lies south of the Dulles airport's main terminal, in Chantilly, Virginia. The doors to the new 760,057-square-foot facility opened in December 2003, timed to coincide with the 100th anniversary of the Wright brothers' first powered flight.

There's been huge interest in this

them close up and view hanging aircraft from the elevated walkways.

Currently, more than **80 aircraft and dozens of space artifacts** are exhibited. The objects include engines, rockets, satellites, helicopters, airliners, ultra-lights, and experimental flying machines, many of them never shown before in a museum. The aircraft are grouped in categories on the basis of business, Cold War, commercial, military, sport, or general aviation use. A Dash 80 prototype of the Boeing 707 and the de Havilland Chipmunk aerobatic plane are just two examples of the many treasures.

The center continues adding artifacts to the displays; eventually more than 200 aircraft and 135 spacecraft will be on view. In the years ahead, it will also be possible to watch as specialists restore planes and spacecraft in the National Air and Space Museum's huge collection. In the past, this work has been done at the Paul E. Gerber Facility in Suitland, Maryland, but the operations will gradually be shifted to the site at Dulles as the new center expands.

Today, the Udvar-Hazy facility has an **observation tower** where you can watch overhead traffic at the Dulles airport. You can climb inside a **simulator** to experience the thrill felt by contemporary pilots, or, in **Space Walk 2004: 3-D,** take an orbital journey around the International Space Station *(fee)*. Other amenities include an **IMAX theater** *(fee)*, food services, and a museum store.

Outside, along an entryway to the building, is a **Wall of Honor** memorial bearing the names of tens of thousands of people who have contributed to aviation and space exploration. You might want to take a close look to see if you can find the name of someone you know. ∎

new museum and its exhibits, despite the out-of-the-way location. By June 2004, only six months after it opened, the center had already attracted a million visitors.

VISITING

A shuttle bus service *(fee)* runs several round trips a day between the National Air and Space Museum building on the Mall in Washington and the new annex in Virginia. The bus tickets are limited and sell out quickly, so it's best to purchase them by calling in advance *(202-633-4629)*. If you plan to arrive on your own by car, paid parking is available nearby.

Inside, all the artifacts are displayed on the floor or suspended from the ceiling, two levels high. The entrance area and lobby are on the second level. Pick up a map showing the relative location of all the objects; tour the floor to see

Potomac River plantations

Mount Vernon

www.mountvernon.org

🅰 217 B2

✉ S end of George
Washington Memorial
Pkwy., Mt. Vernon, VA

☎ 703-780-2000

💲 $$

IN THE 18TH AND EARLY 19TH CENTURIES, LANDOWNERS built magnificent plantation houses along the Potomac south of present-day Washington, D.C. Three—Mount Vernon, Woodlawn, and Gunston Hall—lie within easy reach of the city. A visit to any one of these mansions, each carefully preserved in period detail, immerses you in the early slaveholding aristocratic life.

MOUNT VERNON

The stately Georgian-style home of George Washington sits on 500 acres of smartly kept grounds overlooking the Potomac, about a half hour from Washington by car. This estate richly deserves its ranking as the country's second most visited historic home; only the White House (see pp. 108–113) edges it out.

George Washington moved to Mount Vernon, home of his elder half-brother Lawrence, when he was in his teens; he acquired the estate from Lawrence's widow in 1754 at the age of 22. As commander in chief of the Continental forces, Washington rarely saw his home between 1775 and 1783. He then spent the next six years farming, expanding the plantation to

nearly 8,000 acres. After serving as the country's first President (1789–97), he had only a couple of years left to enjoy his beloved home before his death.

The Mount Vernon Ladies' Association purchased the estate from a Washington relative in 1858 and continues to own and operate it. Both the Confederate and Union Armies considered the estate neutral ground during the Civil War.

Visiting

Pick up a map at the entrance gate and check the schedule for various free tours around the estate. You can also rent audio tour cassettes here. Plan on at least two hours to see everything.

The 30-acre main area includes

**Washington
enlarged Mount
Vernon—once
a modest 1.5-
story farm-
house—to its
present
appearance.**

the mansion, numerous outbuildings, formal flower and kitchen gardens, and woodlands. Most people head straight for the house, a white mansion looking somewhat like a huge red-roofed barn with symmetrical wings; the wood exterior has the look of stone—sand thrown onto wet paint does the trick. All the details pertaining to the appearance of the house—down to the exact color of the interiors—are authentic.

The crowd of visitors is usually large, and the line to enter forms at the servants' hall on the left. Inside, the house is a treasure. Many of the furnishings are original to the house, others 18th-century duplicates. You may tour at your own pace; docents offer a steady patter of information about each of the 12 rooms.

Each room provides an interesting glimpse into life at Mount Vernon. The large two-story green **dining room,** which appears much as it did in the Washingtons' lifetime, was used for many different functions so it held chairs and sideboards but formal tables were usually installed only when the family entertained.

Washington's study and personal sanctuary sits at the other end of the house. The personal artifacts, including a telescope, globe, and an 884-volume library, reflect his varied interests. A small staircase connects the study to the **master bedroom** on the second floor. This simply decorated bedroom contains the four-poster bed in which Washington died in 1799. After his death, his wife, Martha, could not bear to stay in the room—she moved to a room on the third floor.

Back on the first floor, before you step onto the piazza, take note of the framed key hanging on a wall in the passageway; it's the key to the Bastille's west portal, which the Marquis de Lafayette sent as a gift to Washington in 1790. The piazza, looking east over a lawn that sweeps down toward a deer park, offers a grand view of the Potomac River.

Return to the house's west side to explore the formal grounds and various outbuildings. The walled-in upper and lower gardens flank the long, rolling bowling green. Tall trees edge the green—Washington planted the two 130-foot-tall tulip poplars, along with a dozen or so others.

The **outbuildings** sit along the perimeter of the formal grounds. The smokehouse, kitchen, washhouse, servant's hall, and other buildings offer a look at what it took to run a large, profitable 18th-century estate. A nearby building houses the **George Washington Museum.** You'll find silver, china, jewelry, swords, and other family heirlooms here, including the Houdon bust. French sculptor J.A. Houdon made this likeness in 1785 from a plaster mold of Washington's face. The **Archaeology & Restoration Museum,** in the reconstructed greenhouse-slave quarters complex next door,

George Washington Museum

Archaeology & Restoration Museum

Mansion

Entrance

Upper Garden

MOUNT VERNON ESTATE & GARDENS

Woodlawn

www.woodlawn1805.org

216 B2

9000 Richmond Hwy. (US 1), 3 miles W of Mount Vernon

703-780-4000

Closed Jan.–Feb.

$$

displays unearthed artifacts that reveal details of daily life. Other exhibits explain the estate's building techniques and craftsmanship.

Next, circle around the fruit garden and nursery to the iron-gated brick tomb that holds the remains of George and Martha and other family

members. A nearby memorial marks the estate's slave burial ground.

Downhill from here you'll find the wharf. This restored version dates from the 1800s, replacing an earlier wharf that Washington used to transport his goods to Alexandria.

If you have time, stroll over to the **George Washington: Pioneer Farmer Site,** a 4-acre demonstration area. Costumed interpreters explain, in an appealing and comprehensible fashion, Washington's experimentation with various crops and techniques.

Dogue Run gristmill

George Washington built this gristmill in 1771 to grind corn and wheat into meal. He deeded it to his step-grand-daughter, Nelly Custis, in 1799 as part of her wedding gift. By 1850 the mill had ceased functioning. First reconstructed in the 1930s, it was inoperable until a recent renovation. A professional miller explains how water power is used to grind wheat into flour. The mill lies just off Va. 235, south of Woodlawn. ∎

WOODLAWN

George Washington gave Nelly Custis, his step-granddaughter, and Maj. Lawrence Lewis, his nephew, 2,000 acres of his estate in 1799 as their wedding present and asked William Thornton, first architect of the U.S. Capitol, to design a house for them. Thornton completed the late Georgian/early federal-era two-story mansion in 1805.

Wharf

**George Washington
Pioneer Farm Site**

**Fruit Garden
and Nursery**

Slave Memorial

Lower Garden

Typical of the period, the house is arranged symmetrically according to a five-part Palladian plan. There is no "front" or "back," rather two formal facades for approach by land or river.

The Lewis family and over 90 slaves lived on the estate for more than 40 years. The family sold the estate in 1846 to a Quaker community, which used the house as a nucleus for their growing abolitionist organization. The National Trust for Historic Preservation acquired the house and some of the land in 1951; the estate now comprises about 120 acres. The house is furnished much as it was during the Lewises' occupation, with some furnishings that the Lewises brought from Mount Vernon.

The refined **first-floor interior** includes a dining room, a family sitting room, and a parlor, where formal entertaining took place. The ceilings soar 13.5 feet high—the parlor excepted, which is a foot higher, in keeping with the grand

proportions of the space. The second floor is divided into four graciously appointed chambers. In honor of its first patron, Woodlawn's **main hall** features a bust of George Washington commissioned by Nelly Custis Lewis; it stands on a pedestal at 6 feet 2 inches, the general's actual height.

Outside in the **formal garden** bloom lilacs, azaleas, and roses. From the riverside portico you can make out the Potomac, although silting over the past two centuries has pushed the river back. On the eastern horizon, tall trees block your view of Mount Vernon.

Before leaving Woodlawn, you can also walk over to view the 1940 **Pope-Leighey House** *(703-780-4000, www.popeleighey1940.org)*. This Frank Lloyd Wright-designed house was moved here in 1964 from Falls Church, Virginia, to save it from destruction. The small, low-ceilinged, flat-roofed dwelling is a classic example of Wright's Usonian style.

GUNSTON HALL

Gunston Hall
www.gunstonhall.org
🏛 216 B1
✉ Lorton, VA, on Va.
242, 4 miles E of
US 1
☎ 703-550-9220
💲 $$

The farthest south of the three plantation houses, Gunston Hall anchors 550 magnificently lush acres, with tree-lined lanes, formal gardens, and farm animals. Its owner was Virginian George Mason (1725–1792), a lesser known but brilliant patriot and statesman.

Mason tried to quit public life after his wife's death in 1773, but the fledgling country would need him in the years ahead. Mason penned the 1776 Virginia Declaration of Rights, advocating religious tolerance and freedom of the press. Thomas Jefferson picked up, in some cases almost word for word, the same sentiments for the Declaration of Independence. Mason holds distinction as one of three delegates who refused to sign the Constitution in 1787. His passionate orations objecting that the Constitution gave the government too much power helped pave the way for the Bill of Rights.

Begin your tour at the **visitor center,** which holds several interesting exhibits, including family objects; a 12-minute film presents

Mason as a paradoxical man. Although an ardent supporter of human rights and intellectually opposed to slavery, Mason's 5,500 acres were tended by up to 90 slaves. He could not reconcile his desire to end slavery with a means to ensure the continued prosperity of his plantation.

Then head over to the two-story Georgian **brick house.** Designed in 1755 by indentured servant and soon-to-be-prominent architect William Buckland, each room has its own distinctive style. The Chinese-style formal parlor and the neoclassic, Palladian-style dining room, with arches and painstaking embellishments, are works of art. The rooms are furnished with family and period pieces.

In the **gardens,** a boxwood allée, likely dating from Mason's time, runs between formal plantings to the brow of a hill that provides a glimpse of the distant Potomac. You can take a 1-mile trail through coastal plain woods to the river, perhaps spotting deer, herons, and geese along the way. ■

A rudimentary curtsying lesson at Gunston Hall

Annapolis

YACHTS, MIDSHIPMEN IN CRISP UNIFORMS, STREETS LINED with colonial architecture, and restaurants serving world-famous crabcakes: The colorful port of Annapolis, less than an hour's drive east of Washington, offers big-time history in a small-town setting.

Puritans escaping persecution first settled at the strategic mouth of the Severn River, just off the Chesapeake Bay, in 1649. Named the Capital of the Proprietary of Maryland in 1694, the settlement grew to become one of the Colonies' most sophisticated towns by the eve of the American Revolution. As tobacco flowed out of its port, in flowed European luxuries to adorn beautiful Georgian homes and their elegant inhabitants.

Annapolis's political high point occurred between November 1783 and August 1784, when it served as the fledgling nation's working capital. After the capital was moved to Trenton, New Jersey, in 1784, however, the city dozed for two centuries.

The U.S. Naval Academy came in 1845, turning Annapolis into a sort of company town that catered to its guest institution. In the 1960s, interest in historic preservation brought about new life, as taverns, shops, restaurants, and museums moved into restored structures.

Today Annapolis showcases more than a dozen architectural styles spanning three centuries; some 1,300 buildings—all meticulously maintained—predate 1900. Much of the small city's charm owes to the fact that it preserves its 1695 radial street plan, which gives the highest elevations for the church (St. Anne's) and state (State House)—and offers many vistas of the picturesque waterfront. ■

Annapolis
🅰 217 E4
Visitor information
www.visit-annapolis.org
✉ Annapolis & Anne Arundel County Conference & Visitors Bureau, 26 West St.
☎ 410-280-0445

Ego Alley in the heart of Annapolis is the place to show off your yacht.

The Maryland State House (1779) anchors Annapolis's 18th-century downtown.

Walking around Annapolis

The narrow streets and brick sidewalks in the historic center of Annapolis will enchant you. Plan to spend at least half a day strolling around and visiting its sights. With limited street parking available, your best bet is to park in one of the garages near the visitor center.

Start your stroll at the friendly, information-packed **visitor center** ❶ *(Annapolis & Anne Arundel County Conference & Visitors Bureau, 26 West St., 410-280-0445)*. Just to the east, Church Circle features the Romanesque **St. Anne's Episcopal Church** ❷ *(410-267-9333)*, built in 1858–59 as the third church on this site. The church still uses the communion silver set sent by King William III in 1696. Standing at the intersection of Church Circle and Main Street, the venerable 1772 **Maryland Inn** *(410-263-2641)* features wood balconies and a posh, award-winning restaurant, the Treaty of Paris. Proceed six blocks down Main Street, attractively lined with two-story brick and wood buildings harboring boutiques, restaurants, galleries, and bars.

At end of the street awaits Market Space and its busy waterfront, the **City Dock** ❸. No longer a thriving working dock, it's still the heart of the city, bustling with cafés, shops, and restaurants. The number of yachts moored here year-round attests to Annapolis's standing as one of the East Coast's great sailing centers; visiting boaters often cruise down the narrow, alleylike waterway fronting the dock to show off their boats (hence its local name, Ego Alley). Stop by the dockside 1858 **Market House** for a sandwich and join a life-size bronze of *Roots* author Alex Haley by the water's edge, where he sits telling a story to a group of children on the same spot where his ancestor, Kunta Kinte, arrived in 1767 on a slave ship. For fancier dining, head across Market Space to **Middleton Tavern** *(Randall & Pinkney Sts., 410-263-3323)*, a cozy, dark-paneled establishment dating from 1750 that has welcomed the likes of George Washington, Thomas Jefferson, and Benjamin Franklin.

Just up Pinkney Street, step into the **Waterfront Warehouse** (ca 1815) and take a look at the scale model of the waterfront as it appeared in the 1700s. A few doors up, **Ship-lap House 4** (*18 Pinkney St.*) dates from 1715; an exhibit inside details the worldwide trade network of slaves, china, linens, and cotton operated by Nathan Hammond, who ran a dry goods store here from 1759 to 1773.

Now go back down Pinkney and turn left on Randall; in two blocks turn right for the gates to the **U.S. Naval Academy 5** (*410-263-6933*) and follow signs to the visitor center. Established in 1845, the academy is now a 338-acre, four-year coed college attended by 4,000 midshipmen. Flanking the tree-dotted central green to the southeast is the enormous

🅰	See area map pp. 216–17
▶	Visitor center
⬌	1.8 miles
🕓	4 hours
▶	Maryland State House

NOT TO BE MISSED
- City Dock
- U.S. Naval Academy Chapel
- Hammond-Harwood House

Sandy Point State Park

For a change of scenery, drive out to this Chesapeake Bay park *(9 miles E of Annapolis on US 50, 410-974-2149).* A sandy beach is great for swimming, as well as for views of the Bay Bridge and of freighters far out on the bay. Rowboats and motorboats are available for rent, and 5 miles of trails wind through woods and marshes. ∎

beaux arts **Bancroft Hall,** one of the world's largest dormitories. All of the midshipmen live and eat here. Step inside the palatial entrance hall to see paintings of historic sea battles. The nearby copper-domed **Navy Chapel** features a long, shiplike nave; don't miss the lavishly displayed marble tomb of Revolutionary War naval hero John Paul Jones in the chapel's crypt. Just to the northwest, Preble Hall houses the **Naval Academy Museum,** containing one of the world's finest collections of model warships. (Note: Visitors are allowed within the academy only on foot and must show a photo ID at the entrance gate.)

Back at the entrance gate turn northwest on King George Street, then southwest on Maryland Avenue. The 1774–75 **Hammond-Harwood House ❻** *(19 Maryland Ave., 410-269-1714, $$)* stands on the left, just beyond King George Street. This national historic landmark house was the last project of

The U.S. Naval Academy Band stays crisply in line and in tune.

architect William Buckland, once an indentured servant, who also designed Gunston Hall in Northern Virginia (see p. 226) and the interiors of the Chase-Lloyd House across the street. Many consider this house to be the finest example of Georgian architecture in colonial America. The furnishings date from the mid-18th and early 19th centuries.

Continue down Maryland Avenue to Prince George Street and turn left to the Georgian **William Paca House and Garden** *(186 Prince George St., 410-263-5553, $),* built in 1765. Paca was a signer of the Declaration of Independence and a three-term governor of Maryland. Inside and out, the house has been meticulously restored to its colonial appearance. Two acres of gardens have also been returned to their former glory, down to the terraced rose beds, brick canal, and Chinese Chippendale bridge.

Walking a block west on East Street brings you to State Circle, upon which sits the **Old Treasury Building** and the **Maryland State House ❼** *(State Circle, 410-974-3400).* Completed in 1779, the state house is the nation's oldest continuously used capitol building. Two events of national importance took place in its old Senate Chamber during the nine months when Annapolis served as the new country's working capital: George Washington resigned his commission as commander in chief of the Continental Army on Dec. 23, 1783, and, three weeks later, Congress ratified the Treaty of Paris, officially ending the Revolutionary War. Return to your starting point via School Street and Church Circle. ∎

Baltimore

ONLY AN HOUR AWAY, BALTIMORE SEEMS LIKE AN ALTO-gether different place than Washington, its brick buildings, puffing factories, older ethnic neighborhoods, and active ship traffic giving it more of a "real city" feel. But it also has its share of world-class museums, including the Baltimore Museum of Art and the Walters Art Museum. And the Inner Harbor, a showcase of urban revitalization, ranks as one of the East Coast's top tourist destinations.

Strategically placed at the mouth of the Patapsco River at Chesapeake Bay, the Inner Harbor has long been a major port for coal and grain. Also considered an urban eyesore, it was targeted for demolition and renewal as far back as 1963. Buildings began coming down in the late 1960s, and the first sky-scrapers appeared in the early '70s. Restaurants, tourist attractions, and Oriole Park at Camden Yards followed thereafter, contributing to the harbor's vitality.

A wide promenade lined with shops and restaurants edges the waterfront and offers a delightful stroll past the harbor's various museums. Water taxis will ferry you from sight to sight if you'd rather ride than walk.

On the harbor's north side, at Pier 3, the seven-story **National Aquarium** *(410-576-3800, $$$$)* is Baltimore's biggest tourist draw. Inside, bottlenose dolphins perform feats in a 1.2-million-gallon ocea-narium; an Atlantic coral reef teems with colorful tropical fish; and sharks and manta rays glide effort-lessly through a pool that you cross on bridges.

The submarine U.S.S. *Torsk* and the lightship *Chesapeake* are moored alongside the aquarium. They, along with the Coast Guard cutter *Taney* and Seven Foot Knoll Lighthouse on Pier 5, form the **Baltimore Maritime Museum** *(410-396-3453, $$)*. Exhibits aboard World War II veterans *Taney* and *Torsk* tell about U.S. naval history; the other two focus on local maritime history.

The last Civil War-era vessel still

Baltimore

🔼 217 D6

Visitor information

www.baltimore.org

✉ Baltimore Area Convention & Visitors Association, 100 Light St.

☎ 888-BALTIMORE

Led by the Inner Harbor, Baltimore has stepped into the limelight of urban revitalization.

The wonderful world of fish eyes at Baltimore's National Aquarium

Baltimore Museum of Art
www.artbma.org
✉ Corner of N. Charles & 31st Sts.
☎ 410-396-7100
🕐 Closed Mon.–Tues.
💲 $$

Walters Art Museum
www.thewalters.org
✉ 600 N. Charles St.
☎ 410-547-9000
🕐 Closed Mon.-Tues.
💲 $$

Fort McHenry National Monument and Historic Shrine
www.nps.gov/fomc
✉ End of E. Fort Ave.
☎ 410-962-4290
💲 $

afloat, the **U.S.S. Constellation** is moored at Pier 1 *(410-539-1797, $$)*. Climb aboard to learn about her many commissions. Launched in 1854, she has caught slave traders off the coast of Africa, blockaded ports during the Civil War, and served as a relief flagship of the U.S. Atlantic Fleet in World War II.

Walk past the cruise ship docks toward the harbor's south side and the **Maryland Science Center** *(601 Light St., 410-685-5225, $$$)*. You can easily spend half a day here exploring three floors of hands-on exhibits, seeing an IMAX film, and picking out constellations in the planetarium.

Located inland, on the harbor's north side, is the interactive **Port Discovery** *(35 Market Pl., 410-727-8120, $$$)*. Exhibits let you decipher hieroglyphics, create musical instruments, and make chewing gum; the highlight is a three-story "urban treehouse," in which kids climb and crawl like monkeys. Outside, ride in the swaying gondola of a helium balloon, anchored by a steel cable, and take in breathtaking city and harbor views.

Within a short driving distance of the harbor are a number of other sights. Impressionist lovers will not want to miss the Cone Collection—works by Henri Matisse, Pablo Picasso, and others—on display at the **Baltimore Museum of Art.** The fascinating **Walters Art Museum** offers a broad look at over 55 centuries of world art, including Roman sarcophagi, Asian ceramics, Old Master paintings, and art deco jewelry.

Fort McHenry sits southeast of the harbor. During the War of 1812, as American forces valiantly defended the fort against the British, a young lawyer named Francis Scott Key felt inspired to pen some words as he saw its flag still waving in the early dawn light; later, these words became our national anthem. A tour of this restored monument to American freedom is illuminating.

At the end of the day, consider a jaunt to historic **Fells Point,** where the city took root in the early 1700s. Located east of the Inner Harbor, this salty waterfront district's brick row houses, congenial pubs, and snug restaurants have an enduring charm. ■

Travelwise

**The soaring lines of Eero
Saarinen's Dulles
International Airport**

TRAVELWISE INFORMATION.

PLANNING YOUR TRIP

WHEN TO GO/ CLIMATE

Until well into the 20th century, Washington was, because of its reputation for heat and humidity, classified as a hardship post for British diplomats. It is true that July and August in the capital are frequently hot and steamy, but Washington has relatively brief winters and often long and lovely springs and falls. Rain is fairly evenly divided throughout the year (an average of 3.21 inches per month), but after-noon thunderstorms in June, July, and August make rain more likely during those months.

The busy season for tourism starts in April with school spring vacation, when busloads of schoolchildren visit the museums, monuments, and U.S. Capitol. Spring is also the time of the annual cherry blossoms display around the Tidal Basin, and when the blossoms are at their peak, the area around the monuments is packed with sightseers. Summer, despite the heat, is family vacation time.

The average high and low temperatures are as follows:

January—42°F/26°F
February—45°F/29°F
March—56°F/37°F
April—66°F/46°F
May—76°F/56°F
June—84°F/66°F
July—88°F/71°F
August—86°F/70°F
September—80°F/62°F
October—69°F/50°F
November—58°F/41°F
December—47°F/31°F

WHAT TO BRING

Heavy winter coats are usually essential only in December, January, and February, but a light coat or jacket can come in handy in the cooler spring or fall months. Government buildings and museums have miles of cor-ridors with marble floors—com-fortable shoes are a good idea.

TRAVELING TO WASHINGTON, D.C.

BY PLANE

Washington is served by three major airports: **Ronald Reagan Washington National Air-port** (DCA), in Virginia about 4 miles from the city center; **Washington Dulles Interna-tional Airport** (IAD), 26 miles west of Washington; and **Baltimore/Washington International Airport** (BWI), about 25 miles northeast of Washington.

Ronald Reagan Washington National Airport is the closest to the city and the most con-venient to reach, because Washington's state-of-the-art Metro system has a station located there, adjacent to ter-minals B and C. (A shuttle bus connects terminal A to the Metro station.) Taxi fare to downtown Washington is about $12. Reagan National is also served by SuperShuttle, which picks up from and delivers passengers to their homes, hotels, and offices. Call 800/BLUEVAN or 202/296-6662 for reservations.

Dulles International Airport is served by its own Washington Flyer taxi fleet, which provides 24-hour service to and from the airport. For information, call 703/661-6655. Taxi fare to down-town Washington is approxi-mately $50 to $55. Washington Flyer also operates a coach service (703/572-8400) connect-ing Dulles to the West Falls Church Metro station. An express bus, operated by the Washington Metropolitan Area Transit Authority, connects Dulles to L'Enfant Plaza down-town. For information call 202/637-7000. SuperShuttle, which operates on a shared ride-on-demand basis, also serves the airport (800/BLUEVAN).

BWI Airport is served by SuperShuttle (800/BLUEVAN), by taxi 410/859-1102 (about $55 to downtown Washington), or by train. Both MARC's Penn Line (800/325-RAIL) and Amtrak (800/872-7245) provide frequent service between Union Station in downtown Washington and BWI's own rail station; a free shuttlebus connects the station and the airport terminal. (MARC runs only during rush hours but is much cheaper than Amtrak.)

AIRPORT INFORMATION

For airport information (not information about specific flights), for Reagan National airport, call 703/417-8000; for Dulles airport, 703/572-2700; and for Baltimore/Washington airport, 410/859-7100.

AIRLINES

The Washington, D.C., metropolitan area is served by the following airlines. They fly into DCA, IAD, and BWI unless otherwise indicated.
Aeroflot 888/340-6000, www.aeroflot.com (IAD only)
Air Canada 888/247-2262, www.aircanada.com
Air France 800/321-4538, www.airfrance.com
Air Tran 800/247-8726, www.airtran.com
Alaska Airlines 800/252-7522, www.alaskaair.com (DCA & IAD only)
America West Airlines 800/235-9292, www.americawest.com (DCA & BWI only)
American Airlines 800/433-7300, www.aa.com
American Trans Air 800/435-9282, www.ata.com (DCA only)

ANA 800/235-9262, www.fly-ana.com (IAD only)

Atlantic Coast Airlines 800/241-6522 www.atlanticcoast.com (IAD only)

British Airways 800/247-9297, www.britishairways.com (IAD & BWI only)

Continental 800/525-0280, www.continental.com

Delta Air Lines 800/221-1212, www.delta.com

Frontier Airlines 800/432-1359, www.fly frontier.com

Icelandair 800/223-5500, www.icelandair.com (BWI only)

Independence Air 800/359-3594 www.flyi.com (IAD only)

JetBlue Airways 800/538-2583, www.jetblue airways.com (IAD only)

KLM 800/225-2525, www.klm.com (IAD only)

Korean Air 800/438-5000, www.koreanair.com (IAD only)

Lufthansa 800/645-3880, www.lufthansa.com (IAD only)

Midwest Express 800/452-2022 www.midwestexpress.com (DCA & IAD)

Northwest Airlines 800/225-2525, www.nwa.com

SAS 800/221-2350, www.scandinavian.net (IAD only)

Southwest Airlines 800/435-9792, www.southwest.com (BWI only)

Spirit Airlines 800/772-7117 www.spiritair.com (DCA only)

Swiss 877/359-7947, www.swiss.com (IAD only)

Ted 800/225-5833, www.flyted.com

United Airlines 800/241-6522, www.ual.com

US Airways 800/428-4322, www.usairways.com

Virgin Atlantic 800/862-8621, www.virgin atlantic.com (IAD only)

BY TRAIN

Amtrak (800/872-7245) trains arrive at Washington's spectacu-larly refurbished Union Station on Capitol Hill. The station, with shops, restaurants, and a downstairs food court, is worth a visit for its own sake.

Although locals use the train mostly as a fast, convenient way to get to New York on the Acela and Metroliner trains, Washington is a major rail hub, and it is connected by train to most U.S. destinations with rail service.

The Metro station at Union Station provides easy access to the rest of the city. The taxi stand at the station sometimes has long lines, and riders are frequently expected to share cabs with others going to nearby destinations.

GETTING AROUND

BY PUBLIC TRANSPORTATION

METRO

The Washington Metropolitan Area Transit Authority operates the bus and subway systems in the metropolitan area. The impressively clean and efficient system was designed primarily to enable commuters to travel easily to the downtown area. Metrorail stations are marked by large brown columns with colored stripes that indicate the lines served by the station.

Metro farecards are purchased at vending machines in the stations. The minimum fare is $1.35, the maximum is $3.90, based on the distance traveled and time of day. Fare information is available near the ticket machines. Metrorail opens at 5:30 a.m. on weekdays and 7 a.m. on weekends. It closes at midnight Sunday through Thursday. On Friday and Saturday nights, it runs until 3 a.m.

Route information: Call 202/637-7000 or log onto www.metroopensdoors.com

METRO TIPS

Plan your trip before arriving at the station by visiting www.metroopen doors.com.

The farecard machines bear step-by-step illustrated explanations of how to buy a farecard. New Metro patrons can even push a button—designed primarily for the vision impaired—to hear the purchase instructions.

Ask the station manager (usually posted in the glass kiosk near the farecard machines) for help if you continue to have difficulty purchasing a card.

Carry plenty of one-dollar bills for the farecard machines. If not, you will likely be saddled with a Vegas-style payoff, since the machines give change—up to $6.25—in quarters only.

If making numerous trips after 9:30 a.m., consider buying a One Day Pass—at $6.50 an excellent bargain.

On the escalators, stand right, walk left. Otherwise you risk being trampled by others in a hurry.

If traveling in a group, designate one person to buy the farecards (one per rider) for the entire group; that way only one person needs to learn how to operate the station's farecard machine.

BUS

Metrobus service covers the city and the suburbs, with some lines running 24 hours. The fare for any destination within Washington is $1.25. Exact fare is required. Drivers do not make change. For route and fare information, call 202/637-7000.

BY TAXICAB

Washington's taxi fleet may not be the most modern in the country, and the fares are determined by a mysterious—to visitors and sometimes to locals as well—zone system, but cabs are plentiful and fairly inexpensive. It's usually possible to hail a cab on major streets.

The fare is $5 in the central zone, which covers the downtown from the Capitol on the east to 23rd Street on the west. There are frequent surcharges—$1.50 for each extra passenger, $1 for rush hour, $1.25 for an airport pickup. The driver may pick up extra passengers if it does not take the original passenger more than five blocks out of his or her way.

BY CAR

Visitors should consider the possibility that a car will be more an annoyance than a convenience. Parking is difficult, parking garages are expensive, and the most efficient branch of the city government is the one that gives parking tickets.

Should you find on-street parking, check the signs, since many streets become no parking zones during rush hour. If your car is not where you left it, call 202/541-6074 for information on its location.

Some streets are two-way most of the time, but during rush hour become one-way—including Rock Creek and Potomac Parkway and 17th Street, N.W.

CAR RENTALS

All three airports are served by the following national car rental companies:

Alamo	800/327-9633
Avis	800/831-2847
Budget	800/527-0700
Dollar	800/800-4000
Enterprise	800/325-8007
Hertz	800/654-3131

National	800/227-7368
Thrifty	800/847-4389

BY TOUR

Old Town Trolley Tours, 202/832-9800. This two-hour tour allows you to visit monuments and museums at your own pace, by simply getting off the bus to see what you want for as long as you want, and reboarding at will.

Tourmobile, 202/554-5100. Narrated shuttlebus tours of major monuments, museums, and attractions. You can get off the bus to visit any of these, and simply get on the next bus when it comes along.

DC Ducks: The Boats On Wheels, 202/832-9800. DC Ducks' amphibious vehicles allow you to tour the Mall by land, then splash into the Potomac River on the boats with wheels. Fully narrated 90-minute tours depart regularly 10 a.m.–4 p.m. from Union Station.

More tours: For specialty tours, please see pp. 263-64.

NEGOTIATING THE CITY

When seeking a site, first check the quadrant address, which indicates where it lies vis-a-vis the Capitol. Are you looking for N.W., N.E., S.W., or S.E.? The city is laid out in these four quadrants, with the Capitol building in the center. North Capitol, South Capitol, and East Capitol Streets radiate from this nucleus, separating the quadrants (the Mall runs west from the Capitol building).

Beware that many addresses can be found in more than one quadrant, and therefore are not the same place (for instance, there is a 400 M St. in N.E., S.E., S.W., and N.W.).

After locating the quadrant, note that there are three types of streets in Washington. First are the numbered streets—those that run in a north–south direction from the Capitol. First Street, for instance, is located one block east or west of North or South Capitol Street, respectively.

The second street type is the lettered or named streets laid out in an east–west direction. Starting from East Capitol Street or the Mall, the streets run through the alphabet (with the exceptions of J, X, and Z). The ones nearest the Capitol are one-syllable words; when the alphabet has been run through, they become two syllables, then three. As such, you can tell how far a certain street is from the Capitol by the letter with which it begins and how many syllables it contains.

Finally, the avenues that are named after states run diagonally across the grid.

PRACTICAL ADVICE

COMMUNICATIONS

NEWSPAPERS

Washington, D.C., is a city of news. Most national and international news agencies have Washington bureaus. The Washington-based daily newspapers are the *Washington Post* and the *Washington Times.*

For upcoming local events, check the Weekend section of the *Washington Post,* published on Fridays, and the Washington Weekend section of the *Washington Times.* Both provide excellent suggestions for making plans. Also of interest is the free weekly publication, the *Wash-ington CityPaper,* published on Thursdays. It provides an up-to-date listing of what's happening in the clubs and theaters around town.

RADIO

WTOP (AM 1500) News, traffic

WXTR (AM 820) All news

WKDV (AM 1460) Asian

WDCT (AM 1310) Korean

WACA (AM 1540) Spanish

WAMU (FM 88.5) National Public Radio

WPFW (89.3) Pacifica, non-commercial jazz

WCSP (FM 90.1) CSPAN/Public Affairs

WETA (FM 90.9) National Public Radio

WKYS (FM 93.9) Urban

WARW (FM 94.7) Classic rock

WASH (FM 97.1) Soft rock

WMZQ (FM 98.7) Country

WIHT (FM 99.5) Top 40

WBIG (FM 100.3) Oldies

WGMS (FM 103.5) Classical

WJZW (FM 105.9) Pop, jazz

TELEPHONE

Local and long-distance information, 411
Toll-free directory information, 800/555-1212
Public telephones are located in all hotels, at tourist attractions and other public places, at most restaurants, and along some city streets. Local calls cost 50 cents. Long-distance calls are easier and cheaper if you use your home carrier's telephone calling card or purchase a prepaid calling card (available at post offices and larger drug-stores).

Area codes: The area code of Washington, D.C., is 202; for Maryland it's 301; and for Northern Virginia it's 703. For all Virginia calls, even local, you must always dial the area code with the number.

CRIME

Washington has a reputation as a dangerous city, but crimes of all sorts have been on the decrease in the last few years. Reduce your risk by following a few common-sense rules:

Don't wander onto deserted or ill-lighted streets or parks, particularly at night. If a neighborhood looks dangerous, it probably is. Stay with the crowds. There's safety in numbers.

If someone tries to rob you, give the robber whatever he or she asks. Your life is more valuable than your belongings.

Keep your wallet in a front trouser pocket—they're less vulnerable to pickpockets than rear pockets or breast pockets. Women should keep their purses close and not wear expensive jewelry. Don't carry large amounts of cash. Leave credit cards you don't plan to use at home.

Don't leave valuables in your car. The trunk is more secure than the space under the seats.

MONEY MATTERS

ATM LOCATIONS

Cirrus, 800/424-7787
Plus, 800/843-7587

Banks and automatic tellers (ATMs) are located throughout the city, and most major attractions and shopping centers also have them. Check with your home bank to find out which system accepts your card. Credit cards, debit cards, and traveler's checks are accepted almost everywhere; make sure you have an official I.D. on you as some places require it before you can make a transaction.

NATIONAL HOLIDAYS

New Year's Day; Martin Luther King, Jr., Day (3rd Mon. in Jan.); President's Day (3rd Mon. in Feb.); Easter Sunday; Memorial Day (last Mon. in May); Fourth of July; Labor Day (1st Mon. in Sept.); Thanksgiving Day (4th Thurs. in Nov.); Christmas Day.

PLACES OF WORSHIP

The citizens and churches in Washington welcome people of all faiths and practices. With more than 2,000 established churches in the area, you will be able to find a service of your choice. Check with your hotel concierge or the local yellow pages for a listing of times and locations. The *Washington Post* and *Washington Times* also publish listings of services in the religion sections in their Saturday editions.

SALES TAX

The price tags are misleading. Taxes will increase your hotel bill by 14.5 percent, restaurant bill by 10 percent, and rental car bill by 10 percent.

SECURITY

Security has become a major issue in many places worldwide, but is especially a concern in and around Washington's public areas and main buildings. Sreets sometimes close with or without notice, and may be blocked by concrete barriers.

Government buildings are generally open to the public, but they may close for security reasons with little or no notice. Be flexible, and call ahead.

Metal detectors are standard equipment in most public buildings. Be prepared for searches. If you have a pacemaker or other medical device that might be affected, let the guards know. And do not carry anything that could be considered a weapon and might be confiscated—e.g. Grandpa's pocketknife.

TIPPING

Leave at least 15 percent of the bill at restaurants (20 percent at upscale places). Taxi drivers should receive 10-15 percent, bartenders 10 percent, hairdressers 15 percent, porters at least a dollar a bag, valet parking attendees $2 or more, parking attendees $2 or more, and doormen a couple of dollars every time they whistle you a cab. Tip the hotel concierge or restaurant maitre d' at your discretion, depending upon services performed.

TRAVELERS WITH DISABILITIES

Washington is a very accessible city for travelers with disabilities. The Washington, D.C. Convention & Tourism Corporation (www.washington.org) publishes a fact sheet detailing general accessibility of Washington hotels, restaurants, shopping malls, and attractions. For a free copy, call 800/422-8644.

The Washington Metropolitan Area Transit Authority also publishes a free pamphlet on Metro's bus and rail system accessibility for the elderly and physically disabled. Call 301-562-5360 to order the guide, or visit the Metro's Web site at www.metroopensdoors.com.

Smithsonian museum buildings are accessible to wheelchair visitors. A comprehensive free publication called "Smithsonian Access" lists all services available to visitors with disabilities, including parking, building access, sign language interpreters, and more. To obtain a copy, call 202/357-2700.

VISITOR INFORMATION

The best source of visitor information is the **Washington, D.C. Visitor Information Center,** located in the Ronald Reagan International Trade Center at 1300 Pennsylvania Ave., N.W. (202/328-4748; www.dcvisit.com). Here you can obtain tickets, tour information, and maps. For details on events, pick up the weekly *Washington CityPaper,* free at cafés, restaurants, and bookstores.

EMERGENCIES & HEALTH CARE

USEFUL NUMBERS

- Emergencies (police/fire/ambulance) 911
- Washington, D.C., Police (non-emergency) 202/737-4404
- Metro Transit Police (emergency) 202/962-2121
- U.S. Park Police (emergency) 202/619-7300
- Travelers Aid 202/371-1937
- International Visitors Information Desk (offers multilingual information and assistance; located at Dulles) 703/572-2536

LOST CREDIT CARDS

American Express, 800/327-2177
Diners Club, 800/234-6377
Discover Card, 800/347-2683
MasterCard, 800/307-7309
Visa, 800/847-2911

ANNUAL EVENTS

JANUARY
Martin Luther King Jr.'s Birthday Mid-January. Lincoln Memorial, 202/619-7222. A military color guard salute at the site where King delivered his famous "I have a dream" speech.

Presidential Inauguration January 20, every fourth year. After the swearing-in on the Capitol steps, a parade follows down Pennsylvania Avenue to the White House.

FEBRUARY
Chinese New Year Parade 202/638-1041. Late January or early February, depending on the moon. Chinatown, H St., N.W., between 5th and 8th Sts. Colorful parade with firecrackers and dragons.

Abraham Lincoln's Birthday February 12. Lincoln Memorial, 202/619-7222. A reading of the Gettysburg Address and a wreath-laying ceremony at the memorial.

George Washington's Birthday February 22. Wreath-laying ceremonies at Mount Vernon (703/780-2000) and at the Washington Monument (202/619-7222).

MARCH
Smithsonian Kite Festival Late March or early April. 202/357-2700, http://kitefestival.org. Professional and amateur kitemakers and kite flyers compete for prizes at a contest on the Washington Monument grounds.

APRIL
National Cherry Blossom Festival Late March or early April. 202/547-1500. The annual display of blossoms around the Tidal Basin doesn't always coincide with the festival, but the city celebrates with two weeks of performances, exhibitions, and activities. The Cherry Blossom Parade is usually held on the first Saturday in April. For up-to-date information on when the blossoms will peak, consult the National Park Service at www.nps.gov/nacc/cherry.

Filmfest DC 202/724-5613, www.filmfestdc.org. Two weeks of international and American films, shown at local theaters and other auditoriums.

White House Easter Egg Roll Monday after Easter. 202/456-7041. This annual event dates back to 1878 during the Rutherford B. Hayes Administration. Children, ages three to six, have a chance to play on the South Lawn of the White House. The event includes storytelling, music, and costumed characters.

White House Spring Garden and House Tour April. 202/456-7041. A chance to tour the lovely spring gardens of the White House's South Lawn.

MAY
Georgetown Garden Day 2nd Sat. in May. 202/965-1950,

ANNUAL EVENTS/FURTHER READING

www.gtowngarden.org. A chance to visit the private gardens of some beautiful, historic homes.

Evening Parade Friday nights, May–Aug. U. S. Marine Barracks, 8th and I Sts., S.E., 202/433-6060. The evening begins with a concert by the United States Marine Band, followed by a demonstration of precision marching by Marine Drum and Bugle Corps, and the Marine Corps Silent Drill Platoon.

Memorial Day Celebrations Events on Memorial Day weekend include ceremonies at the Vietnam Veteran's Memorial (703/697-2131), the Tomb of the Unknowns at Arlington National Cemetery (703/607-8052), usually with an address by the President, and a concert by the National Symphony Orchestra on the West Lawn of the Capitol (202/619-7222).

Washington National Cathedral Flower Mart Early May. Massachusetts and Wisconsin Aves., N.W., 202/537-6200. An annual flower and crafts show and sale on the cathedral grounds.

JUNE
Dupont-Kalorama Museum Walk Weekend 1st weekend in June. Dupont Circle neighborhood, 202/667-0441, www.dkmuseums.com. Visit museums and enjoy textile-weaving demonstrations, interactive tours, hands-on workshops, and concerts.

Capital Pride Festival Along Pennsylvania Ave. between 3rd and 9th Sts., N.W., 202/797-3510. A week-long celebration of the area's gay, lesbian, bisexual, and transgender residents, culminating in a parade through Washington and a festival on Pennsylvania Ave., N.W.

JULY
Smithsonian Folklife Festival Late June/early July. On the Mall, 202/357-2700. An annual two-week celebration of folk cultures, American and foreign, with music, food, and handicraft demonstrations.

Fourth of July Celebrations The National Independence Day Parade takes place at 11:45 a.m. on Constitution Ave. between 7th and 17th Sts., N.W. The National Symphony Orchestra, with guest stars and soloists, performs at 8 p.m. on the West Lawn of the Capitol.

Fourth of July fireworks The show starts about 9:10 p.m. over the Washington Monument grounds (202/619-7222).

AUGUST
Virginia Wine Festival Mid-Aug. weekend. Long Branch Estate, Millwood, Va. 888/453-9746. A chance to sample the wares of Virginia's emerging wine industry with music, food, and entertainment.

SEPTEMBER
Labor Day Concert 202/619-7222. The National Symphony Orchestra closes its summer season with a concert on the West Lawn of the Capitol.

Kalorama House and Embassy Tour 202/387-4062. Get inside looks at some of the mansions and stately homes in this distinguished neighborhood.

Washington National Cathedral Open House Massachusetts and Wisconsin Aves., N.W., 202/537-6200. Washington National Cathedral holds its annual open house, with special tours, tower climbs, and entertainment.

OCTOBER
Taste of D.C. Festival 202/789-7002. 2nd weekend in Oct. Pennsylvania Ave., N.W., between 7th and 14th Sts. Outdoor stages with live entertainment and food from many area restaurants are featured at this festival. Admission is free, but there's a charge for food tastings.

Marine Corps Marathon 800/786-8762, www.marinemarathon.com. Thousands of runners take part in this annual marathon. It starts at 8:30 at the Iwo Jima memorial in Arlington and follows a course in Washington past monuments on the Mall.

NOVEMBER
Washington Craft Show Mid-Nov. Washington Convention Center, 203/254-0486. A juried show of American crafts, including basketry, ceramics, fiber decorative and wearables, furniture, glass, jewelry, leather, metal, mixed media, paper, and wood.

DECEMBER
Pageant of Peace/Lighting of the National Christmas Tree On the Ellipse south of the White House, 202/619-7222. The official kickoff of the Christmas season in Washington, with concerts and a Christmas tree from each of the states.

Washington National Cathedral Christmas Services Massachusetts and Wisconsin Aves., N.W., 202/537-6200. Christmas Eve services at 6 p.m. and 10 p.m. Passes are required.

FURTHER READING

The best book on Washington architecture is E. J. Applewhite's *Washington Itself*. Applewhite, a former CIA officer, has a keen eye for buildings and an ear for the details of history that make his opinions come alive.

To learn where famous and not-so-famous events happened throughout the city, pick up a copy of *On the Spot: Pinpointing the Past in Washington, D.C.* (Douglas E. Evelyn and Paul Dickson, 1999).

Fiction lovers should check out one of Margaret Truman's many murder mysteries set in and around Washington, D.C.

HOTELS & RESTAURANTS

HOTELS & RESTAURANTS

Where you sleep and eat can make all the difference between a good visit and bad. Washington offers a panoply of hotel and restaurant selections in all price categories and styles—something for every taste.

HOTELS

Washington hotels vary from the luxurious and expensive—the Four Seasons in Georgetown and the new Ritz-Carlton in the West End being good examples—to the basic and still fairly expensive—the large downtown hotels that cater mostly to the convention and meeting trade. Small and charming is harder to find, but the new boutique hotels being opened by the Kempton Group in Washington—Topaz is the first of them and more will follow—are a hopeful sign.

Because every major business in the country is affected by government legislation and regulations, Washington hotels cater to business travelers on expense accounts. That means high prices during the week, when businesses are paying the tab, but it also means weekend bargains for the leisure and family traveler. Similarly, prices are higher in the winter, when Congress is in session, and lower in the summer, when much of official Washington takes vacation time and flees the city for cooler climes.

Because hotels in the city are expensive, many visitors prefer to stay in less expensive places in suburban Virginia and travel into the city each day. It's always worth asking a hotel "Is this the best rate you can give me?"

Many hotels routinely offer rates cheaper than their posted rack rates, and many offer discounts through organizations such as AAA or AARP. All know that a room rented for a discounted price is income, but an unrented room is income lost forever.

RESTAURANTS

For many years, Washington was thought to hold little interest as a restaurant city. It's a city obsessed by power, the popular wisdom had it, and people cared more about whom they were eating with than what they were eating. Well, things have changed in the last decade. There's still plenty of meat-and-potatoes power dining—the late '90s and the first year of the new century saw an unprecedented number of steakhouses opening in the city and the suburbs. But a number of distinguished chefs running national-class restaurants now make Washington their home. Roberto Donna at Galileo, Michel Richard at Citronelle, and Gerard Pangaud at Gerard's Place are at the top of the class, but their students, many of whom have stayed in Washington and opened their own restaurants, continue to enrich Washington dining.

In addition to this wonderful but pricey dining, the Washington area has long been an attractive place for exiles from their own countries to locate, and they have brought their food with them. It is said that any upheaval in a foreign country enriches Washington dining. Refugees from Vietnam opened fine restaurants in the Virginia suburbs, particularly in the area surrounding the Clarendon Metro station. Washington has more Ethiopian restaurants than any other city in the country. Thailand, India, Pakistan, Laos, and Malaysia have all given the city fine restaurants.

Unless otherwise noted, all restaurants are air-conditioned and offer non-smoking seating. All restaurants are open daily unless indicated otherwise.

PRICES

HOTELS
An indication of the cost of a double room in high season, excluding tax, is given by **$** signs.

$$$$$	$225+
$$$$	$175–$225
$$$	$125–$175
$$	$85–$125
$	Under $85

RESTAURANTS
An indication of the cost of a three-course dinner without drinks, tax, or tip is given by $ signs.

$$$$	Over $50
$$$	$35–$50
$$	$15–$35
$	Under $15

L=lunch
D=dinner

CREDIT CARDS
Many hotels and restaurants accept all major credit cards. Smaller ones may accept some or none, as shown in their entry. Abbreviations used are: AE American Express, D Discover, DC Diners Club, MC MasterCard, and V Visa.

ORGANIZATION
Hotels and restaurants are listed first by chapter area, then by price category, then alphabetically.

Hotel restaurants of note have been bolded in the hotel entries and indicated by a restaurant icon beneath the hotel icon (if they're unusually special, they are treated in a separate entry within the restaurant section).

HOTELS & RESTAURANTS

CAPITOL HILL

HOTELS

THE HOTEL GEORGE
$$$$–$$$$$
15 E ST., N.W.
TEL 202/347-4200 OR
800/576-8331
FAX 202/347-0359
A completely renovated
building originally built in
1928, the George is convenient to Capitol Hill offices
and attractions. The decor
is striking and modern. The
restaurant **Bistro Bis** (see
below) offers quality updated
French bistro fare. Around-
the-clock cigar-friendly
Billiard Room.
🛏 139 🅿 🚾 🌊 AE, D,
DC, MC, V 🚇 Union Station

HYATT REGENCY
WASHINGTON ON
CAPITOL HILL
$$$–$$$$
400 NEW JERSEY AVE., N.W.
TEL 202/737-1234
FAX 202/737-5773
This large convention hotel
occupies a full city block on
Capitol Hill. The Hyatt
Regency has two in-house
restaurants with a wide
range of American cuisine.
The rooftop **Capitol View
Club** overlooks the U.S.
Capitol and Senate Office
Buildings. The hotel is cen-
trally located to offer access
to museums, monuments,
and government buildings.
🛏 834 🅿 🏊 🚾 🌊 AE,
D, DC, MC, V 🚇 Union
Station

PHOENIX PARK
HOTEL
$$$–$$$$$
520 N. CAPITOL ST., N.W.
TEL 202/638-6900 OR
800/824-5419
FAX 202/393-3236
Named after the park in
Dublin, the Phoenix Park
calls itself "America's center
of Irish hospitality." The
adjoining **Dubliner Pub**
offers good pub cooking and

Irish entertainment.
🛏 150 🅿 🚾 🌊 AE, D,
DC, MC, V 🚇 Union Station

CAPITOL HILL SUITES
$$$
200 C ST., S.E.
TEL 202/543-6000
FAX 202/547-2608
Tucked behind the Library
of Congress on the House
side of the hill, Capitol Hill
Suites offers kitchenettes in
every suite. The hotel was
refurbished in 2000.
🛏 152 🅿 🌊 AE, D, DC,
MC, V 🚇 Union Station,
South Capitol

WASHINGTON COURT
HOTEL
$$–$$$$
525 NEW JERSEY AVE., N.W.
TEL 202/628-2100
FAX 202/ 879 7938
The Washington Court has
a dramatic four-story atrium
lobby with leather furniture
and luxuriant plant life.
The **Cafe and Grill
Restaurant** offers American
cuisine. Billiards and cigars
offered in the Club Room.
🛏 264 🅿 🚾 🌊 AE, D,
DC, MC, V 🚇 Union Station

HOLIDAY INN
WASHINGTON,
D.C. ON THE HILL
$$–$$$
415 NEW JERSEY AVE., N.W.
TEL 202/638-1616
OR 800/638-1116
FAX 202/638-0707
A newly remodeled hotel
with modern decor and
well-appointed guest rooms.
The hotel's **Senators
Grille**, with a huge lineup of
TV sets, is one of the largest
sports bars in Washington.
🛏 343 🏊 🚾 🌊 AE, D,
DC, MC, V 🚇 Union Station

RESTAURANTS

B. SMITH'S
$$$
UNION STATION, 50
MASSACHUSETTS AVE., N.E.
TEL 202/289-6188

This gracious restaurant,
owned by former super-
model B. Smith, occupies
the former presidential
reception room at Union
Station, perhaps the grandest
dining room in Washington.
Chef James Oakley's menu
is a combination of tradi-
tional Southern, New
Orleans-style, and Mid-
atlantic seafood dishes.
🍴 268 🅿 In rear of station
🌊 AE, D, DC, MC, V
🚇 Union Station

BISTRO BIS
$$$
THE HOTEL GEORGE,
15 E ST., N.W.
TEL 202/661-2700
Chef owner Jeffrey Buben
serves traditional bistro fare
and intelligently updated ver-
sions of it in this sleek, modern Capitol Hill hangout that
is a favorite of many who
work and do business in the
neighborhood. Start with a
galette of chevre, rabbit, and
potato, and for a main
course try the perfect
braised veal stew. The
restaurant's hallmark pastry
desserts are a treat.
🍴 115 🅿 🌊 AE, D, DC,
MC, V 🚇 Union Station

LA COLLINE
$$$
400 N. CAPITOL ST., N.W.
TEL 202/737-0400
Traditional without being
stuffy, La Colline is the kind
of French restaurant that
makes you remember why
French cooking was the
cuisine most responsible for
the current boom in dining
out. The coarse, country-
style pâté is a good starter.
And there's no better place
in town to have a plate of
tripes á la mode de Caen, but
if that's a bit too exotic,
there's always a terrific steak
frites.
🍴 270 🕐 Closed Sun.
🌊 AE, DC, MC, V 🚇 Union
Station

🍴 DUBLINER
$$

520 N. CAPITOL, N.W.
TEL 202/737-3773

There are many things to eat at this lively Irish pub—fish and chips, shepherd's pie, even a burger—but the only thing to drink, particularly if you're Irish, is Guinness on tap, or maybe Irish whiskey. It all goes well with the Irish entertainment, every night after 9 p.m.

🔲 136 ⬥ AE, DC, MC, V 🚇 Union Station

🍴 THE MONOCLE
$$

107 D ST., N.E.
TEL 202/546-4488

Its position as the closest restaurant to the Senate side of the Capitol means that there's no better place in town for sighting politicos, either eating a meal or arriving for one of the frequent political fundraisers in the private rooms upstairs. Run by the Valonos family for 40 years, the Monocle serves an all-American menu of burgers, steaks, and seafood.

🔲 110 🕐 Closed Sat.–Sun. ⬥ AE, DC, MC, V 🚇 Union Station

🍴 TWO QUAIL
$$

320 MASSACHUSETTS AVE., N.E.
TEL 202/543-8030

A quirky but romantic place located in three town houses near Union Station, Two Quail draws its flea-market decor and its menu from eclectic sources. The cooking is basically Modern American—portobello mushrooms or duck and orange salad to start, pasta and grilled meats for main courses.

🔲 80 🕐 Closed all Sat., & Sun. L ⬥ AE, DC, MC, V 🚇 Union Station

🍴 BANANA CAFÉ
$

500 8TH ST., S.E.
TEL 202/543-5906

This cheap and cheerful Mexican and Cuban restaurant has a bar and dining room on the main level and a piano bar above. You can order from a small selection of tapas to start, but the really interesting part of this menu is the Cuban specialties—*ropa vieja* (shredded flank steak cooked with tomato and spices), *carnitas Cubanas* (pork roasted with bitter oranges), and stuffed plantains. Don't miss the mango margaritas, a house specialty. Piano bar on Saturday evenings.

🔲 100 ⬥ AE, D, DC, MC, V 🚇 Eastern Market

SOMETHING SPECIAL

🍴 MARKET LUNCH

On Saturdays, the line for breakfast at the Market Lunch starts forming before the tiny restaurant opens, and it doesn't let up until noon. It's good Chesapeake Bay fare—pancakes and eggs for breakfast, maybe with a side of grits or scrapple, crab-cake sandwiches for lunch. The Market Lunch is one of those bits of an earlier Washington that locals hope will never change.

$

EASTERN MARKET
225 7TH ST., S.E.
TEL 202/547-8444

🔲 25 inside, 50 outside (in summer) 🕐 Closed L, Sun. D, & all Mon. ⬥ Cash only 🚇 Eastern Market

THE MALL

HOTELS

🏨 LOEW'S L'ENFANT PLAZA
$$–$$$$$

480 L'ENFANT PLAZA, S.W.
TEL 202-484-1000
FAX 202/646-5060

Close to the Smithsonian museums, Loew's L'Enfant Plaza is attractive to both business and leisure travelers. The American Grill serves both Mediterranean and Pacific food.

ⓘ 370 🔲 ⬥ AE, D, DC, MC, V 🚇 L'Enfant Plaza

🏨 MANDARIN ORIENTAL
$$$$$

1330 MARYLAND AVE., S.W.
TEL 202/554-8588
FAX 202/554-8999

This super-luxury hotel opened in 2004 near the southeastern end of the Mall, overlooking the Potomac Tidal Basin and the Jefferson Memorial. The lush carpets, marble baths, lacquered furniture, silk furnishings, and extensive spa services make for a soothing stay. **Café MoZu** offers Asian-inspired cuisine all day, while the **Signature Restaurant** is open for dinner and the **Empress Lounge** features live music.

ⓘ 400 🅿 ⬥ AE, D, DC, MC, V 🚇 L'Enfant Plaza

RESTAURANTS

🍴 LES HALLES
$$$$

1201 PENNSYLVANIA AVE., N.W.
TEL 202/347-6848

No restaurant in Washington feels more like Paris than this bustling French steakhouse. Service can be abrupt, but Washingtonians throng here to eat the flavorful *onglet*, hearty *cassoulet*, heaping platters of *choucroute garnie*, and the best French fries in town. The wine list is well-chosen and inexpensive.

🔲 186 🅿 Valet ⬥ AE, D, DC, MC, V 🚇 Metro Center, Federal Triangle

🍴 TENPENH
$$$

1001 PENNSYLVANIA AVE., N.W.
TEL 202/393-4500

Asian-American fusion cooking is everywhere these days, but few places do it more intelligently than this strikingly attractive downtown place. Chefs Jeff Tunks and Cliff Wharton have put together a menu that ranges from Vietnam to the Philippines, from Hong Kong to Thailand. Tunks's specialty, a Chinese-style smoked lobster, is a perfect marriage of East and West. Pastry chef David Guas's desserts are superb.
🍴 166 🅿 Valet
🕐 Closed Sat. L, & all Sun.
🈂 AE, D, DC, MC, V
🚇 Metro Center

🍴 CAFÉ ATLANTICO
$$
405 8TH ST., N.W.
TEL 202/393-0812
With an attractive three-level dining space tucked into an old power plant, Café Atlantico serves a fascinating menu of nuevo Latino dishes and other cuisines, including an interesting take on feijoada, Brazil's national dish. The tiny minibar offers a prix fixe menu of about 30 tiny courses and other innovative food. At the bar here, you'll find the best caipirinhas in town, and the wine list offers well-chosen South American wines at fair prices.
🍴 105 🅿 Valet 🕐 Closed Sun. L 🈂 AE, DC, MC, V
🚇 Archives/Navy Memorial

🍴 SMITHSONIAN CASTLE, COMMONS RESTAURANT
$$
1000 JEFFERSON DR., S.W.
TEL 202/ 357-2957
The best food on the Mall is found in the impressive, high-ceilinged Commons Restaurant in the Smithsonian Castle. However, it is open to the public only for lunch on Saturday and brunch on Sunday; reservations are recommended. The lunchtime buffet has good meat and

fish dishes and a generous salad bar.
🍴 120 🈂 AE, D, MC, V
🚇 Smithsonian

🍴 NATIONAL GALLERY OF ART CAFES
$
6TH ST. & CONSTITUTION AVE.
TEL 202/737-4215
The **Garden Café** offers a daily lunch buffet, while the large **Cascade Café**, in the concourse between the two buildings, has a varied cafeteria menu. The **Sculpture Garden Pavilion Café** seres pizzas, sandwiches, desserts, wine, and beer. Check out the weekend jazz brunches, and for a treat, don't miss the great gelato at the **Espresso Bar.**
🕐 Closed Sat.-Sun. D
🚇 Archives/Navy Memorial

WHITE HOUSE & AROUND

HOTELS

🏨 THE HAY-ADAMS 🍴 HOTEL
$$$$$
ONE LAFAYETTE SQUARE,
16TH & H STS. N.W.
TEL 202/638-6600 OR
800/424-5054
FAX 202/638-2716
Built on the site where, alternately, President Lincoln's secretary John Hay and John Adams's grandson Henry Adams lived. The newly renovated hotel is just across Lafayette Park from the White House. The **Lafayette Dining Room** and guest rooms on the south side offer great views of the Executive Mansion.
ℹ 145 🅿 🈂 AE, D, DC, MC, V 🚇 Farragut West, McPherson Square

🏨 PARK HYATT 🍴 $$$$-$$$$$
24TH AT M ST., N.W.
TEL 202/789-1234
FAX 202/419-6795
Located in Washington's

West End, just three blocks from Georgetown, the Park Hyatt is comfortably but strikingly modern. The lobby is decorated with an impressive collection of modern art. Rooms are large and luxurious. The distinguished restaurant **Melrose** serves chef Brian McBride's accomplished Modern American cooking and a lavish Sunday brunch.
ℹ 223 🅿 🔽 🈂 AE, D, DC, MC, V 🚇 Foggy Bottom

🏨 THE ST. REGIS 🍴 $$$$-$$$$$
923 16TH ST. AT K ST., N.W.
TEL 202/638-2626 OR
800/562-5661
FAX 202/638-4231
The posh St. Regis, well located near the White House and museums, is built in Italian Renaissance style with elaborate plasterwork ceilings, European antiques, and ornate chandeliers. **Timothy Dean's** restaurant serves French and American fare. The Library Lounge is one of Washington's coziest bars.
ℹ 193 🅿 🔽 🈂 AE, D, DC, MC, V 🚇 Farragut North

🏨 HOTEL LOMBARDY
$$-$$$$$
2019 PENNSYLVANIA AVE., N.W.
TEL 202/828-2600 OR
800/424-5486
FAX 202/872-0503
This low-key but well-located hotel recently underwent a stylish renovation to reflect the spirit of the 1926 building. The rooms now showcase imported Italian and German fabrics, oriental rugs, local art, stainless steel kitchenettes, and fine bedding. Café Lombardy is a cozy neighborhood bistro with French-inspired cuisine.
ℹ 132 🅿 🈂 AE, D, DC, MC, V 🚇 Foggy Bottom

🏨🍽 WILLARD INTER-CONTINENTAL HOTEL
$$$$-$$$$$
1401 PENNSYLVANIA AVE., N.W.
TEL 202/628-9100 OR
800/327-0200
FAX 202/637-7326

A Willard Hotel has been located on this site since 1850. Abraham Lincoln stayed here before his inauguration; Julia Ward Howe wrote the "Battle Hymn of the Republic" while staying here. The hotel has been thoroughly remodeled and luxuriously decorated. The **Willard Room** is perhaps the grandest dining room in the city. The **Round Robin Bar** is one of the city's most popular gathering places.

🛈 341 🅿 🚇 ⬛ AE, D, DC, MC, V 🚇 Metro Center

🏨🍽 SOFITEL LAFAYETTE SQUARE
$$$$-$$$$$
806 15TH ST, N.W.
TEL 202/730-8800 OR
866/397-8800
FAX 202/730-8500

This new hotel at the corner of Lafayette Square, near the White House, is convenient to museums, monuments, and government buildings. Housed in a 12-story 1880s building, the hotel has the restrained elegance characteristic of its parent, the French Accor chain. **Cafe´ 15**, the hotel's restaurant serving French cuisine, was cited by *Esquire* magazine as one of the top 10 new U.S. restaurants, and **Le Bar** lounge is a popular meeting place for its great location.

🛈 237 🅿 ⬛ AE, D, DC, MC, V 🚇 McPherson Square

🏨 JW MARRIOTT HOTEL
$$$$$
1331 PENNSYLVANIA AVE., N.W.
TEL 202/393-2000
FAX 202/626-6991

Large, centrally located, and connected to the shops and boutiques of National Place, the JW Marriott is a convenient hub for explorations of the city. Two in-house restaurants.

🛈 774 🅿 🚇 ⬛ AE, DC, MC, V 🚇 Metro Center

🏨🍽 FAIRMONT HOTEL
$$$-$$$$$
2401 M ST., N.W.
TEL 202/429-2400 OR
888/353-4040
FAX 202/457-5010

Built around an attractive garden courtyard, the Fairmont (previously the Monarch) is in the West End of town near Georgetown. Rooms are luxurious, service is attentive. The fitness center, with pool, is one of the most complete in the city. **The Bistro** offers good Modern American cooking, while the **Collonade** s offers an elaborate Sunday brunch that's popular.

🛈 415 🅿 🚇 ⬛ AE, D, DC, MC, V 🚇 Foggy Bottom-GWU

🏨🍽 ONE WASHINGTON CIRCLE HOTEL
$$$-$$$$$
ONE WASHINGTON CIRCLE, N.W.
TEL 202/872-1680 OR
800/424-9671
FAX 202/887-4989

Located near George Washington University, One Washington Circle has spacious rooms with private balconies, colorful furnishings, and a small-hotel atmosphere. **Circle Bistro** has very good American food with Mediterranean influences.

🛈 151 🅿 🚇 ⬛ AE, D, DC, MC, V 🚇 Foggy Bottom

🏨🍽 THE WESTIN GRAND
$$$$-$$$$$
2350 M ST., N.W.
TEL 202/429-0100
FAX 202/429-9759

This lovely hotel, located between Georgetown and the White House, is ele-

---

PRICES	
HOTELS	

An indication of the cost of a double room in high season, excluding tax, is given by **$** signs.

$$$$$	$225+
$$$$	$175–$225
$$$	$125–$175
$$	$85–$125
$	Under $85

RESTAURANTS

An indication of the cost of a three-course dinner without drinks, tax, or tip is given by $ signs.

$$$$	Over $50
$$$	$35–$50
$$	$15–$35
$	Under $15

---

gantly decorated and warmly welcoming. Rooms include executive-size desks and all-marble bathrooms with separate shower stalls. The **M Street Grille** features an elaborate morning buffet along with lunch and dinner. **Café on M** serves lunch, dinner, and cocktails in a clubby setting.

🛈 263 🚇 ⬛ 🅿 Valet ⬛ AE, D, DC, MC, V 🚇 Foggy Bottom

🏨 HOTEL WASHINGTON
$$-$$$$$
15TH ST. & PENNSYLVANIA AVE., N.W.
TEL 202/638-5900 OR
800/424-9540
FAX 202/638-1594

Near the White House and the Treasury Department, the Hotel Washington is popular with locals and visitors for its seasonal rooftop bar offering great views (see p. 246). The in-house restaurant Two Continents offers American fare.

🛈 350 ⬛ ⬛ AE, D, DC, MC, V 🚇 Metro Center

WASHINGTON SUITES GEORGETOWN
$$$–$$$$

2500 PENNSYLVANIA AVE., N.W.
TEL 202/333-8060 OR
877/736-2500
FAX 202/338-3818
Located just over Rock Creek from Georgetown, this hotel is popular with performers at the nearby Kennedy Center. Each suite is more than 600 square feet in area and offers a living room with desk and sofabed, a separate bedroom with walk-in closet, two TV sets, and an equipped kitchen.
🛈 124 🅿 📺 AE, D, DC, MC, V 🚇 Foggy Bottom

EMBASSY SUITES, WASHINGTON D.C.
$$$$–$$$$$

1250 22ND ST., N.W.
TEL 202/857-3388 OR
800/EMBASSY
FAX 202/785-2411
Built around an open, tropical atrium with waterfalls and plantlife, this popular hotel has an active lobby bar. The **Panevino Italian Ristorante** provides good basic Italian cooking.
🛈 318 🏊 📺 AE, D, DC, MC, V 🚇 Foggy Bottom

RESTAURANTS

EQUINOX
$$$$

818 CONNECTICUT AVE., N.W.
TEL 202/331-8118
Chef Todd Gray is fascinated by, but never limited by, the food of the Chesapeake Bay region. Many restaurants claim to use the freshest local ingredients, but few have taken the trouble, as Gray has, to research historical recipes and to update them for contemporary tastes while respecting their basic tastes. Gray's recent menus have included Virginia oysters on celery root purée as a starter and wild rockfish on country-style squash as a main course.
🍴 90 🕐 Closed Sat.–Sun. L

AE, DC, MC, V
🚇 Farragut West

GALILEO
$$$$

1110 21ST ST., N.W.
TEL 202/293-7191
The flagship restaurant of one of Washington's most popular and inventive chefs, Galileo offers a number of ways of dining. For a quick lunch or snack, the bar menu of sandwiches and salads is a great bargain. The main dining room has a large selection of dishes from chef Roberto Donna's native Piedmont, but for a real treat (and splurge), make reservations for Donna's Laboratorio, where the chef himself cooks a ten-course tasting menu based on what is available in the market.
🍴 175 🅿 Valet 🕐 Closed Sat.–Sun. L AE, DC, MC, V 🚇 Foggy Bottom, Farragut

SOMETHING SPECIAL

KINKEAD'S

The popularity of this Foggy Bottom seafood restaurant makes reservations a must. Like most Modern American chefs, Robert Kinkead's repertoire includes dishes from a wide range of international cuisines and American regions: pepita-crusted salmon, roasted cod with crab imperial, rockfish with red curry and coconut-milk broth. His cooking is also impressive when he returns to his New England roots—Kinkead's has the best fried clams in town.
$$$$
2000 PENNSYLVANIA AVE., N.W.
TEL 202/296-7700
🍴 190 🅿 Valet AE, D, MC, V 🚇 Foggy Bottom

MARCEL'S
$$$$

2401 PENNSYLVANIA AVE., N.W.
TEL 202/296-1166
Chef Robert Wiedmaier's

Belgian-influenced French cooking is both sophisticated and robust. Start a meal with his wonderfully light *boudin blanc*; continue with a game dish, perhaps loin of venison in a subtle sauce of beats and blackberries. The wine list is particularly strong in red Burgundies and wines from the Côtes du Rhone.
🍴 120 🅿 Valet 🕐 Closed L AE, DC, MC, V
🚇 Foggy Bottom

BOMBAY CLUB
$$$

815 CONNECTICUT AVE., N.W.
TEL 202/659-3727
The dark wooden chairs, ceiling fans, rugs, and leafy palms make this popular Indian restaurant near the White House seem like a trip back in time to the days of the British Raj. Lovers of spicy food might find the offerings here a bit tame, but but the signature tandoori seafood dishes, and anything else from the tandoor clay oven, are wonderful.
🍴 96 🅿 Valet 🕐 Closed Sat. L AE, DC, MC, V
🚇 Farragut West

OVAL ROOM AT LAFAYETTE SQUARE
$$$

800 CONNECTICUT AVE., N.W.
TEL 202/463-8700
Just across Lafayette Square from the White House, the Oval Room is a favorite lunch spot for senior executive branch staffers, drawn by the warm welcome and the innovative cooking of chef Frank Morales. Try the seared sea scallops with chorizo and squid, the loin of pork served with root vegetables, and finish with a selection of the perfectly kept cheeses.
🍴 125 🅿 Valet 🕐 Closed Sat. L & all Sun. AE, DC, MC, V 🚇 Farragut West

HOTELS & RESTAURANTS

🍴 TABERNA DEL ALABARDERO

$$$

1776 I ST., N.W.
TEL 202/429-2200
The small tapas bar at the entrance is a good first stop at this distinguished Spanish restaurant, perhaps for a glass of dry sherry and a plate of Serrano ham to whet the appetite. The main-course selections demonstrate that there is much more to Spanish cooking than paella—maybe lovely garlic soup or stuffed squid to start and a main course of a hearty rabbit stew.

🍽 162 🅿 Valet 🕐 Closed Sat. L & all Sun. 🅰 AE, D, DC, MC, V 🚇 Farragut West

🍴 OLD EBBITT GRILL

$$

675 15TH ST., N.W.
TEL 202/347-4801
Large, casual, and always crowded, the Old Ebbitt Grill feeds Washingtonians and out-of-towners with a large menu that ranges from burgers to grilled fish and meat. There's no better place in town for oysters. The grill always has a large assortment of varieties from waters that are certified safe, and a crew of able shuckers to open them.

🍽 500 🅿 Valet
🅰 AE, D, DC, MC, V
🚇 Metro Center

🍴 SKY TERRACE, HOTEL WASHINGTON

$$

15TH ST. & PENNSYLVANIA AVE., N.W.
TEL 202/638-5900
The Hotel Washington's Sky Terrace, open from May through October, has spectacular views of Washington toward the south and the monuments and toward the west and the White House. It's a favorite summer place for drinks and also serves light American fare such as sandwiches, salads, and fish.

🍽 200 🕐 Closed Nov.–April 🅰 AE, D, DC, MC, V 🚇 Metro Center

🍴 BREAD LINE

$

1751 PENNSYLVANIA AVE., N.W.
TEL 202/822-8900
Owner Mark Furstenburg's popular lunch spot near the White House specializes in bread and bread-based dishes from around the world. Sandwiches are wonderful—if you're lucky enough to be in Washington in tomato season, try the BLT on brioche—but you can also find wonderful pizzas, emapanadas, pirogis, and soups. It's a great place to buy a loaf of bread for a lunchtime picnic, but remember that it closes about 4 p.m.

🍽 100 🕐 Closed Sat.–Sun., & all D 🅰 AE, D, MC, V 🚇 Farragut West

🍴 MALAYSIA KOPITIAM

$

1827 M ST., N.W.
TEL 202/833-6232
Owners Penny and Leslie Phoon are hospitable guides to the food of Malaysia, which is less well known than it ought to be. The menu thoughtfully provides photos of the dishes, but the Phoons are glad to make recommendations—maybe appetizers of fish balls or a spicy lamb satay followed by Malaysian Chili Shrimp or a Chinese noodle dish.

🍽 110 🅰 AE, D, DC, MC, V 🚇 Dupont Circle

DOWNTOWN

HOTELS

🏨 JEFFERSON HOTEL

$$$$$

1200 16TH ST., N.W.
TEL 202/347-2200 OR
800/23-LOEWS
FAX 202/331-7982

Small boutique residential-type hotel, with every room unique. First an apartment house, in 1955 it was converted into a hotel. Oliver North resided here during the Iran Contra trials. During the '80s the Larry King radio program was broadcast live from within the Jefferson. Located four blocks from the White House.

ⓘ 100 🅿 🅰 AE, D, DC, MC, V 🚇 Farragut

🏨 THE MADISON

$$$$-$$$$$

15TH & M STS., N.W.
TEL 202/862-1600
FAX 202/785-1255
The Madison, which opened in 1963, iss filled with works of art and antiques. Federal-period decor is designed to be reminiscent of James and Dolly Madison's stately Virginia home, Montpelier.

ⓘ 353 🅿 🈺 🅰 AE, D, DC, MC, V 🚇 McPherson Square

🏨 MORRISON CLARK 🍴 INN

$$$$

MASSACHUSETTS AVE. & 11TH ST., N.W.
TEL 202/898-1200
OR 800/332-7898
FAX 202/289-8576
The stately Victorian mansion housingthis hotel was built as two separate town homes in 1864, with original turn-of-the-19th-century furnishings. Chefs of the **Morrison Clark Restaurant,** located in the former drawing room, have won many awards for their new American cuisine.

ⓘ 54 🅿 🈺 🅰 AE, D, DC, MC, V 🚇 Mt. Vernon Sq.

🏨 GRAND HYATT WASHINGTON

$$$$-$$$$$

1000 H ST., N.W.
TEL 202/582-1234
FAX 202/637-4781
Located near the Washington Convention Center and

the MCI Center, this large hotel features a parklike atrium, cigar bar, and six dining options, including a martini lounge.

ⓘ 888 P 🔈 🕎 🖾 AE, D, DC, MC, V 🚇 Metro Center

🏨 HENLEY PARK HOTEL
🍴 $$$$-$$$$$

926 MASSACHUSETTS AVE., N.W.
TEL 202/638-5200 OR
800/222-8474
FAX 202/638-6740

Quaint, Tudor-style hotel in the tradition of Europe's finest mall hotels—one of Washington's most charming. One hundred eighteen gargoyles and real lead windows decorate its exterior. The **Coeur de Lion** restaurant offers very good Modern American cooking. The Blue Bar has frequent live music and a menu of small plates.

ⓘ 96 P 🕎 🖾 AE, D, DC, MC, V 🚇 Mount Vernon Square, Gallery Place/Chinatown

SOMETHING SPECIAL

🏨 HOTEL MONACO
🍴 This new luxury boutique hotel is housed in the architecturally stately 1839 Tariff Building in the Penn Quarter. The convenient location is within steps of MCI Center, Washington Convention Center, downtown monuments, and the bustling Seventh Street arts scene. The distinctive rooms with 15-foot ceilings feature neoclassic furnishings and vivid contemporary colors. The Poste restaurant is a brasserie offering American cuisine.

$$$$$

700 F ST., N.W.
TEL 202/628-7177 OR
800/649-1202
FAX 202/628-7277

ⓘ 184 P 🕎 🖾 AE, D, DC, MC, V 🚇 Gallery Place/Chinatown

🏨 RENAISSANCE
🍴 MAYFLOWER HOTEL
$$$$-$$$$$

1127 CONNECTICUT AVE., N.W.
TEL 202/347-3000 OR
800/228-7697
FAX 202/776-9182

Once the home to many members of Congress, the historic Mayflower has been the site of an inaugural ball for every President since its opening in 1925. J. Edgar Hoover had breakfast here every morning. The gracious lobby runs an entire city block from Connecticut Avenue to 17th Street. **Café Promenade** features Mediterranean cooking, and the **Town and Country Lounge** is a favorite gathering spot.

ⓘ 657 P 🕎 🖾 AE, D, DC, MC, V 🚇 Farragut North

🏨 MARRIOTT AT METRO
🍴 CENTER
$$$$-$$$$$

775 12TH ST., N.W.
TEL 202/737-2200
FAX 202/347-5886

Conveniently located at the flagship station of the city's Metro system, the Marriott at Metro Center is attentive to both business and vacation guests. The **Metro Center Grille** features New American cuisine.

ⓘ 453 🔈 🕎 🖾 AE, D, DC, MC, V 🚇 Metro Center

🏨 WASHINGTON
RENAISSANCE HOTEL
$$$$-$$$$$

999 9TH ST., N.W.
TEL 202/898-9000
FAX 202/289-0947

The closest hotel to the Washington Convention Center and the MCI Center, the Washington Renaissance is a fully equipped business hotel well located for leisure travelers.

ⓘ 807 🔈 🕎 🖾 AE, D, DC, MC, V 🚇 Gallery Place/Chinatown

🏨 HOTEL HARRINGTON
🍴 $$-$$$

436 11TH ST., N.W.
TEL 202/628-8140 OR
800/424-8532
FAX 202/393-2311

Low prices, a prime location, and very plain, clean rooms, make the Hotel Harrington popular with bus tours of schoolchildren who come to Washington for their spring breaks. The hotel restaurant serves breakfast, lunch, and dinner. **Ollie's Trolley** on the lobby level is good for burgers and shakes.

ⓘ 250 🖾 AE, D, DC, MC, V 🚇 Metro Center

RESTAURANTS

🍴 GERARD'S PLACE
$$$$

915 15TH ST., N.W.
TEL 202/737-4445

Chef Gerard Pangaud is the only Michelin two-star chef currently cooking in the U.S. In Pangaud's sparely elegant dining room, a mixture of food-loving locals and international officials enjoy classics and improvisations—a perfect roast chicken, his signature lobster in Sauternes, a simple roasted pear with vanilla ice cream.

🍴 55 🕐 Closed Sat. L & all Sun. 🖾 AE, DC, MC, V 🚇 McPherson Square

🍴 OCEANAIRE
$$$$

1201 F ST., N.W.
TEL 202/347-2277

This sophisticated seafood restaurant with curving walls, cozy banquettes, and flattering lighting resembles the inside of an art deco ocean liner. The seafood is pristinely fresh and comes in enormous portions a lot like the gargantuan meals of ocean voyages—good oysters on the half-shell, a Grand Shellfish Platter that is a meal for two, a heaping Fisherman's Platter of fried

HOTELS & RESTAURANTS

seafood, delicious Dover sole boned at tableside. The huge banana split should be attempted only by those with the heartiest appetites.
🔲 500 Ⓟ Valet ⏱ Closed Sat.–Sun. L ◈ AE, D, DC, MC, V 🚇 Metro Center

🍴 TOSCA
$$$
1112 F ST., N.W.
TEL 202/367-1990
Chef Cesare Lanfrancone spent five years in the kitchen at Galileo before starting his own restaurant with a menu based on the food of his native Lake Como region. The sophisticated modern setting with widely spaced tables is designed for privacy and conversation. Signature dishes include the ravioli, roast meats and stews, and a wonderful tiramisu that makes you understand why this dish was popular.
🔲 120 Ⓟ Valet ⏱ Closed Sat.–Sun. L ◈ AE, DC, MC, V 🚇 Metro Center

🍴 LE PARADOU
$$$$
678 INDIANA AVE., N.W.
TEL 202/347-6780
Yannick Cam, who helped introduce Washingtonians to nouvelle cuisine a generation ago, is back with this elegant French restaurant that opened in April 2004. The de´cor is awash in lovely honey tones, and the food is equally sophisticated: lobster and mascarpone cheese in ravioli packets dressed with carrot and ginger sauce, roasted pigeon breast served on red cabbage with foie gras. A three-course prix fixe menu and a chef's tasting menu are options.
🔲 70 (plus private dining for up to 35) Ⓟ Valet ⏱ Closed Sat. L & all Sun. ◈ AE, D, DC, MC, V 🚇 Archives/ Navy Memorial

🍴 JALEO
$$
480 7TH ST., N.W.
TEL 202/628-7949
There are main courses at Jaleo, but most diners choose to make a meal of the large selection of tapas—wonderful Spanish cheeses and cold cuts, eggplant flan, spicy octopus, sausages and beans. It's a great place for a light dinner before a performance at the nearby Shakespeare Theatre.
🔲 145 Ⓟ Valet parking ◈ AE, D, DC, MC, V 🚇 Gallery Place/Chinatown

GEORGETOWN

HOTELS

SOMETHING SPECIAL

🏨 FOUR SEASONS 🍴 HOTEL
Located on the very eastern edge of Georgetown, this luxurious hotel provides a nice link into the rest of the city. Seasons Restaurant, overlooking the C&O Canal, is a favorite power breakfast spot. The three-level fitness center with an adjoining spa is one of the most opulent in town.
$$$$$+
2800 PENNSYLVANIA AVE., N.W.
TEL 202/342-0444
FAX 202/944-2076
ⓘ 259 Ⓟ ♒ 🍴 ◈ AE, DC, MC, V 🚇 Foggy Bottom

🏨 RITZ CARLTON 🍴 GEORGETOWN
$$$$–$$$$$
3100 SOUTH ST., N.W.
TEL 202/912-4100 OR
800/241-3333
FAX 202/912-4199
This Ritz-Carlton opened in 2003 in the heart of Georgetown's main shopping and entertainment district. Built on the former site of a historic brick incinerator building, complete with a 130-foot-

PRICES

HOTELS
An indication of the cost of a double room in high season, excluding tax, is given by **$** signs.

$$$$$	$225+
$$$$	$175–$225
$$$	$125–$175
$$	$85–$125
$	Under $85

RESTAURANTS
An indication of the cost of a three-course dinner without drinks, tax, or tip is given by $ signs.

$$$$	Over $50
$$$	$35–$50
$$	$15–$35
$	Under $15

high smokestack, the hotel offers views of the Potomac waterfront. All the guest rooms and suites are outfitted for luxury and soothing retreat. The top-floor **Fahrenheit Restaurant** features new American cuisine while **Degrees Bar and Lounge** offers classic cocktails and tasting menus.
ⓘ 86 Ⓟ 🍴 ◈ AE, DC, MC, V 🚇 Foggy Bottom

🏨 HOTEL MONTICELLO
$$$$$
1075 THOMAS JEFFERSON ST., N.W.
TEL 202/337-0900 OR
800/388-2410
FAX 202/333-6526
Completely remodeled in 2000, this all-suite hotel is located in the center of Georgetown and is popular with international guests. Rooms are bright, cheery, and spacious, and all have wet bars, microwaves, and refrigerators. It is close to the historic C&O Canal.
ⓘ 47 ◈ AE, DC, MC, V 🚇 Foggy Bottom

THE GEORGETOWN INN
$$$$-$$$$$
1310 WISCONSIN AVE., N.W.
TEL 202/333-8900 OR
800/424-2979
FAX 202/295-2003
Opened in 1961, this pleasant red brick hotel has colonial decor, large rooms, and marble bathrooms. It's conveniently located for Georgetown shopping and entertainment. The **American Grill** is reminiscent of the great American grills of the 1920s.
ⓘ 96 Ⓟ AE, DC, MC, V Foggy Bottom

THE LATHAM HOTEL
$$$$-$$$$$
3000 M ST., N.W.
TEL 202/726-5000 OR
800/368-5922
FAX 202/337-4250
This well located hotel has a variety of rooms and suites. The nearby C&O Canal towpath is convenient for jogging and bicycling. Michel Richard's **Citronelle** restaurant and cocktail lounge (see below) offers exceptional food. **La Madeleine,** a French cafeteria and patisserie, is in front of the hotel, facing M Street.
ⓘ 143 AE, DC, MC, V Foggy Bottom

HOLIDAY INN GEORGETOWN
$$$-$$$$
2101 WISCONSIN AVE., N.W.
TEL 202/338-4600
FAX 202/338-4458
Recently renovated, this moderately priced hotel in upper Georgetown is close to Dumbarton Oaks and Tudor Place.
ⓘ 296 AE, DC, MC, V Foggy Bottom, then bus

RESTAURANTS

CITRONELLE
$$$$
LATHAM HOTEL
3000 M ST., N.W.

TEL 202/625-2150
There's no more imaginative French cook at work in America today than Michel Richard. The open kitchen at Citronelle, with banks of tables rising above it, is a fitting stage for his art. The menu changes frequently, according to the availability of ingredients and the chef's whims. For a sampling, order one of his fixed-price menus, and don't forget dessert—he started as a pastry chef.
100 Ⓟ Valet Closed all L & Sun. July-Aug. AE, D, DC, MC, V Foggy Bottom, then 15-min. walk

1789
$$$
1226 36TH ST., N.W.
TEL 202/965-1789
One of Washington's loveliest and most beloved restaurants, housed in a federal town house. There's no better way to spend a winter evening than at a table by the fireplace in the central dining room enjoying chef Ris Lacoste's rack of lamb, filet of beef, or pinenut-crusted chicken breast. Don't miss the pecan pie with bourbon ice cream for dessert. Downstairs you'll find the **Tombs,** where generations of Georgetown students have drunk countless pitchers of beer.
300 Ⓟ Valet Closed L AE, D, DC, MC, V Foggy Bottom, Rosslyn, then bus

HERITAGE INDIA
$$$
2400 WISCONSIN AVE., N.W.
TEL 202/333-3120
This elegant restaurant offers an unusually wide selection of cooking from the Indian subcontinent. Look for tandoori prawns, Kashmiri lamb curry simmered in a sauce of yogurt and saffron, baby eggplant in sesame sauce, and splendid vegetable curries.
100 Ⓟ Valet AE, D,

MC, V Tenleytown–AU, then bus

SEA CATCH
$$$
1054 31ST ST., N.W.
TEL 202/337-8855
The Carrera marble oyster bar at the entrance to this dependable seafood restaurant hints at what to order first—a selection of oysters and clams on the half-shell. The seafood selection, always perfectly fresh, is based on market availability. Chef Jeff Shively, a Louisiana native, has a way with New Orleans-style seafood dishes, but his repertory is by no means limited to them. Try the steamed shellfish platter, seared sea scallops paired with lentils, or, in season, yellow snapper from Florida.
200 Ⓟ Closed Sun. AE, D, DC, MC, V Foggy Bottom

BISTRO FRANCAIS
$$
3128 M ST., N.W.
TEL 202/338-3830
In a city where restaurants close early, this lively French bistro serves until 3 a.m. on weekdays and 4 a.m. on weekends. The classics of bistro cooking are dependably done: roast chicken with *pommes frites;* a hearty *cassoulet;* rabbit in mustard sauce.
150 AE, DC, MC, V Foggy Bottom, then walk

CLYDE'S
$$
3236 M ST., N.W.
TEL 202/333-9180
The founder of the small Clyde's group of restaurants had the idea that he'd "rather eat in a bar than drink in a restaurant." This Georgetown original of the chain is built around a bar business, but offers an impressive menu of bar food, particularly in the summer when Clyde's makes a point of sending trucks to local farms for

HOTELS & RESTAURANTS

fresh produce. It's a good place for a restorative drink and light meal while shopping in Georgetown.
🛏 188 🅿 Georgetown Park Mall lot 🚇 AE, D, DC, MC, V 🚇 Foggy Bottom, Rosslyn, then bus

🍴 PATISSERIE POUPON
$
1645 WISCONSIN AVE., N.W.
TEL 202/342-3248
Primarily a bakery that makes wonderful fruit tarts, cakes, and Washington's best croissants, Patisserie Poupon has a small dining area and a small menu of sandwiches, soups, and salads.
🛏 26 🕐 Closed Mon. L & all D 🚇 AE, MC, V 🚇 Tenleytown–AU, then bus

DUPONT CIRCLE & ADAMS MORGAN

HOTELS

🏨 THE CHURCHILL
🍴 $$$$-$$$$$
1914 CONNECTICUT AVE., N.W.
TEL 202/797-2000 OR
800/424-2464
FAX 202/462-0944
Located just north of the vibrant Dupont Circle area in Kalorama, an area known for its stately residences and embassies, the Churchill offers a variety of suites and room with separate baths. The **Trocadero Café** offers French-inspired cuisine, and the Pullman Bar is a relaxing place for a drink.
ℹ 144 🅿 🍽 🚇 AE, D, DC, MC, V 🚇 Dupont Circle

🏨 JURYS WASHINGTON
🍴 HOTEL
$$$-$$$$$
1500 NEW HAMPSHIRE AVE., N.W.
TEL 202/483-6000
FAX 202/328-3265
Owned and operated by Jurys Doyle Hotels, Ireland's largest hotel group, this recently remodeled hotel

on Dupont Circle is one of the city's liveliest areas. Biddy Mulligan's Bar is a traditional Irish pub. **Dupont Grille** blends Spanish, French, and Asian flavors.
ℹ 309 🅿 🍽 🚇 AE, D, DC, MC, V 🚇 Dupont Circle

🏨 RADISSON BARCELO
🍴 HOTEL
$$$$$
2121 P ST., N.W.
TEL 202/293-3100
FAX 202/857-0134
Located between Georgetown and Dupont Circle, the Radisson Barcelo boasts some of Washington's largest guest rooms. The rooms have climate control, 3 phones, color cable TV, and radio. The restaurant **Gabriel** (see p. 249) serves Nuevo Latino cuisine and has one of the most popular Sunday brunches in the city.
ℹ 301 🅿 🍽 🚇 AE, D, DC, MC, V 🚇 Dupont Circle

🏨 HOTEL HELIX
$$$-$$$$$
1430 RHODE ISLAND AVE., N.W.
TEL 202/462-9001
FAX 202/332-3519
This boutique hotel in the city's Logan Circle neighborhood of stately old townhouses and mansions is convenient to downtown. Pop-art is the decorating theme here, with a Magritte-like mural welcoming you and lots of cherry red, royal blue, lime green, pink, orange, and purple inside. An example of the amenities designed to create an atmosphere of fun are "bunk beds" for grown-up slumber parties: a sofa-cum-twin-bed that converts to a regular-sized double bed. **Helix Lounge** features politically inspired cocktails, contemporary American cuisine, and mood lighting.
ℹ 178 🅿 🍽 🚇 AE, D, DC, MC, V 🚇 Dupont Circle

🏨 TOPAZ HOTEL
$$$-$$$$$
1733 N ST., N.W.
TEL 202/393-3000 OR
800/775-1202
FAX 202/785-9581
This new boutique hotel, created from an older hotel on the site, is doing its best to spice up the hotel scene around Dupont Circle. It promises "cosmic energy and good karma." Decorated in a dazzling array of shapes and colors, all rooms are equipped with flat-screen Sony TVs, down comforters, and cordless speakerphones. A yoga exercise room provides instruction videos, and you can even get an energy drink on your way out in the morning. The **Topaz Bar** is open for meals and drinks.
ℹ 99 🅿 🚇 AE, D, DC, MC, V 🚇 Dupont Circle

🏨 WASHINGTON
🍴 COURTYARD
MARRIOTT
$$$$$
1900 CONNECTICUT AVE., N.W.
TEL 202/332-9300 OR
800/842-4211
FAX 202/328-7039
This pleasant Dupont Circle hotel is popular with conventioneers, and business- and vacation travelers. The lobby is welcoming with lush plantlife, the rooms gracious and modern. **Clarets** restaurant serves American cuisine.
ℹ 147 🅿 🍽 🚇 AE, D, DC, MC, V 🚇 Dupont Circle

🏨 WESTIN FAIRFAX
🍴 $$$$$
2100 MASSACHUSETTS AVE., N.W.
TEL 202/293-2100
FAX 202/293-0641
Opened in 1924 as the Fairfax Hotel, it was for many years the residential hotel favored by members of Congress. Former Vice President Al Gore grew up here. Guest rooms are luxurious, as one would

expect from a hotel on Massachusetts Avenue's Embassy Row. **Cabo** restaurant, which replaced the Jockey Club, offers California cuisine.

📱 206 **P** 🏨 🔊 AE, D, DC, MC, V 🚇 Dupont Circle

🏨 HOTEL MADERA
🍴 $$$-$$$$$
1310 NEW HAMPSHIRE AVE., N.W.
TEL 202/296-7600 OR
800/430-1202
FAX 202/293-2476

This pampering metro hideaway is like a B&B tucked in a quiet location near downtown office buildings and embassies, with good views of the city, Georgetown, and Rock Creek Park. Part of the Kimpton chain, it has a sophisticated decor and the amenities of a big hotel. **Firefly** restaurant offers American bistro fare.

📱 82 **P** 🔊 AE, D, DC, MC, V 🚇 Dupont Circle

🏨 TABARD INN
🍴 $$$
1739 N ST., N.W.
TEL 202/785-1277
FAX 202/785-6173

This small hotel is greatly loved by those who consider it quaint and love the Victorian clutter. Others hate it for the same reason. Locals love the hotel's restaurant (see below), which has a charming outdoor garden and imaginateive food. The rooms vary widely in size, so it's wise to look before you commit.

📱 40 **P** 🔊 AE, D, DC, MC, V 🚇 Dupont Circle

RESTAURANTS

🍴 THE PALM
$$$$
1225 19TH ST., N.W.
TEL 202/293-9091

The downtown branch of this steakhouse chain is the epicenter of Washington power dining. You'll see polit-ical figures, faces familiar from the news talk shows, and a flock of lesser Washington lights who like to be seen there. The main attractions are the Palm's steaks and five-pound lobsters, served by an efficient and irreverent crew of wisecracking waiters, but the Italian food is also very good.

🍽 185 **P** Valet 🕐 Closed Sat.–Sun. L 🔊 AE, DC, MC, V 🚇 Dupont Circle

🍴 VIDALIA
$$$$
1990 M ST., N.W.
TEL 202/659-1990

Named after the sweet Georgia onion, Vidalia is one of the city's leading exponents of Southern cooking. In season, there's a large variety of Vidalia onion dishes. At other times of the year, onion offerings are likely to be limited to a dish of onion relish with your bread and the wonderful Five Onion Soup. The shrimp and grits is a signature dish, as is roasted sweetbreads with lobster. For dessert, don't miss lemon chess pie.

🍽 115 **P** Valet 🕐 Closed Sat.–Sun. L 🔊 AE, D, DC, MC, V 🚇 Farragut West

🍴 CASHION'S EAT PLACE
$$$
1819 COLUMBIA RD., N.W.
TEL 202/797-1819

Chef Ann Cashion's Adams Morgan restaurant offers distinguished Modern American cooking in a setting that's casual enough for a week-night dinner and attractive enough for a special occasion. The menus change frequently, but you'll usually find a perfectly roasted free range chicken, and if you're lucky, roast leg of pork with creamed collard greens, a *fritto misto* of crisply fried seafood, or a venison chop with aromatic vegetables. Desserts are a treat, particularly the chocolate cake and the frozen lemon tart.

🍽 100 **P** Valet 🕐 Closed Mon. 🔊 MC, V 🚇 Woodley Park/Zoo–Adams Morgan, plus 15-minute walk

🍴 ETRUSCO
$$$
1606 20TH ST., N.W.
TEL 202/667-0047

Chef Francesco Ricchi is a native of Tuscany, and the cooking of his native region is reflected on the menu of this moderately priced Dupont Circle restaurant. Join neighborhood regulars for *ribolita*, a hearty Tuscan bread soup with Parmesan; rabbit sausage; a signature ragu of duck on pappardelle; and main courses such as roast rabbit or braised veal shank. Desserts include Grandfather's Cake, a chocolate treat, and a delicious pear cake.

🍽 130 🕐 Closed L & Sun. 🔊 AE, MC, V 🚇 Dupont Circle

🍴 GABRIEL
$$$
RADISSON BARCELO HOTEL
2121 P ST., N.W.
TEL 202/956-6690

Gabriel has the best Sunday brunch in Washington, and one of the most popular. Chef Greggory Hill's groaning buffet tables feature a whole roast suckling pig surrounded by a selection of hot and cold vegetable dishes, and for the less adventurous, a traditional breakfast bar. The regular menu is an intelligent combination of Spanish cooking and the more robust flavors of Latin America. Start with a selection of tapas, then move on to more substantial dishes—perhaps bison tenderloin, a braised lamb shank, or rotisserie chicken with garlic mashed potatoes.

🍽 70 **P** Valet 🕐 Closed L, Sun. D & all Mon. 🔊 AE, D, DC, MC, V 🚇 Dupont Circle

---

HOTELS & RESTAURANTS

🍴 NORA RESTAURANT

$$$

2132 FLORIDA AVE., N.W.

TEL 202/462-5143

Chef Nora Pouillon was a pioneer advocate of organic farming, and her restaurant is the first locally to be certified organic by Oregon Tilth, an organization that promulgates standards for organic growers. This means that 95 percent of the ingredients at the restaurant comes from certified organic sources. But the handsome appearance and polished service at Nora Restaurant belie our '60s preconceptions of what an organic restaurant might be. The menu changes daily, but you will find wonderful first course salads, beautifully cooked organic chicken, fresh seafood, and spectacular pies for dessert.

🪑 80 🅿 Valet 🕐 Closed L, & all Sun. 🚫 AE, MC, V 🚇 Dupont Circle

🍴 OBELISK

$$$

2029 P ST., N.W.

TEL 202/872-1180

At Obelisk, everything is small in scale except flavor. This tiny Italian restaurant holds fewer than 40 people, which makes it one of the hardest-to-get reservations in town. The $55 fixed-price menu, which changes too often to recommend specific dishes, offers two or three choices of antipasto, pasta, main course, and dessert. Chef Peter Pastan's cooking is simple but never precious and is likely to be a memorable culinary experience, based on fresh ingredients in the hands of a skilled chef.

🪑 36 🕐 Closed L, & all Sun.–Mon. 🚫 DC, MC, V 🚇 Dupont Circle

🍴 TABARD INN

$$$

1739 N ST., N.W.

TEL 202/833-2668

The restaurant of this quaint hotel south of Dupont Circle serves New American cuisine in a well-worn dining room that's a popular lunch spot for the offices nearby. Sunday brunch is a favorite with the neighborhood, and the pleasant brick-walled garden is a good place for a drink and dinner on a spring evening. Similary, the fireplace-cozy lounge with creaky wood floors is cozy on winter evenings.

🪑 80 (30 summer patio) 🅿 Valet Fri. & Sat. 🚫 AE, MC, V 🚇 Dupont Circle

🍴 BISTROT DU COIN

$$

1738 CONNECTICUT AVE., N.W.

TEL 202/234-6969

It's not a place for quiet conversation, particularly in the evenings when locals from the neighborhood crowd around the zinc-topped bar and fill the trestle tables, but Bistrot du Coin is a lot of fun. Owner Michael Verdun and chef Yannis Felix strike a good balance between good cheer and good cooking. Mussels are a good way to start a meal here, particularly the curried *mouclade de Charantes*. For a main course, it's hard to go wrong with *steak frites*, but the more adventurous can order *tripes à la Niçoise* or a delicious stew of rabbit and mushrooms. The house wines—a Beaujolais, a Rhone, and an Alsatian white—are good value.

🪑 100 🚫 AE, D, DC, MC, V 🚇 Dupont Circle

🍴 LAURIOL PLAZA

$$

1835 18TH ST., N.W.

TEL 202/387-0035

There's almost always a wait to get into this well-run Mexican restaurant, but there are good margaritas and baskets of chips and salsa to help you while away the time. The Mexican side of the menu is more interesting than the selection of international dishes—great fajitas, good enchiladas and burritos. The roof deck is a wonderful place to spend a summer evening over a pitcher of sangria or a few bottles of Dos Equis.

🪑 340 🅿 🚫 AE, D, DC, MC, V 🚇 Dupont Circle

PRICES

HOTELS

An indication of the cost of a double room in high season, excluding tax, is given by **$** signs.

$$$$$	$225+
$$$$	$175–$225
$$$	$125–$175
$$	$85–$125
$	Under $85

RESTAURANTS

An indication of the cost of a three-course dinner without drinks, tax, or tip is given by **$** signs.

$$$$	Over $50
$$$	$35–$50
$$	$15–$35
$	Under $15

SOMETHING SPECIAL

🍴 IRON GATE INN

There's no more charming spot in Washington for outdoor dining than the terrace at the Iron Gate Inn, with its overhead trellis and cooling fountain. The menu is Mediterranean-inspired and the kitchen does a good job on Middle Eastern dishes—stuffed grape leaves, braised lamb shank, shish kebobs with grilled vegetables.

$$

1734 N ST., N.W.

TEL 202/737-1370

🪑 120 🕐 Closed Sun., & Sat. L 🚇 Dupont Circle

HOTELS & RESTAURANTS

JOHNNY'S HALF SHELL
$$
2002 P ST., N.W.
TEL 202/296-2021
Washington has a dearth of good seafood restaurants, particularly moderately prices ones. Johnny's Half Shell, with its menu of mid-Atlantic and New Orleans-style seafood, was a hit from the day it opened. Oysters are a treat here, either raw on the half-shell or crisply fried with an accompaniment of pickled vegetables. The gumbo, dark and filled with seafood, is delicious. Main dishes include a perfectly cooked filet of rockfish, or chicken with slippery dumplings. Two of Johnny's real treats are available only at lunchtime—a wonderful fried oyster po' boy sandwich (a half is enough for a normal appetite) and the best hot dog in town. Don't miss the chocolate angel-food cake for dessert.
54 Closed Sun. L
AE, MC, V Dupont Circle

MESKEREM
$$
2434 18TH ST., N.W.
TEL 202/462-4100
Washington has one of the largest concentrations of Ethiopian restaurants outside Addis Ababa, and Meskerem is a good place for an introduction to this appealing culture and cuisine. *Alechas* and *wats,* and spicy stews of meats, vegetables, and pulses form the center of this cooking. Eat with your hands, picking up small bites with pieces of *injera,* a large, floppy pancake. It's inexpensive and an unusual treat.
200 AE, DC, MC, V
Dupont Circle

PERRY'S
$$
1811 COLUMBIA RD., N.W.
TEL 202/234-6218
Despite its meat-and-potatoes name, Perry's serves

sushi and new takes on familiar fare such as scallops and soft-shell crabs. The Sunday drag brunch, with lip-synched entertainment by glamorous drag queens, is an Adams Morgan institution. The roof deck is pleasant for dinner.
90 outdoors, 90 indoors
Valet Closed
Mon.–Sat. L AE, D, DC, MC, V Woodley Park/Zoo–Adams Morgan

SKEWERS
$$
1633 P ST., N.W.
TEL 202/387-7400
The food at this small Dupont Circle eatery, popular with the locals, is Middle Eastern with an overlay of pastas, salads, and sandwiches. Kebobs, both meat and vegetable, are very well done here and are available as an entrée or atop a salad, making for a light, healthy meal.
65 AE, MC, V
Dupont Circle

COPPI'S ORGANIC
$$
1414 U ST., N.W.
TEL 202/319-7773
Long a neighborhood favorite for its pizzas from a wood-burning oven, this modest restaurant also offers an excellent selection of Italian fare made from the best ingredients chef Elizabeth Bright can find. There's also a good selection of inexpensive Italian wines.
50 Closed L AE, D, MC, V U Street–Cardozo

BEN'S CHILI BOWL
$
1213 U ST, N.W.
TEL 202/667-0909
A fixture on the U Street corridor since 1958, Ben's has served chili dogs, chili burgers, and chili half-smokes to a generation of Washingtonians and visitors. Bill Cosby, a frequent visitor when he's in town, loves the

chili half-smokes.
60 Cash only
U Street–Cardozo

PIZZERIA PARADISO
$
2029 P ST., N.W.
TEL 202/223-1245
This small pizza parlor, which you will be able to recognize by the line reaching out the front door and down the steps, makes simply the best pizza in Washington, maybe in the country. The crust, which tastes like good bread, is thin but supports the sparely applied toppings. This is not the place for a sweep-the-kitchen pizza. Order one of the set toppings—the spicy Atomica, the potato-and-pesto Genovese, or the delicious five-cheese combination. If you don't want pizza, there are also superb panini, Italian sandwiches, and salads.
40 DC, MC, V
Dupont Circle

CLEVELAND PARK & BEYOND

HOTELS

MARRIOTT WARDMAN PARK HOTEL
$$$$-$$$$$
2660 WOODLEY RD., N.W.
TEL 202/328-2000 OR
800/228-9290
FAX 202/234-0015
Still Washington's largest, the Wardman Park is set on six acres of flower-planted gardens within walking distance of the National Zoo. **Perle's** restaurant, an American café, serves breakfast, lunch, and dinner.
1340 AE, D, DC, MC, V
Woodley Park/Zoo–Adams Morgan

OMNI SHOREHAM HOTEL
$$$$-$$$$$
2500 CALVERT ST., N.W.

TEL 202/234-0700
FAX 202/265-7972
Opened in 1930 on 11 land-scaped acres near Rock Creek, the Shoreham is a frequent convention site and location for large events. Its location gives it convenient access to the jogging trails and paths of Rock Creek Park. **Robert's Restaurant** provides elegant dining, or you can rub elbows with the international mix of guests at the Marquee Bar and Lounge. [i] 835 🔲 📺 🔲 AE, D, DC, MC, V 🚇 Woodley Park/Zoo–Adams Morgan

RESTAURANTS

🍴 YANYU
$$$–$$$$
3435 CONNECTICUT AVE., N.W.
TEL 202/686-6968
A beautifully designed, upscale pan-Asian restaurant, Yanyu cooks fewer dishes than most traditional Chinese restaurants, but what it does, it cooks well and presents beautifully. Start with little dragon buns, soup-filled Shanghai dumplings meant to be eaten whole to release their rich stock in the mouth. The lily bulb dumplings, stuffed with shrimp, chicken, and lily buds, are equally delicious. Yanyu serves a wonderful Peking duck, one of the best in the area, and the server does the business of wrapping and rolling it for you. 🍴 150 🅿 Valet 🔲 Closed L 🔲 AE, DC, MC, V 🚇 Cleveland Park

🍴 NEW HEIGHTS
$$$
2317 CALVERT ST., N.W.
TEL 202/234-4110
A gracious second-floor dining room with large windows overlooking Rock Creek and a menu of creative New American cooking make this restaurant a perennial

favorite. Sunday brunch, the only time the restaurant is open during the day, is particularly pleasant—almost, in the spring and summer, like eating in a tree house. 🍴 92 🅿 Valet 🔲 Closed Mon.–Sat. L, Sun. D 🔲 AE, D, DC, MC, V 🚇 Woodley Park/Zoo–Adams Morgan

🍴 PALENA
$$–$$$$
3529 CONNECTICUT AVE., N.W.
TEL 202/537-9250
Chef Frank Ruta and pastry chef Ann Americk met when both were working in the White House kitchen. Ruta's style is a combination of French, Italian, and Modern American. You might find tiny ravioli stuffed with oxtail almonds, raisins, and spinach, or veal cheeks paired with sweetbreads. The menu changes frequently, and the prix fixe menus of three, four, or five courses are good value. Amernick's homey desserts are legendary. The newly upgraded bar room offers a light café menu. 🍴 68 🔲 Closed Sun. & L 🔲 AE, D, DC, MC, V 🚇 Cleveland Park

🍴 ARDEO
$$
3311 CONNECTICUT AVE., N.W.
TEL 202/244-6750
This sophisticated neighborhood restaurant, with its warm woods, white tablecloths, and lively bar, has become a hangout for media types who live in Cleveland Park. It's the creation of restaurant entrepreneur Ashok Bajoj, who also owns the wine bar Bardeo next door. The kitchen starts with top-quality ingredients, and when it stumbles, it's because of bad combinations or faulty execution. So it's best to order simply—diver scallops, fresh fish, braised lamb shanks—and you'll eat well. 🍴 40 🅿 Valet 🔲 Closed

Mon.–Sat. L, open Sun. brunch 🔲 AE, D, DC, MC, V 🚇 Cleveland Park

🍴 CACTUS CANTINA
$$
3300 WISCONSIN AVE., N.W.
TEL 202/686-7222
This many-chambered cantina, usually noisy and crowded, serves very good Tex-Mex food, both large combination platters and specialties from its mesquite grill. The tamales are a terrific way to begin, but for a main course, order from the grill: crispy quail, great grilled shrimp, or full-flavored spareribs. 🍴 130 inside, 30 outside 🅿 🔲 AE, D, DC, MC, V 🚇 Tenleytown–AU

SOMETHING SPECIAL

🍴 LEBANESE TAVERNA
There's no better place in Washington to experience the legendary hospitality of the Middle East—and its wonderful cooking—than at this busy Lebanese restaurant. It's possible to order a traditional three-course meal here, but you'll get to try a larger variety of dishes if your party makes a meal from mezze, the small appetizer plates that precede a Middle Eastern meal: spicy beef sausages, stuffed vine leaves, tart hummous, babaganoush, Lebanese "pizzas"—count on about three dishes per person.
$$
2641 CONNECTICUT AVE., N.W.
TEL 202/265-8681
🍴 100 🅿 🔲 Closed Sun. L 🔲 AE, DC, MC, V 🚇 Woodley Park/Zoo–Adams Morgan

🍴 LAVANDOU
$$
3321 CONNECTICUT AVE., N.W.
TEL 202/966-3002
A sunny, cheerful bistro with a loyal neighborhood follow-

ing, Lavandou features the Provençal cooking of owner/chef Francis Devilliers. Soups are a good beginning here, the *soupe au pistou* with vegetables, basil, and garlic, or a country soup of leeks and beans. For a main course, try the daube of beef, cooked in wine to a melting tenderness, or the *carbounado* of lamb, a deeply flavorful stew of lamb, artichokes, and beans.

🏛 80 🕐 Closed Sat.–Sun. L 🌐 AE, DC, MC, V 🚇 Cleveland Park

EAST OF THE CAPITOL

RESTAURANT

🍴 COL. BROOKS' TAVERN
$
901 MONROE ST., N.E.
TEL 202/529-4002
A good place for a casual meal while visiting the nearby Shrine of the Immaculate Conception, Col. Brooks's Tavern has a Southern-inspired menu of steak and chicken dishes, burgers, and other sandwiches, all complemented by a large selection of beers. Live Dixieland Jazz on Tuesday nights.

🏛 100 🅿 🌐 AE, D, MC, V 🚇 Brookland–CUA

ACROSS THE POTOMAC

HOTELS

ARLINGTON, VA

🏨 RITZ-CARLTON 🍴 PENTAGON CITY
$$$$$
1250 S. HAYES ST., 22202
TEL 703/415-5000 OR
800/241-3333
FAX 703/415-5061
A part of the Fashion Centre mall, this hotel offers traditional Ritz-Carlton luxury with the added advantage of

shopping. It is minutes from Reagan National airport. Dinner is offered in the club-like atmosphere of the **Grill**. Afternoon tea is popular.

🛈 366 🅿 🖼 🍸 🌐 AE, D, DC, MC, V 🚇 Pentagon City

🏨 CRYSTAL CITY MARRIOTT
$$$–$$$$
1999 JEFFERSON DAVIS HWY., 22202
TEL 703/413-5500
FAX 703/413-0192
Located a mile from Reagan National airport, this hotel connects to the Crystal City Metro stop, so access to the memorials and Smithsonian museums is easy.

🛈 345 🖼 🍸 🌐 AE, D, DC, MC, V 🚇 Crystal City

🏨 KEY BRIDGE 🍴 MARRIOTT
$$$–$$$$
1401 LEE HWY., 22209
TEL 703/524-6400
FAX 703/524-8964
Another hotel just across the river from Georgetown, the Key Bridge Marriott offers easy access by Metro to downtown and its sites. **The View**, which overlooks Georgetown University and the National Cathedral in the distance, serves steak and Continental cuisine.

🛈 585 🖼 🍸 🌐 AE, D, DC, MC, V 🚇 Rosslyn

🏨 RESIDENCE INN BY MARRIOTT PENTAGON CITY
$$$–$$$$
550 ARMY NAVY DR., 22202
TEL 703/413-6630 OR
800/331-3131
FAX 703/418-1751
All rooms have fully equipped kitchens with cooking and eating utensils, microwave, and refrigerator with icemaker. Ronald Reagan Washington National Airport is a half-mile away.

🛈 299 🍸 🌐 AE, D, DC, MC, V 🚇 Pentagon City

🏨 DAYS INN CRYSTAL CITY
$$
2020 JEFFERSON DAVIS HWY., 22202
TEL 703/920-8600
FAX 703/920-2840
A mile from downtown Washington, the Pentagon, and Reagan National airport, this Days Inn (which was undergoing renovations in 2004) is within walking distance of the Crystal City Metro stop, two shopping malls, and many restaurants.

🛈 247 🍸 🌐 AE, D, DC, MC, V 🚇 Crystal City

🏨 HOLIDAY INN 🍴 ROSSLYN
$$$–$$$$
1900 N. FORT MYER DR., 22209
TEL 703/807-2000 OR
800/368-3408
FAX 703/522-8864
An impressive orange-brick structure, this hotel is located in Rosslyn, just across the Key Bridge from Georgetown. For dinner, guests can go to one of the many restaurants in Rosslyn, cross the bridge to Georgetown, or stay in and enjoy dinner at the hotel's own **Vantage Point** restaurant.

🛈 306 🖼 🍸 🌐 AE, D, DC, MC, V 🚇 Rosslyn

🏨 BEST WESTERN PENTAGON
$$
2480 S. GLEBE RD., 22206
TEL 703/979-4400 OR
800/426-6886
FAX 703/685-0051
This Best Western provides a courtesy shuttle to Reagan National airport, Pentagon City Metro station, and the Fashion Centre Mall. The restaurant **Monuments** has traditional American cuisine.

🛈 206 🅿 🖼 🍸 🌐 AE, D, DC, MC, V 🚇 Pentagon City, then courtesy shuttle

---

🌐 Nonsmoking 🌐 Air-conditioning 🖼 Indoor/🖼 Outdoor swimming pool 🍸 Health club 🌐 Credit cards **KEY**

🏨 QUALITY INN IWO JIMA
$$
1501 ARLINGTON BLVD. (US 50) AT FAIRFAX DR., 22209
TEL 703/524-5000
FAX 703/522-5484
It's easy to get to downtown D.C. and Old Town Alexandria from this modest hotel; and the Marine Corps War Memorial is just down the street. More than 100 restaurants within a 1-mile radius.
🛏 140 ☎ 🍽 🏊 🚭 🕸 AE, D, DC, MC, V 🚇 Rosslyn

ALEXANDRIA, VA

🏨 EMBASSY SUITES
$$$$-$$$$$
1900 DIAGONAL RD., 22314
TEL 703/684-5900
FAX 703/684-0653
Located at King Street's north end, this all-suite hotel is convenient to Old Town Alexandria. All suites have two rooms and a variety of amenities to allow for comfort and working space.
🛏 268 ☎ 🚭 🕸 AE, D, DC, MC, V 🚇 King Street

🏨 MORRISON HOUSE
$$$$$
116 S. ALFRED ST., 22314
TEL 703/838-8000 OR 866/834-6628
FAX 703/684-6283
A modern hotel designed to evoke the atmosphere of Old Alexandria, the Morrison resembles an 18th-century manor house. Guest rooms are furnished in federal-period reproductions. Dinner offered at the hotel's very good **Elysium** restaurant.
🛏 45 🅿 🕸 AE, MC, V 🚇 King Street, then bus to Old Town

RESTAURANTS

ARLINGTON, VA

🍴 MAESTRO
$$$$

RITZ-CARLTON HOTEL, 1700 TYSONS BLVD., TYSONS CORNER
TEL 703/821-1515
Maestro is one of the most ambitious restaurants to open in Northern Virginia in the last few years, the successful collaboration of a team that includes chef Fabio Trabocchi and wine steward Vincent Feraud. Trabucchi divides his Italian menu in traditional and contemporary sections. The setting is sumptuous, the food is frequently dazzling, and the experience is worth the charge on the credit card. Where else might you be served sea urchin in its shell; lobster-and-black-truffle pasta; and three different preparations of lamb in the same meal?
🍽 86 🅿 Valet 🕔 Closed all Sun., Mon., & L 🕸 AE, D, DC, MC, V

🍴 QUEEN BEE
$$
3181 WILSON BLVD.
TEL 703/527-3444
Of the cluster of Vietnamese restaurants that surround the Clarendon Metro station, Queen Bee is the most dependable and popular. The spring rolls are the standard by which others should be judged. The shrimp and pork rolls are also delicious, as is the green papaya salad with beef jerky and spicy sausage. Good main course choices are the Hanoi-style grilled pork, the Saigon pancake, and the whole fried fish served with spicy sauce. Vietnamese iced coffee, sweetened with condensed milk, is the perfect dessert.
🍽 98 🕸 AE, DC, MC, V 🚇 Clarendon

ALEXANDRIA, VA

🍴 LA BERGERIE
$$$-$$$$
218 N. LEE ST.
TEL 703/683-1007
This dependable French

restaurant has long been Old Town Alexandria's favorite place for special occasions. Vincent Damman, who recently took over the kitchen, offers an excellent $65 tasting menu. A recent meal starter was celery root with apples and lobster, and main courses have included *ris de veau* with chanterelle mushrooms and brandy cream sauce. La Bergerie is one of the few restaurants that still go to the trouble to make dessert soufflés (order at the beginning of the meal). Hazelnut is the best.
🍽 70 🕔 Closed Sun. L 🕸 AE, D, DC, MC, V 🚇 King Street, then bus

🍴 BLUE POINT GRILL
$$$
600 FRANKLIN ST.
TEL 703/739-0404
The casually elegant dining room at Blue Point Grill is a wonderful place for a dozen oysters and a glass of wine, a shopping lunch on weekends, or a full-scale special occasion dinner. The prime draw is immaculately fresh fish and shellfish. You have to pass the impressive raw bar to get to your table, so let that be a clue to the best first courses. Main course selections depend on availability, but good picks have included sea bass margherita with black beans, tomato-corn relish, and cilantro; and seared halibut with creamy polenta.
🍽 66 🅿 🕸 AE, D, MC, V 🚇 King Street, then bus

🍴 MAJESTIC CAFÉ
$$$
911 KING ST.
TEL 703/837-9117
Chef Susan Lindeborg reopened this landmark Alexandria restaurant, which had been standing vacant for many years, and the result is impressive. The place has been modernized and many of its art deco elements preserved. Lindeborg's forte is

home cooking—moist chicken breast served with cornbread dressing; a simple gratin of oysters, Virginia ham, and cracker crumbs; richly satisfying spoonbread. And don't leave without a piece of the fabulous buttermilk pie.

🛏 72 🕐 Closed Mon.
🅰 AE, D, DC, MC, V
🚇 King Street, then DASH bus or Metro shuttle

🍴 EVENING STAR CAFÉ
$$
2000 MT. VERNON AVE.
TEL 703/549-5051
An ambitious American comfort-food menu and an impressive wine program raise this appealing eatery out of the neighborhood restaurant category. A new bar offers wines by the glass and small plates for snacking. In fair weather, there's outdoor seating.

🛏 70 🕐 Closed Mon. L
🅰 AE, D, DC, MC, V
🚇 Braddock Road

🍴 LE GAULOIS
$$
1106 KING ST.
TEL 703/739-9494
Loyal diners have followed this popular French restaurant from its former home in Washington to its present one in Alexandria. What keeps them coming back is a menu of familiar classics of French bourgeois cooking, all done very well. You can get a comforting *pot-au-feu* in cool weather, a well-made omelet at lunch, and dinner specials such as chicken fricassée Normandy-style with a sauce made from apples, mushrooms, calvados, and cream.

🛏 100 🅰 AE, D, DC, MC, V 🚇 King Street, then walk six blocks

🍴 ECCO CAFE
$
220 N. LEE ST.
TEL 703/684-0321
A large and popular Italian-

American neighborhood pizza and pasta place.

🛏 150 🅰 AE, D, DC, MC, V 🚇 King Street; then bus

EXCURSIONS

RESTAURANTS

ANNAPOLIS, MD

🍴 TREATY OF PARIS
$$$
16 CHURCH CIRCLE
TEL 410/216-6340
The menu at this historic inn in the heart of Old Annapolis is not groundbreaking, but it's well prepared. Crab is king here. Crab Louis with a Cajun remoulade sauce is a good starter, as are the fried crab cakes. Seafood *en papillote* contains a mixture of fish, scallops, shrimp, and clams, and if you haven't had your fill of crab in the first course, the Crab Imperial is traditional and good. There is also a good selection of meat dishes—beef Wellington, veal Oscar, rack of venison.

🛏 75 🅿 Valet 🅰 AE, D, DC, MC, V

🍴 CANTLER'S RIVERSIDE INN
$$
458 FOREST BEACH RD.
TEL 410/757-1467
A short drive from downtown Annapolis, Cantler's—owned by a family of watermen—is one of the city's most popular seafood restaurants. You eat at benches at communal tables, or at picnic tables on the deck, overlooking the docks and beautiful creek. Begin with a Styrofoam cup of she-crab soup. There are meat and chicken dishes, but the best main courses feature seafood from Maryland waters—crab cakes, softshell crabs, and rockfish.

🛏 318 🅿 🅰 AE, D, DC, MC, V

BALTIMORE, MD

🍴 CHARLESTON
$$$$
1000 LANCASTER ST.
TEL 410/332-7373
Chef Cindy Wolf's Charleston place on the Inner Harbor is Baltimore's most praised restaurant. As the name suggests, the specialty is low-country Southern cooking. Starters have included Charleston she-crab soup, cornmeal-crusted oysters, and fried green tomatoes with lobster and crab hash. Wolf frequently features traditional Carolina dishes such as seafood Perlau, or southern improvisations such as venison medallions with spoonbread or duck breasts with Madeira-poached pears and pecan rice. The wine selection is well chosen and well priced.

🛏 130 🅿 Valet 🕐 Closed Sun. & all L 🅰 AE, D, DC, MC, V

SOMETHING SPECIAL

🍴 OBRYCKI'S CRAB HOUSE
Don't leave Baltimore without eating at one of the city's traditional crab houses. Tables are covered with paper; steamed crabs coated with Old Bay Seasoning are dumped in the middle; and if you don't know how to eat them, your friendly server gives you a quick lesson in the art of opening crabs with a knife and wooden mallet. Obrycki's is closed for the winter and opens with crab season about the middle of March. You can also order crab cakes or softshell crabs, or crabmeat sautéed in butter, which require less work to eat.
$$$
1727 EAST PRATT ST.
TEL 410/732-6399
🕐 Closed Dec.–Feb.

SHOPPING

Washington is the place to pick up that perfect political souvenir—from campaign buttons to White House Easter eggs to Presidential seal mousepads. But just as there is more to the city than what goes on atop Capitol Hill, there is more to Washington shopping than political paraphernalia. The museum stores, for starters, have wonderful inventories of unique books, arts and crafts, jewelry, and artifact reproductions. It's natural that in such a highly educated city you'll find countless excellent bookstores. And local markets feature interesting bric-a-brac.

For a real shopping experience, however, wander into the neighborhoods, which harbor neat little one-of-a-kind shops and boutiques. Georgetown's two main arteries—M Street and Wisconsin Avenue—has many fashionable boutiques, bookstores, art galleries, antique stores, and contemporary clothing stores. Dupont Circle is much funkier, with its eclectic boutiques, vintage clothing stores, antique furniture shops, plus stores catering to the neighborhood's gay population. Adams Morgan resembles Berkeley, California, more than anything found on the East Coast, with its down-to-earth selection of African goods and curious New Age paraphernalia. Across the river, Old Town Alexandria's historic core along King Street showcases a slew of antique shops, galleries, and carpet stores in 18th-century buildings.

This listing covers some of the more unique shopping experiences in the Washington, D.C., area.

ANTIQUES

Georgetown overflows with antique shops, especially on Wisconsin Avenue between P and S Streets, and along M and O Streets. Store after store features gorgeous furniture and such accessories as grandfather clocks, 19th-century paintings, and sterling tableware. **Adams Morgan** and **Dupont Circle** also offer a good selection of antiques. In **Kensington, Maryland,** Howard Avenue is one of the foremost antique districts in the mid-Atlantic, with prices being better than those in Georgetown. Head to the lower, warehouse end of the street for serious antique shopping. The downtown Antique Row has cute, smaller shops full of collectibles. **Old Town Alexandria** has dozens of antique shops, purveying real Persian rugs, as well as French, English, and American period furniture.

ARTS & CRAFTS, GALLERIES

The best places to look for handmade works of art are Adams Morgan, Georgetown, Dupont Circle, and Old Town Alexandria. Seventh Street, N.W., between D Street and the MCI Center, has become a mecca of galleries.

Addison/Ripley Fine Art, 1670 Wisconsin Ave., N.W. (Georgetown), 202/338-5180. One of Washington's foremost galleries, established in 1981, featuring painting, sculpture, photography, and fine arts prints.

Appalachian Spring, 1415 Wisconsin Ave., N.W. (Georgetown), 202/337-5780; & Union Station (Capitol Hill), 202/682-0505. Traditional and contemporary crafts, including jewelry, gorgeous pottery, quilts, and woodcarvings.

Canal Square, 31st & M Sts. (Georgetown) Art galleries galore.

Torpedo Factory Art Center, 105 N. Union St., Alexandria (Across the Potomac), 703/838-4565. 84 working artists' studios (each one selling their works) and five galleries showcase sculpture, pottery, paintings in watercolor, acrylic, and oil, plus much more.

BOOKS

Chapters, 445 11th St, N.W. (White House & around), 202/737-5553. Metro: Metro Center. Independent literary bookstore with current events, contemporary fiction, classics, and poetry.

Government Printing Office Bookstore, 710 N. Capitol St., N.W. (between G and H Sts.), 202/512-0132, closed weekends. Metro: Union Station. The largest general printing plant in the world, the GPO serves the printing needs of Congress. With nearly 16,000 titles (books and pamphlets) covering every conceivable area, from Cardiac Rehabilitation to the Dictionary of American Naval Fighting Ships, you should be able to find something that relates to any new hobby, interest, or activity. Also photography books, CD-ROMS and diskettes, prints, lithographs, and posters.

Kramerbooks & afterwords, 1517 Connecticut Ave., N.W., (Dupont Circle & Adams Morgan), 202/387-1400, open 24 hours on weekends. Metro: Dupont Circle. Small but good selection of books, including political, fiction, and religion. Late-night dining and entertainment at the café.

Olsson's Books & Records, 1307 19th St., N.W., 202/785-1133; 418 7th St., N.W., 202/638-7610; www.olssons.com. Large and varied collection of books and a good selection of classical and folk records, tapes, and CDs.

**Politics and Prose
Bookstore & Coffeehouse,**
5015 Connecticut Ave., N.W.,
(Cleveland Park & beyond),
202/364-1919. Metro: Friendship
Heights. Topical novels and literary nonfiction, frequented often
by Washington's intelligentsia.
Frequent author readings. Café.

Second Story Books,
2000 P St., N.W. (Dupont Circle
& Adams Morgan), 202/659-
8884. Metro: Dupont Circle.
Used and rare books, including
first editions, fine bound volumes, and just plain used. Stays
open late.

DEPARTMENT STORES & MALLS

**The Shops at Chevy Chase
Pavilion,** 5335 Wisconsin Ave.,
N.W., 202/686-5335. Metro:
Friendship Heights. Stores at
this popular mall include Pottery
Barn, Joan and David, and
Talbots. Food court.

Crystal City Shops, Crystal
Dr. between 15th & 23rd Sts.,
Arlington (Across the Potomac),
703/922-4636. Metro: Crystal
City. More than 125 stores with
clothing, gifts, and more. Dining.

**Fashion Centre at Pentagon
City,** 1100 S. Hayes St.,
Arlington (Across the Potomac),
703/415-2400. Metro: Pentagon
City. Four-story mall with 163
shops, including Macy's and
Nordstrom. Dining and cinema
as well.

Mazza Gallerie, 5330
Wisconsin Ave., N.W. Metro:
Friendship Heights. This complex
of exclusive shops, restaurants,
and theaters showcases Neiman
Marcus, Saks Fifth Avenue Men's
Store, and Filene's Basement.

Old Post Office Pavilion,
1100 Pennsylvania Ave., N.W.
(Downtown), 202/289-4224.
Metro: Federal Triangle.
Clothing, souvenirs, gifts in a

historic 19th-century building.
Dining. Entertainment.

Potomac Mills Outlet Mall,
2700 Potomac Mills Circle,
Woodbridge, VA (Excursions),
703/490-5948. Off I-95 about 30
miles south of Washington.
Said to be Virginia's number one
tourist attraction, the 152-acre
shoppers' paradise has some
220 discount and outlet stores,
including Nordstrom Rack,
Ralph Lauren, Laura Ashley,
Coach, and L.L. Bean. IKEA, a
popular Swedish furniture store,
has recently expanded to twice
its original enormous space.

Shops at Georgetown Park,
3222 M St., N.W. (Georgetown),
202/298-5577. More than 100
upscale shops and boutiques in a
restored tobacco warehouse.

Shops at National Place,
13th & F Sts., N.W. (Downtown),
202/662-1250. Metro: Metro
Center. Three levels of shops,
including men's and women's
clothing, jewelry, gifts, shoes, and
an enormous food court.

Tyson's Corner Center,
1961 Chain Bridge Rd., McLean,
VA (Excursions), 703/827-7700.
Washington's largest mall, with
more than 230 shops and bou-
tiques, including Nordstrom,
Bloomingdale's, and Lord &
Taylor's. Dining.

Union Station,
50 Massachusetts Ave., N.E.
(Capitol Hill), 202/371-9441.
Metro: Union Station. 125-plus
stores on 3 levels, plus a food
court and cinema multi-plex, in
an active train station.

FARMER & FLEA MARKETS

**Alexandria Farmer's
Market,** 301 King St.,
Alexandria (Across the
Potomac), Sat. a.m. only.
Traditional farmer's market with
the freshest fruit and vegetables,
preserves, pastries, and flowers.

Eastern Market, 225 7th St.,
S.E. (Capitol Hill), closed Mon.
Washington's last remaining
public market, where butchers
and greengrocers purvey
cheeses, meats, fish, baked
goods, flowers, and such local
delicacies as pigs' feet, baby back
ribs, and homemade jams in a
big redbrick building dating from
1870. Outside unfolds a farmers'
market (Sat.) and flea market
(Sun. March-Dec.). Popular
breakfast grill.

Georgetown Flea Market,
34th St. & Wisconsin Ave., N.W.
(Georgetown), Sun. only
March–Dec. A museum's worth
of antique musical instruments,
rugs, clothes, furniture, new jewelry and sunglasses, old cameras
and books, and much more. This
being Georgetown, don't expect
great bargains.

**Maine Avenue Seafood Mar-
ket,** Washington Channel, S.W.
A dozen canopied dockside
barges hold beautiful, gleaming
piles of the recently swimming
rockfish, bluefish, shad, catfish,
swordfish, pompano, crabs,
clams, and just about any other
catch you can name. A couple of
stands sell hot cooked crabs, for
those who can't wait.

GOURMET FOODS & WINE

Dean & Deluca, 3276 M St.,
N.W. (Georgetown), 202/342-
2500. Gourmet foods in the historic Markethouse building, plus
kitchen accessories and gifts. Its
café is a wonderful place to pick
up a quick bite, including sandwiches on your choice of
baguette, focaccia, or onion roll;
sushi; and salads with such
clever touches as dried cranber-
ries in wild rice.

Marvelous Market, 5035
Connecticut Ave., N.W., 202/686-
4040; 1511 Connecticut Ave.,
N.W., 202/332-3690; 1800 K St.,
N.W., 202/828-0944; 3217 P St.,
N.W., 202/333-2591. Inventive

sandwiches, small yet impressive selection of prepared foods, and wonderfully crusty bread.

Sutton Place Gourmet, 5 locations in the Washington area, including 3201 New Mexico Ave., N.W., 202/363-5800. Modeled on European markets, featuring specialty foods and wines.

MUSEUM SHOPS

Bureau of Engraving & Printing, 14th and C Sts., S.W. (The Mall), 202/874-3019, closed weekends. Metro: Smithsonian. Engravings of Presidents, Washington landscapes, and government seals. Buy sheets of uncut $1 and $2 bills.

Decatur House museum shop, 1600 H Street, N.W. (White House & around), 202/842-1856. Reproductions of home accessories from the 18th and 19th centuries, including Presidential china. Books, jewelry, and children selections.

Hillwood Museum, 4155 Linnean Ave., N.W. (Cleveland Park & beyond), 202/686-8500 The former residence of Marjorie Merriweather Post, cereal heiress, includes a gift shop purveying French and Russian decorative arts and reproductions.

Hirshhorn Museum, 950 Independence Ave., S.W. (The Mall) 202/357-1300. Metro: Smithsonian.Contemporary jewelry that's fun and quirky.

John F. Kennedy Center for the Performing Arts, Rock Creek and Potomac Pkwy. & New Hampshire Ave., N.W. (White House & around), 202/467-4600, Metro: Foggy Bottom. Good selection of gifts with music, dance, theater, and opera themes.

Mount Vernon Inn Gift Shop, George Washington Memorial Pkwy., Alexandria (Across the Potomac), 703/780-0011. Reproductions of the Washingtons' belongings, including china and silver, as well as toys and souvenirs.

National Air and Space Museum, 7th St. & Constitution Ave., N.W. (The Mall), 202/357-1300. Freeze-dried ice cream (like what the astronauts eat), kites, books, and videos for aspiring pilots and astronauts.

National Archives Museum Store, 7th St. & Constitution Ave., N.W. (Downtown), 202/501-5000. Replicas of the Charters of Freedom, posters, and postcards.

National Building Museum, 401 F St., N.W. (Downtown), 202/272-2448. Architecture-related books, prints, posters, toys, and gifts.

National Gallery of Art, 600 Constitution Ave., N.W., (The Mall), 202/737-4215. Metro: Archives, Judiciary Square. Several shops in the museum feature quality prints and posters, art reproductions, gifts, and art books.

National Geographic Society, 1145 17th St., N.W. (White House & around), 800/638-6400. Metro: Farragut North, Farragut West. Wall maps, books, globes, and educational children's toys.

National Museum of African Art, 950 Independence Ave., S.W. (The Mall), 202/786-2147. Books for adults and children on African culture and history. Also African crafts, posters, dolls, jewelry, records, and tapes.

National Museum of Women in the Arts, 1250 New York Ave., N.W. (Downtown), 202/783-5000. Unique jewelry, decorative objects, books, and other gifts.

Phillips Collection, 1600 21st St., N.W. (Dupont Circle & Adams Morgan), 202/387-2151. Jewelry, ceramics, glassware, and other objects by contemporary artists, plus hand-painted scarves, reproductions, books, and more.

Renwick Gallery, Pennsylvania Ave. at 17th St., N.W. (White House & around).Features contemporary crafts of fiber, metal, ceramic, and wood, plus books, toys, posters, and more.

White House Gift Shop, National Press Bldg., 529 14th St., N.W. (Downtown), 202/662-7280.Gifts and collectibles, including glassware, jewelry, and clothing.

OTHER

The Map Store, 1636 I St., N.W. (White House & around), 202/628-2608, closed Sun. Metro: Farragut West. More than 5,000 maps from around the world, plus guidebooks, narratives, and globes.

Counter Spy Shop, 1027 Connecticut Ave., N.W. (White House & around), 202/887-1717, closed Sun. Metro: Farragut North. Gadgets for spies & aspiring 007s.

Washington National Cathedral, Wisconsin & Massachusetts Aves., N.W., 202/537-5766. Gothic- and Medieval-inspired ware, including window decorations, scarves, and stuffed gargoyles. Don't miss the Herb Cottage on the grounds.

ENTERTAINMENT

After traipsing around all day from site to site, be sure to save some energy for Washington after dark. Your choices are many: theater, a movie, dancing, or just hanging out at one of the local bars. Check the Friday Weekend section of the *Washington Post* for goings-on; as well as the weekly *Washington CityPaper*. *Washingtonian* magazine is another good source of information.

DANCE

Dance Place, 3225 8th St., N.E., 202/269-1600. Metro: Brookland. Dance Place presents programs of modern and ethnic dance most weekends.

Washington Ballet, 202/362-3606. The nationally recognized Washington Ballet presents a full season between September and May at the Kennedy Center and also presents the *Nutcracker* each Christmas at the Warner Theater and the Center for the Arts at George Mason University.

FILM

American Film Institute, The AFI (www.afi.com) screens hundreds of films every years at its new AFI Silver Theatre and Cultural Center at 8633 Colesville Rd., Silver Spring, Md. (301/495-6720) and at the Kennedy Center in Washington (202/833-2348). Actors and directors often discuss their work at these showings.

Filmfest DC, 202/724-5613; www.filmfestdc.org. The DC International Film Festival, held in late April and early May, screens American and international films in a variety of local theaters and auditoriums.

National Gallery of Art East Building, 4th St. and Constitution Ave., N.W., 202/737-4215. The National Gallery shows free classic films and films relating to exhibitions in the galleries.

Reel Affirmations, 202/986-1119. D.C.'s gay and lesbian film festival, held for ten days in October each year, shows films of gay and lesbian interest at Lincoln Theatre (1215 U St., N.W.), the Jewish Community Center (16th and Q Sts., N.W.), and at the Goethe-Institut Inter Nationes (814 7th St., N.W.).

MUSIC

CHAMBER MUSIC
Corcoran Gallery of Art, 17th St. and New York Ave., N.W., 202/639-1700. Metro: Farragut West. Well known quartets appear in the Corcoran's musical evenings series from October to May.

Library of Congress, 1st St. and Independence Ave., S.E., 202/707-5502. Metro: Union Station, Capitol South. Both the Julliard String Quartet and the Beaux Arts Trio are in residence at the Library of Congress and present frequent free concerts.

Phillips Collection, 1600 21st St., N.W., 202/387-2151. Metro: Dupont Circle. Free Sunday-afternoon concerts in the Phillips mansion's wood-paneled music room.

CHORAL MUSIC
Choral Arts Society of Washington, 202/244-3669. Between September and May, this 180-voice ensemble, directed by Norman Scribner, presents frequent classical programs in the Kennedy Center Concert Hall.

OPERA
Washington Opera, Kennedy Center Opera House, 202/295-2400. Metro: Foggy Bottom. During the November to March season, the Washington Opera, directed by Placido Domingo, produces eight operas, sung in their original languages with English subtitles.

ORCHESTRA
National Symphony Orchestra, Kennedy Center Concert Hall, 202/416-8100. Metro: Foggy Bottom. From September to June, the NSO performs at the Kennedy Center. In the summer, there are concerts at Wolf Trap (703/225-1800) and at Carter Barron Amphitheatre.

NIGHTLIFE

The Birchmere, 3701 Mount Vernon Ave., Alexandria, 703/549-7500; www.birchmere.com. The Birchmere takes music very seriously—the club's no-talking policy is strictly enforced. But the performers and the sound are terrific; the food, from Alexandria's King Street Blues, is very good; and there's also a pool hall, a brewery, and a large bar.

Blues Alley, 1073 Wisconsin Ave., N.W., 202/337-4141; www.bluesalley.com. Metro: Foggy Bottom, then walk or bus. All the legends of blues have played at this small club—Dizzy Gillespie, Wynton Marsalis, Nancy Wilson, Charlie Byrd. Tickets are $18 to $60—and there's a $9 minimum plus a $2.25 per-person surcharge for the Blues Alley Music Society. There are usually 8 and 10 p.m. shows, and sometimes on weekends a midnight set. Reservations are essential.

Bohemian Caverns, 2003 11th St., N.W., 202/299-0800. Metro: U Street–Cardozo. Bohemian Caverns was once a Washington institution, hosting Duke Ellington, Billie Holiday, Louis Armstrong, Jelly Roll Morton, Thelonious Monk, and others. The fake-cavern decor itself is worth seeing.

Chi-Cha Lounge, 1624 U St., N.W., 202/234-8400. Metro: U Street–Cardozo. Modern Andean cooking, Latin folkloric music, and a house drink called the Chi-Cha Morada, made of red corn, pineapple, cinnamon, cloves, and alcohol make this late-night lounge a favorite on U Street.

HR-57 Center for the Preservation of Jazz and Blues, 1610 14th St., N.W., 202/667-3700; www.hr57.org. Named for the House of Representatives resolution that honored jazz as a national treasure, this non-profit music cultural center holds jazz jam sessions and performances four evenings a week.

IOTA Club & Cafe, 2832 Wilson Blvd., Arlington, 703/522-8340. Metro: Clarendon. Iota consistently books some of the best folk, alternative country, and rock music in the area, and the food's good, too.

Kramerbooks & afterwords café, 1517 Connecticut Ave., N.W., 202/387-1462; www.kramers.com. Metro: Dupont Circle. Serving latte´ to the literati, this bookstore with attached café is the informal community center for the Dupont Circle neighborhood. It's open all night Friday and Saturday nights, and has live music Wednesday through Saturday.

Madam's Organ, 2461 18th St., N.W., 202/667-5370; www.madamsorgan.com. The popular Madam's Organ has a full schedule of bluegrass,

R&B, and blues. Try to arrive before 10 Thursday through Saturday—after 11, you'll probably wait in line.

Modern, 3287 M St., N.W., 202/338-7027. Metro: Foggy Bottom, then walk or bus. You may not be sure if it's a bar or a retro furniture store, but this handsome, friendly bar with couches, coffee tables, a hardwood dance floor, and a dress code is a delightful exception to the rule that Georgetown bars are only for students.

9:30 Club, 815 V St., N.W., 202/265-0930; www.930.com. Metro: U Street–Cardozo. A great sound system makes this crowded club the best place in Washington to hear top-tier rock, punk, hip-hop, and country shows.

Strike Bethesda, 353 Westbard Ave., Bethesda, MD, 301/652-0955. Bowling is hip again. Sister establishment to New York's wildly popular Bowlmor Lanes, Strike Bethesda features 34 lanes, a VIP room, state-of-the-art sound and video systems, and a restaurant serving New American cuisine. It's open until 1 a.m. weeknights, and 2 a.m. weekends.

Visions, 1927 Florida Ave., N.W., 202/667-0090; www.visionsdc.com. Metro: Dupont Circle. An art movie house theater cum coffeehouse, it has a full bar with a funky coffeehouse atmosphere—plus a bistro that serves Mediterranean, Middle Eastern, and Indian tapas-style food; a bar; and a coffee selection worthy of the Pacific Northwest. Two narrow theaters show the latest independent and foreign films.

THEATER

Arena Stage, 6th St. and Maine Ave., S.W., 202/488-3300; www.arenastage.com. This respected resident theater

company presents a busy season on its three stages.

Ford's Theatre See p. 132.

Howard Theatre See p. 174.

Lincoln Theater See p. 174.

National Theatre See p. 143.

Shakespeare Theatre, 450 7th St., N.W., 202/393-2700. Metro: Gallery Place/Chinatown Widely acknowledged as one of the best Shakespeare companies in America, the Shakespeare Theatre stages four plays a year in a custom-built, state-of-the-art theater. See p. 134.

Signature Theatre, 3806 S. Four Mile Run Dr., Arlington, 703/218-6500; http://www.sig-online.org. Especially known for its productions of modern musical theater.

Source Theatre, 1835 14th St., N.W., 202/462-1073. Metro: U Street–Cardozo. The Source Theatre company specializes in new plays, contemporary works, and bold reinterpretations of the classics.

Studio Theatre, 1333 P St., N.W., 202/332-3300. Metro: Dupont Circle. The third largest producing theater in Washington, Studio Theatre presents the best of contemporary theater. It is the home of Studio Theatre Acting Conservatory, which runs a widely-respected school for the theater.

Warner Theatre See p. 144.

Woolly Mammoth, 917 M St., N.W., 202/393-3939; www.woollymammoth.net. *Variety* comments on Woolly Mammoth's "fierce dedication to the offbeat," a dedication that is pursued with genuine devotion and solid production values.

ACTIVITIES

From boating to golfing to ice skating, Washington offers an amazingly diverse selection of options for outdoor enthusiasts. If you're in the mood to watch others do the work instead, you have a number of big-name sports teams from which to choose, including Michael Jordan's Wizards. For something a little different, join one of the many specialty tours—a chance to see the city from a different point of view, by walking, boating, or even by bike.

OUTDOOR ACTIVITIES

BOATING
Jack's Boats, 3500 K St., N.W., 202/337-9642.
Open April–Oct.
Located under Key Bridge in Georgetown, Jack's rents canoes, kayaks, and row boats.

Thompson Boat Center,
2900 Virginia Ave., N.W., 202/333-9543. Open April–Oct.
Canoes, rowing shells, and kayaks for rent. Lessons available. Also, all-terrain and cruiser bike rentals.

GOLF
East Potomac Park Golf Course, 972 Ohio Dr., S.W., 202/554-7660. This public course near the Mall consists of one 18-hole, par-72 course and two 9-hole courses. Open daily from dawn until dusk. Daily cart fees.

Langston Golf Course,
268 Benning Rd., N.E., 202/397-8638. The Langston Golf Course is an 18-hole, par-72 public course that also offers a golf school, golf shop, driving range, putting green, and snack bar.

Rock Creek Park Golf Course, 16th and Rittenhouse Sts., N.W., 202/882-7332.
This 4,798-yard, par-65 public course has a hilly and challenging terrain. Amenities include a golf school, golf shop, a putting green, and a snack bar. The course is open every day from dawn to dusk.

ICE SKATING
National Gallery of Art Sculpture Garden Ice Skating Rink, 7th St. and Constitution Ave., N.W., 202/737-4215. Beautifully designed, this rink on the Mall affords skaters views of the wonderful works of modern sculpture in the museum garden. The state-of-the-art sound system provides uniform sound to skaters without distracting other visitors to the garden.

TENNIS
East Potomac Tennis Center, 1090 Ohio Dr., S.W., 202/554-5962. Indoor and outdoor courts, seasonal membership or walk-in court rental, tennis lessons, and racquet stringing.

Rock Creek Park Tennis Center, 16th and Kennedy St., N.W., 202/722-5949.
The facility has a total of 25 outdoor tennis courts: 10 hard courts and 15 clay courts. Five indoor courts are heated and available in winter.

SPECTATOR SPORTS

Baltimore Orioles, tickets through TicketMaster, 888-848-2473. Baseball at Oriole Park at Camden Yards, Baltimore.

Baltimore Ravens,
410/261-7283. NFL football in Baltimore.

DC United, 703/478-6600. Professional soccer at RFK Stadium.

Washington Capitals,
202/266-2277. Professional hockey at the MCI Center.

Washington Mystics,
202/432-7328.
Professional women's basketball at the MCI Center.

Washington Power,
301-324-1755. Lacrosse.

Washington Redskins,
301-276-6050. NFL football at FedEx Field.

Washington Wizards,
202/661-5050;
www.nba.com/wizards.
Professional basketball at the MCI Center.

SPECIALTY TOURS

WALKING TOURS
Anecdotal History Walks,
301/294-9514.
Author Anthony Pitch leads tours around Georgetown; around the White House; the Capitol to the White House; Adams Morgan; and sites relating to the Lincoln assassination. Most Sundays. Private tours any day by appointment.

U Street Walking Tours,
202/232-2915.
Long before the Harlem Renaissance, the U Street area was known as Black Broadway, the city's African American social, cultural, and intellectual center. Among the 14 stops included on this 90-minute guided walk through that neighborhood are the block where Duke Ellington lived, the city's first black YMCA, and the African American Civil War Memorial. Monthly tours on first and third Saturdays begin at 10 a.m. at the Thurgood Marshall Center for Service, 1816 12th St., N.W.

Georgetown & Dupont Circle Walking Tours
301/588-8999. In her popular neighborhood walking tours, writer and tour guide Mary Kay Ricks serves up a lot of scandal and history.

ACTIVITIES

Washington Walks,
202/484-1565. Among the walks offered are Capital Hauntings, which seeks out the ghosts that frequent the area around Lafayette Square and the White House; Embassy Row, Washington's grandest boulevard; and Goodnight, Mr. Lincoln, in which families clad in pajamas learn about the 16th President at the base of the Lincoln Memorial.

BOAT TOURS & CRUISES
Dandy Restaurant Cruise Ship, Zero Prince St., Alexandria, VA, 703/683-6076. The *Dandy* cruises from Old Town Alexandria to Georgetown, under the Potomac River bridges and past the monuments and memorials. Dinner is served aboard, and there's a marble dance floor.

***Odyssey* Cruises, Gangplank Marina,** 600 Water St., S.W., 888/822-5991. The 2- to 3-hour *Odyssey* cruises feature innovative meals, a top wine list, and live music, while taking in the sites of the nation's capital.

Spirit of Washington, Pier 4, 6th & Water Sts., S.W., 866/211-3811. With three interior decks and roomy outdoor observation decks, the *Spirit of Washington* can accommodate up to 450 people for leisurely afternoon or evening cruises. Food, entertainment, and dancing are available.

OTHER
BeyondGuide, 301/816-0303. Beyond Guide offers self-guided tours over your cell phone, allowing you to see what you want at your own pace.

Scandal Tours, 202/783-7212. This irreverent tour of Washington's infamous scandal sites is hosted by the critically acclaimed comedy group, Gross National Product, who give you an impudent commentary on

Washington's embarrassing moments. Reservations required. Offered from April Fool's Day through Labor Day weekend on Saturdays at 1 p.m., pick-up at the Post Office Pavilion.

SpyDrive, 866/SPY-DRIVE. Former intelligence officers (U.S. and foreign) host this two-plus-hour bus tour of sites where spies operated.

Washington Photo Safari, 202/537-0937. Professional photographer David Luria offers half-and full-day workshops in landmark photography. Tours are given in English, French, and Spanish.

You and Me Travel, 202/841-8106. Shopping trips to Potomac Mills and Leesburg discount malls.

HEALTH CLUBS

Some fitness clubs in Washington offer guest passes to anyone accompanying a member, or one-time guest passes, ranging from $15 to $25. Call the individual locations for information.

Bally Total Fitness
Call 800/695-8111 for information on all locations, or visit www.ballyfitness.com. No daily guest rate; must be a Bally Total Fitness member. The dozen clubs in the Washington area include, in the city: 2000 L St., N.W., #1B (202/331-7788).

Fitness Company
www.fitnesscompany.com There are 15 clubs in the Washington area, including the following: downtown, at 1875 I St., N.W. (202/833-2629); and near Georgetown, 1010 Wisconsin Ave., N.W. (202/625-9100).

Gold's Gym
www.golds gym.com There are nine Gold's Gyms in the Washington area, including the following; on Capitol Hill, 409 3rd St., S.W. (202/554-4653); and downtown, at 1120 20th St., N.W. (202/293-4200).

Sport and Health Clubs
Call 800/88-CLUBS for information on all locations; www.sportandhealth.com. There are two dozen Sport and Health Clubs in the Washington area, including, in the Watergate area: 2620 Virginia Ave., N.W. (202/298-4460); and in the Tenleytown area, 4000 Wisconsin Ave., N.W. (202/362-8000).

Washington Sports Club
Visit www.washingtonsports .com for information on all locations.
The five clubs in the Washington area include the following: downtown, at 1211 Connecticut Ave., N.W. (202/296-7733); also at 1835 Connecticut Ave., N.W. (202/332-0100).

ILLUSTRATIONS CREDITS

Cover: Richard T. Nowitz; except (left), Karen Ballard

Photographs by Richard T. Nowitz, except 1, Karen Ballard; 9, Bob Rowan / CORBIS; 14-15, Karen Ballard; 19, Bettmann / CORBIS; 20-21, Tom Freeman, White House Historical Association; 22, White House Collection, White House Historical Association; 23, CORBIS; 24-25, Marie Louise Brimberg; 27, Bettmann / CORBIS; 28-29, Hulton I Archive by Getty Images; 31, SABA / CORBIS; 32, Karen Ballard; 35, Karen Ballard; 40-41, Little Girl in a Blue Armchair, Mary Cassatt, Collection of of Mr. and Mrs. Paul Mellon, National Gallery of Art, Washington; 43, Hulton I Archive by Getty Images; 56-57, Artwork by Maltings Partnership, Derby, England; 58-59, Christie's Images / CORBIS; 72, Photograph by Franko Khoury, Courtesy National Museum of African Art, Smithsonian Institution; 75, Courtesy National Air and Space Museum, Smithsonian Institution, Artwork by Rob Wood / Wood, Ronsaville and Harlin, Inc.; 76, CORBIS / Sygma; 78-79, Artwork by Maltings Partnership, Derby, England; 82, Kay Hankins; 83, Ernest Amoroso, ©Smithsonian Institution/National Museum of American Indians; 86-87, Artwork by Maltings Partnership, Derby, England; 87, Self-Portrait, Vincent van Gogh, Collection of Mr. and Mrs. John Hay Whitney, National Gallery of Art, Washington; 88, The Annunciation, Jan van Eyck, Andrew W. Mellon Collection, National Gallery of Art, Washington; 89, Typewriter Eraser, Claes Oldenburg and Coosje van Bruggen, Gift of The Morris and Gwendolyn Cafritz Foundation, National Gallery of Art, Washington; 94, Karen Ballard; 99, Everett C. Johnson / Folio; 100, ©Kevin Lamarque/Reuters/CORBIS; 104, Karen Ballard; 110-111, Artwork by Maltings Partnership, Derby, England; 112-113, Courtesy White House Collection, White House Historical Association; 113, CORBIS / Sygma; 114, Kay Hankins; 118, Kay Hankins; 119 (t), Courtesy of Corcoran Gallery of Art, Washington, D.C.; 119 (b), Albert Bierstadt, The Last of the Buffalo, 1888, oil on canvas, 71-1/8 x 118-3/4 in. Gift of Mary (Mrs. Albert) Bierstadt. Courtesy of Corcoran Gallery of Art, Washington, D.C. 120, Bettmann / CORBIS; 125, Karen Ballard; 126, Taylor Kennedy; 131, Karen Ballard; 133, Courtesy National Museum of Women in the Arts. Gift of the Honorable Clare Booth Luce; 134-135 (all), John Skowronski; 138, ©Richard T. Nowitz/CORBIS; 140, Kay Hankins; 148, Karen Ballard; 149, Karen Ballard; 150-151, Karen Ballard; 159 (upper), Karen Ballard; 159 (lower left), Bettmann / CORBIS; 159 (lower right), Karen Ballard; 166, Interior with Eqyptian Curtain, Henri Matisse, Courtesy The Phillips Collection, Washington, DC; 167, Woman with Dog, Pierre Bonnard, Courtesy The Phillips Collection, Washington, DC; 168, John Skowronski / Folio; 171, Karen Ballard; 174, Bettmann / CORBIS; 174-175, Karen Ballard; 175, Bettmann / CORBIS; 185, Courtesy Hillwood Museum & Gardens; 186 (both), Courtesy Hillwood Museum & Gardens; 192, Karen Ballard; 194 (upper), Hulton I Archive by Getty Images; 214, Richard T. Nowitz / CORBIS; 220-221, ©David Sailors/CORBIS; 224–225, Artwork by Maltings Partnership, Derby, England; 232, Kevin Fleming / CORBIS.

One of the world's largest nonprofit scientific and educational organizations, the National Geographic Society was founded in 1888 "for the increase and diffusion of geographic knowledge." Fulfilling this mission, the Society educates and inspires millions every day through its magazines, books, television programs, videos, maps and atlases, research grants, the National Geographic Bee, teacher workshops, and innovative classroom materials. The Society is supported through membership dues, charitable gifts, and income from the sale of its educational products. This support is vital to National Geographic's mission to increase global understanding and promote conservation of our planet through exploration, research, and education.

For more information, please call 1-800-NGS LINE (647-5463) or write to the following address:

National Geographic Society
1145 17th Street N.W.
Washington, D.C. 20036-4688
U.S.A.

Visit the Society's Web site at www.nationalgeographic.com.

Special Offer! Order today and get one year of National Geographic Traveler, the magazine travelers trust, for only $14.95. Call 1-800-NGS-LINE and mention code TRAC3A6.

Travel the world with National Geographic Experts: www.nationalgeographic.com /ngexpeditions

Published by the National Geographic Society
John M. Fahey, Jr., *President and Chief Executive Officer*
Gilbert M. Grosvenor, *Chairman of the Board*
Nina D. Hoffman, *Executive Vice President,*
    President, Books and School Publishing
Kevin Mulroy, *Vice President and Editor-in-Chief*
Elizabeth L. Newhouse, *Director of Travel Publishing*
Charles Kogod, *Director of Photography*
Marianne Koszorus, *Design Director*
Cinda Rose, *Art Director*
Carl Mehler, *Director of Maps*

Staff for this book:
Barbara A. Noe, *Senior Editor and Project Manager*
Melissa G. Ryan, *Illustrations Editor*
Kay Hankins, *Designer*
Allan Fallow, *Senior Editor*
Jane Sunderland, Carolina E. Averitt, Jarelle Stein, *Text Editors*
Caroline Hickey, *Senior Researcher*
Victoria Garrett Jones, *Editorial Researcher*
Matt Chwastyk, Joseph F. Ochlak, Nicholas P. Rosenbach, Gregory
    Ugiansky, XNR Productions, *Map Edit, Research, and Production*
R. Gary Colbert, *Production Director*
Richard S. Wain, *Production Project Manager*
Janet Dustin, *Illustrations Assistant*
Connie D. Binder, *Indexer*
Lise Sajewski, *Editorial Consultant*
Lawrence Porges, *Editorial Coordinator*
Elizabeth Erskine, Kay Kobor Hankins, Marianne G. Koszorus,
    Contributors

Diana Parsells, *Editorial Consultant for 2005 edition*

Map art drawn by Chris Orr & Associates, Southampton, England
Artwork by Maltings Partnership, Derby, England

Second edition 2005.

Copyright © 2002, 2005 National Geographic Society. All rights reserved. No part of this book may be reproduced or transmitted in any form or by any means, electronic or mechanical, including photocopying, without permission in writing from the National Geographic Society, 1145 17th Street N.W., Washington, D.C. 20036-4688.

ISSN 1538-5515

ISBN: 0-7922-3887-7 (2nd edition)

Printed and Bound by Cayfosa Quebecor, Barcelona, Spain. Color separations by North American Color, Portage, MI.

Visit the society's Web site at http://www.nationalgeographic.com

The information in this book has been carefully checked and to the best of our knowledge is accurate. However, details are subject to change, and the National Geographic Society cannot be responsible for such changes, or for errors or omissions. Assessments of sites, hotels, and restaurants are based on the author's subjective opinions, which do not necessarily reflect the publisher's opinion. The publisher cannot be responsible for any consequences arising from the use of this book.

NATIONAL GEOGRAPHIC
TRAVELER

A Century of Travel Expertise in Every Guide

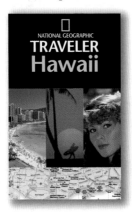

- **Amsterdam** ISBN: 0-7922-7900-X
- **Arizona** ISBN: 0-7922-3888-5
- **Australia** ISBN: 0-7922-3893-1
- **Barcelona** ISBN: 0-7922-7902-6
- **Boston & Environs** ISBN: 0-7922-7926-3
- **California** ISBN: 0-7922-3885-0
- **Canada** ISBN: 0-7922-7427-X
- **The Caribbean** ISBN: 0-7922-7434-2
- **China** ISBN: 0-7922-7921-2
- **Costa Rica** ISBN: 0-7922-7946-8
- **Cuba** ISBN: 0-7922-6931-4
- **Egypt** ISBN: 0-7922-7896-8
- **Florence & Tuscany** ISBN: 0-7922-7924-7
- **Florida** ISBN: 0-7922-7432-6
- **France** ISBN: 0-7922-7426-1
- **Germany** ISBN: 0-7922-4146-0
- **Great Britain** ISBN: 0-7922-7425-3
- **Greece** ISBN: 0-7922-7923-9
- **Hawaii** ISBN: 0-7922-7944-1
- **Hong Kong** ISBN: 0-7922-7901-8
- **India** ISBN: 0-7922-7898-4
- **Ireland** ISBN: 0-7922-4145-2
- **Italy** ISBN: 0-7922-3889-3
- **Japan** ISBN: 0-7922-3894-X
- **London** ISBN: 0-7922-7428-8
- **Los Angeles** ISBN: 0-7922-7947-6
- **Mexico** ISBN: 0-7922-7897-6
- **Miami and the Keys** ISBN: 0-7922-3886-9
- **New Orleans** ISBN: 0-7922-3892-3
- **New York** ISBN: 0-7922-7430-X
- **Paris** ISBN: 0-7922-7429-6
- **Prague & Czech Republic** ISBN: 0-7922-4147-9
- **Provence & the Côte d'Azur** ISBN: 0-7922-9542-0
- **Rome** ISBN: 0-7922-7566-7
- **San Diego** ISBN: 0-7922-6933-0
- **San Francisco** ISBN: 0-7922-3883-4
- **Sicily** ISBN: 0-7922-9541-2
- **Spain** ISBN: 0-7922-3884-2
- **Sydney** ISBN: 0-7922-7435-0
- **Taiwan** ISBN: 0-7922-6555-6
- **Thailand** ISBN: 0-7922-7943-3
- **Venice** ISBN: 0-7922-7917-4
- **Washington, D.C.** ISBN: 0-7922-3887-7

AVAILABLE WHEREVER BOOKS ARE SOLD